Indian Education in Emerging Society

Published by :
Lotus Press Publishers & Distributors

Indian Education in Emerging Society

C.P. Singh

4735/22, Prakash Deep Building
Ansari Road, Darya Ganj,
New Delhi - 110002

Lotus Press : Publishers & Distributors
Unit No. 220, 2nd Floor, 4735/22, Prakash Deep Building,
Ansari Road, Darya Ganj, New Delhi- 110002
Ph.: 23280047, 98118-38000
• E-mail : lotuspress1984@gmail.com
www.lotuspress.co.in

Indian Education in Emerging Society

ISBN: 81-8382-089-1

Printed & Published by : **Lotus Press Publishers & Distributors,** New Delhi-02

PREFACE

Indian Education in Emerging Society is a complete text-cum-reference book for teachers, teacher-trainers, and teacher-trainees of all pedagogical institutes and departments of Education of different universities.

The present book is designed to highlight the important aspects of education, philosophy, phychology, educational thinkers, learning psychology, physical growth and development of children. In the chapters of this book guidance regarding curriculum, audio-visual aids, laboratory and text books, teaching planning has been given in a very impressive manner. This book can prove an effective guide to teachers and teacher-trainees for understanding the psychology of students and their problems and show the right path in the field of teaching.

This book deals with the topics of Introduction to Education; Philosophy of Education; Educational Psychology; Educational Thinkers; Education in Indian Constitution; National Integration and Socialisation; New Educational Policy; Learning Psychology; Physical Growth and Development etc.

All the fundamentals of Teaching of Social Studies has been given in this book which have been drawn from authoritative sources. Yet the simple interpretation makes it an ideal text-cum-reference book.

I am thankful to various authors and educational researchers whose works are consulted, cited or reproduced here. Last but not the least, I owe a deep sense of gratitude to my publisher for materialising my present endeavour.

EDITOR

Contents

1

Introduction to Education

There have been variations in the very concept of education. Eastern and Western concepts have differed to some extent.

Indian Concept of Education. Education being an important social activity, its meaning has been changing through the ages due to change in social and physical conditions. Different educationists have interpreted it differently.

According to **Rigveda,** "Education is that which makes a man self-reliant and selfless." The Rigveda regarded creating confidence in the person as the only function of education whereas the function of education is unlimited.

The Upanishad explains, "Education is that whose end product is salvation." The Upanishad regards attaining salvation as the function of education whereas education develops a person physically, intellectually, socially, economically and culturally.

According to **Kautilya,** "Education means training for the country and love for the nation."

According to **Vivekanand,** "Education is the manifestation of Divine Perfection already existing in man."

According to **Tagore,** "Education makes man's life in harmony with all existence."

According to **Gandhiji,** "By education I mean an all-round drawing out of the best in child and man, body, mind and spirit."

WESTERN CONCEPTS OF EDUCATION

Western thinkers have given following definitions:

According to **Aristotle,** "Education is the creation of a sound mind in a sound body." Aristotle has regarded the meaning of education complete by mentioning physical and spiritual development.

According to **Frobel,** "Education is unfoldment of what is already enfolded in the seed. It is the process through which a child expresses his internal abilities."

Frobel called education as a process through which internal abilities are expressed.

According to **T.P. Nunn,** "Education is the complete development of individuality so that man can make an original contribution to human life according to his best capacity."

According to **Pestalozzi,** "Education is the natural, harmonious and progressive development of man's innate powers". Pestalozzi has talked about the development of innate powers whereas education also brings about personal, social, moral, cultural, economic, national and international development.

Nunn and James have also stressed individual and social development but their definitions are also vague.

According to **James,** "Education is the organisation of acquired habits of such action as will fit the individual to his physical and social environment."

According to **Dewey,** "Education is the development of all those capacities in the individual which enable him to control his environment and fulfil his possibilities."

According to **Bossing,** "The function of education is conceived to be the adjustment of man to his environment, to the end that the most enduring satisfaction may accrue to the individual and to the society."

According to **Redden,** "Education is the deliberate and systematic influence exerted by the mature person upon the immature through instruction, discipline and harmonious development of physical, intellectual, aesthetic, social and spiritual powers of human being."

Redden has not considered the non-formal and economic aspects of education.

According to **Ruskin,** "Education does not mean teaching people what they do not know. It means teaching them to behave as they do not behave."

Ruskin has mentioned the function of education only to make man a social animal. He has not bothered for other aspects.

After studying the interpretation given by various educationists, we can classify the meaning of education into two categories—Narrower and Broader. In the narrow sense, education is regarded as equivalent to instruction, imparted in school or college. Education is believed to begin with the entrance of a child to the school and end with his departure from the university. Education includes those specific influences which are brought to bear upon the child with a definite purpose in a pre-planned, suitable, and methodical manner, by parents, teachers and other members of the community, for the preservation of the cultural heritage. According to this view education is limited to classroom teaching and readymade materials. Education is given in a formal way, under set and controlled conditions and environment. It is pre-planned and is given by teachers in the classroom.

According to **Lodge,** "In the wider sense, all experiences are said to be educative. Even the bite of mosquito and the taste of water melon experiences have a directly educative effect on us." The child educates his parents, the pupils educate their teacher. Every thing that we say, think or do educates us.

According to **J.S. Mill,** Education in its narrower sense means, "The culture which each generation purposely gives to its successor in order to qualify, to keep up and to improve the level attained. Thus education becomes a purposeful activity which is planned deliberately for the purpose of the child's individual and social development. This activity is organised through the school as the chief agency of education.

According to **Dumvile,** "Education includes all the influences which act upon an individual during his passage from the cradle to the grave."

In this wider sense life is education and education is life. Whatever broadens our horizon, deepens our insight, refines our reactions and stimulates our thoughts and feelings educates us. Life is a long process of education and education is synonymous with the act of living.

ANALYTICAL MEANING OF EDUCATION

Education is the Harmonious Development of Child. Education is the harmonious development of the child. Through education all aspects—physical, mental, spiritual and moral are developed.

Education is the Development of Innate and Acquired Powers of the Child. Every child has innate capacities. Education helps in developing those natural qualities of the child. It provides every person with the opportunity of developing according to his capacities.

Education is a Dynamic Process. Education is a dynamic and progressive process. It reconstructs a new and better social pattern according to the changing needs of time, place and society.

Education is a Process of Adjustment with the Environment. Education helps the individual in making adjustment with his own self, parents, peers and society etc.

Education is a Life Long Process. It starts in mother's womb and ends in tomb. The sequence of learning through experiences goes on up to death.

INDIVIDUAL AIMS OF EDUCATION

Some of the most important individual aims of education are:

1. The Knowledge Aim. Knowledge is power. Achievements of all kinds are made possible only through knowledge. An ignorant man can do nothing for himself or for anyone else; and is like an animal. Knowledge is basic for living a rich and happy life. It is for this reason that many educationists consider imparting of knowledge to the people as an important aim. That is why all the schools have graded syllabus for children of different ages and classes. Different subjects are taught in the schools as different aspects of knowledge. In fact acquisition of knowledge is the nucleon around which most of the activities of the schools in the whole world revolve. Most of the teaching strategies developed for teaching aim at imparting knowledge alone. The examination systems in all countries measure, by and large, only knowledge. In fact, education and knowledge giving have become synonymous. Teachers, students and parents all think that good education and good schools are only those which make their children knowledgeable.

There is no doubt that knowledge-giving should be considered an important aim of education. In the past many philosophers like Plato, Aristotle, the Sophists and many others emphasized this aim very much. Comenius said that an ideal school should impart knowledge of all subjects to all men and women. Knowledge and intellectual development go together; and cultivation of intelligence is an importance of education according to Bertrand Russel. Bacon's slogan was "all knowledge for all", knowledge was virtue for Socrates. To Cicero knowledge was a means of mental development. Even the development of other aspects of human personality is dependent largely on acquisition of knowledge. Thus, it is an important aim of education to impart knowledge. But where are we wrong?

We commit a serious error when we accept and say that it is the only aim of education, when we say that nothing else is important. Knowledge alone is not enough and sufficient for living a happy and complete life. Knowledge is a tool which has to be used for achieving many more things. So these many more things should also be brought within the purview of aims of education. Hence, the right way is to say that among many aims of education, knowledge aim is also very important.

2. Harmonious Development Aim. It means harmonious development of child's personality. Child's personality is one word but many things. Intellectual and cognitive development is one aspect. Emotional development including emotional control is another. Feelings, attitudes, interests, values etc., also fall within this component of emotional development. Similarly, development of skills, desirable habits and actions constitute still another aspect of personality development. Adjustment to the environment and many social behaviours come under this. Equal development of all these aspects, balanced development of these, is considered an aim of education. If it happens that a person is very knowledgeable, but socially maladjusted, this would mean a lap-sided development of the personality. Education should provide opportunities to all children for developing all aspects or their personalities.

3. Vocational Aim. This is also known as the 'bread-and-butter" aim of education. Thus no doubt should be considered an important aim of education. It simply means that education received by an individual should enable him to earn his bread, should enable him to get a job, some work that pays him sufficient money regularly so that the individual is able to buy bread, clothes, house, and other things necessary for living a decent and comfortable life. This has led in many countries, to a slogan by the people and educators which is "job-oriented education". Vocationalisation of education is another dimension of the same. Gandhiji's basic education concept had this implication. When he said that true education should be, for the boys and girls, a kind of insurance against employment, he meant to emphasise vocational aim of education.

Again, although we all accept that vocational aim is very important, yet we commit a mistake when we say that it is the only aim to which education should cater. We should always think that along with vocational aim there are other aims which are equally important. We should neither ignore or belittle the importance of vocational aim, nor we should consider this only important aim. Nehru struck the balance between vocational and cultural aims of education when he said that cultural and vocational or productive aspects of education both are essential. "Everybody should be a producer as well as a good citizen and not a sponge on another person," said he. Mahatma Gandhi also emphasised the same point when he said that body, mind and spirit all should be developed by education. Although many philosophers from the ancient times to the present day have insisted upon the satisfaction of the soul belittling the importance of vocation in life, yet their view cannot be the conscious of opinion. These should be taken as the extreme views and one-sided opinions. The majority of the people in the world feel that education should make individual self-dependent and capable of earning their livelihood. An educated man without a job or some work to earn is a curse, a blot on the system of education.

4. Complete Living Aim. This aim means that education should enable the individuals to live a life which is full and complete. In other words it means preparing the individuals for life. Living a full and complete life means exercising and using all capacities and abilities in the interest of one's well-being. Keeping good health, developing a sound mind and using it for the benefit of life's amenities, enjoying life and enriching it culturally, living like a good citizen and gainfully employed may be considered some important features of full or complete living. In other words it is the same as harmonious development of personality. According to this aim education should enable the individual to carry out all necessary activities of life successfully. He should be an enlightened citizen and an efficient man. Herbert Spencer seems to be the advocate of this aim. It is in a way laying an emphasis on liberal education which emphasises teaching the pupils everything that is needed in life. It may be termed as life-centred education or education for life.

The main difficulty with this aim is how to define "completeness of life". When is life complete? Even it is possible to define completeness of life it becomes more difficult to identify what will make it so.

5. The Moral Aim. This aim lays stress on the ethical development of the people. Character-formation and learning of social and moral values are the focus of this aim. Gandhiji termed this as "purity of heart". Vivekananda's "man-making" function of education also means the same thing. Dewey said "all education forms character—moral and mental". This, in other words, means emphasising the moral aim of education. Raymont also considered "cultivation of strength and purity of character" as an important aim of education. Herbart said "the whole work of education could be summed up in the concept of morality." All the idealist philosophers supported the moral aim as an ultimate aim of education. National Policy on Education of 1986 also said that education should be made a "forceful tool for the cultivation of social and moral values".

There can be no gain saying that education should teach morality to children. It is an universally accepted aim of education. But, the difficulty with this aim is how to define character and morality, what are its behavioural components, are these behavioural components acceptable universally, does morality help the individual in actual situations of life, is there any standard way of teaching morality. These questions have no set and unambiguous answers. Morality is good, but very difficult to be taught, particularly in today's materialistic world. Yet, the aim cannot be scored out simply for these difficulties. In a democratic country where the assumption is that the human being is perfect and given the freedom he will make the best use of it in the interest of the society and his own interest, it becomes still more important to teach morality to people. Education alone can play this role.

6. Education for Leisure. This aim asserts that children in the schools should be taught to utilise their leisure time such as their holidays, summer vacation and week days constructively for enjoyment and developing their potentialities. This may add to their happiness and development of creative powers. The educators, for this reason, plead that provisions for hobby centres, recreation centres, social service camps, scouting, NCC etc., should be made in which students can participate and use their leisure time fruitfully. Thus, there are a number of educational aims which fall within the category of individual aims of education. They are said to be individual aims because they all focus on the life of the individual. All round development of the individual is their only concern. They are all complimentary and should not be considered competitive.

7. Aesthetic Aim. This aim emphasises that education should develop in the pupil an aesthetic sense which means a taste for good and beautiful things. They feel that excellence of taste and fairness of feeling can form the basis of good character and genuine morality. By developing in the child sensitivity to what is beautiful and excellent ideals may be generated which play an important role in being a moral person. Aesthetic development is, in fact, a part of the education of the whole man. It is a sort of emotional training. In the past the Athenians considered this important. They aimed, through education, to develop a well-rounded individual, one whose physical, moral, intellectual and aesthetic powers were developed. For developing aesthetic sense of the child the educators stressed that while teaching pupils love of beauty and art should be fostered. The students should be presented with a large variety of art forms such as paintings, drawings, beautiful sceneries both real and painted, songs, poetry, etc. They should be taught to appreciate them and realise the beauty inherent in them.

8. Individual Happiness Aim. Happiness is essentially the purpose of all that an individual does in life. He goes to school, tries to build good health, tries to get a job, serves well, does something which brings him name and fame. All these activities of his are goal-directed. This goal is to derive happiness out of them. Happiness is the basic goal-life. It is asserted, therefore, that education should help the individuals in achieving this goal. All educators have considered health and well-being of the child important and that education must cater to this. For this reason athletics and games form a part of the curriculum of education in every country. For the same reason it is also emphasised that knowledge of the laws of health and right living and knowledge of laws of bodily grace and harmony should be taught to the children in the schools. Happiness of the individual very much depends on sound mind and sound body. So recreational activities should be included in the curriculum.

AIMS OF EDUCATION IN THE PRESENT MODERN INDIAN SOCIETY

Different ideologies such as political, social, economic, religious, psychological, scientific and philosophical and present problems affect the aims of education. Aims of education are laid down keeping them in view. To know this problem it is essential to throw light on various conditions, which are as follows:

Economic Conditions. In India economic conditions are not good. India is a country where large number of people are under poverty line. There is no equitable distribution of wealth, which increases the gap between rich and poor. Unemployment is increasing day by day. We are not economically sound.

Social Conditions. Social conditions of India are also badly affecting the Indian society. Many social evils are prevailing in Indian society such as dowry system, illiteracy, early marriage etc. Diversity of religion, caste, culture and language is assuming the form of serious problem.

Political Conditions. Political environment is also becoming polluted day by day. India wants such leaders who can guide people in right directions. Indian electorate are not properly educated, they are unable to choose the right people for governance. To preserve freedom is becoming a great problem. The existence of freedom is in danger.

Religious Conditions. India is a secular state. Here all religions have equal importance. But it is pity that people do not understand the meaning of religion, they are misusing the concept of religious freedom. There is lack of religious toleration among people due to which anarchism is increasing. It has become a great danger for national integration.

On the basis of these conditions, the aims of education have been patronised by different Commissions from time to time which are as follows:

After independence, democratic view point was adopted. At that time education made its contribution and tried to bring prosperity in country. According to Rajendra Prasad, "India has to choose for herself a culture that derives inspiration from what is noble in our ancient culture and at the same time does not ignore the demands of the present age."

Aims of Education According to University Education Commission, 1948

Pandit Nehru had Observed: "Great changes have taken place in the country and the educational system must also be in keeping with them. The entire basis of education must be revolutionised."

According to University Education Commission, 1948, the aims of education are as follows:

(a) Development of leadership

(b) Preservation and transfer of culture

(c) Vocational efficiency

(d) Emphasis on human and spiritual training

(e) Development of democratic qualities in school

(f) Character development.

Aims of Education According to Secondary Education Commission, 1952-53

This Commission has stated that education which is national in character must develop in its citizens habits, attitudes and qualities of character and equip them to bear the burden of life in the changing economic structure.

According to Secondary Education Commission aims of education are as follows:

(a) Development of democratic citizenship

(b) Development of sense of patriotism

(c) Development of vocational efficiency

(d) Development of personality

(e) Development of leadership.

Development of Democratic Citizenship. It is a challenging responsibility with education to carefully train every citizen for democratic citizenship. Such a training develops following qualities:

(a) ***Clear Thinking.*** A democratic citizen should have the understanding and the intellectual integrity to distinguish truth from falsehood and facts from propaganda. Education should train the child for this purpose.

(b) ***Clearness in Speech and Writing.*** This quality is essential for successful living in democracy which is based not on force but on free discussion and persuasion.

(c) ***Receptivity to New Ideas.*** Education must aim at broadening the intellectual horizon of young scholars to enable them to accept new ideas that can help in strengthening democratic forces.

Development of Sense of Patriotism. Another important aim which the secondary school must foster is the development of a sense of true patriotism. True patriotism involves a sense of appreciation of the social and cultural achievements, a readiness to recognise its weaknesses and an earnest desire to serve one's country.

Development of Vocational Efficiency. Education must aim at increasing the productive or vocational efficiency of young students.

Development of Personality. Education should develop literary, artistic and cultural interests of the students. These are necessary for self-expression and for the full development of human personality. For this purpose subjects like art, craft, music, dance etc. should be included in the scheme of studies.

Aims of Education According to Indian Education Commission, 1964-66

According to Dr. Radha Krishnan, "It is my earnest desire that the Commission should survey all aspects of educational system at all levels and give suggestions that may help the educational system in progressing at all levels."

According to Kothari Commission, "One of the important social objectives of education is to equalise opportunity, enabling the backward or underprivileged classes and individuals to use education as a tool for improvement of their social and economic condition".

The most important and urgent reform needed in education is to transform it, to relate it to the life, needs and aspirations of the people and thereby make a powerful instrument of social, economic and cultural transformation, necessary for realization of the national goals. For this purpose the commission has suggested the following objectives of education:

(a) Increasing productivity.

(b) Social and national integration.

(c) Acceleration the process of modernisation.

(d) Developing social, moral and spiritual values.

These objectives are discussed below.

Education for Increasing Productivity. Though India is a land of vast resources, yet it has not become self-sufficient. For this purpose, the resources must be exploited and education must be related to productivity to increase national income. In order to create a link between education and productivity the following programme has been suggested by Kothari Commission:

Science Education. Science education must become an integral part of school education and ultimately some study of science should become a part of all courses in the humanities and social sciences at university level also. The quality of science teaching must also be improved considerably so as to promote a deep understanding of basic principles, to develop problem solving and analytical skills and to promote the spirit of enquiry and experimentation.

Work Experience. In the programme of relating education to life and productivity, work experience must be introduced as an integral part of all education—general and vocational. To Commission work experience implies participation in productive work in school, in the home, in a workshop, on a farm, in a factory or in any productive situation. All purposeful education should include study of languages, humanities and social sciences, study of mathematics and natural sciences, work experience and social services.

Work experience is a method of integrating education with work. In the present education system work experience and social services have almost been totally neglected. Along with other elements of education work experience should be greatly emphasised for the following reasons:

(a) It will bridge the gap between intellectual and manual work.

(b) It will decrease the over academic nature of formal education.

(c) It will make the entry of youth into the world of work and employment easier by enabling them to adjust themselves to it.

(d) It will relate education to productivity and also as a means of social and national integration.

Vocationalisation. Every attempt should be made to give a vocational bias to secondary education and to increase the emphasis on agricultural and technological education at the university level.

This will surely bring education into closer relationship with productivity. In the modern Indian society which is heading towards industrialisation, it is essential to considerably expand professional education at the university level, especially in agricultural and technological fields.

Education for National Integration. India is a land of diverse social groups. Unity and harmony among these groups is the basis of national integration. Social and national integration is an important objective of a national system of education. The Commission has suggested the following steps for strengthening the nation through education.

The Common School System. The present educational system in our country instead of bringing social groups and classes together is tending to increase social segregation and class distinctions. The schools for the masses (generally maintained by the government) are of poorer quality than those run by private bodies. Good schools are not within the reach of a common man's pocket. This is one of the major weaknesses of the existing educational system. In the opinion of the Commission, "If our educational system is to become a powerful instrument of national development in general, and social and national integration in particular, we must march toward the goal of a Common School System of public education." The common school must be opened to all children irrespective of caste, creed, community and economic or social status.

— It should charge no tuition fee.

— It should maintain a good standard of education in order to meet the needs of average parents so that they may not ordinarily feel the need of sending their children to other expensive schools.

Social and National Service. Social and national service should be made obligatory for all students at all levels. It should form an integral part of education at secondary school and university levels. This programme will prove an effective instrument for building character improving discipline, inculcating a faith in the dignity of labour and developing a sense of social responsibility, if it is organised concurrently with academic studies in schools and colleges. The following are the main forms of organising such a programme:

(a) At the primary stage this programme should be developed in all schools on the lines of Basic Education.

(b) At the lower secondary stage social service should be made compulsory for all students for thirty days a year, at the higher secondary for twenty days and at the under-graduate stage it should be made obligatory for all students or sixty days a year, to be done in one or more stretches. Every educational institution should develop a programme of social and community service of its own in which all students must be involved for the periods as indicated above.

(c) Labour and social service camps or N.C.C. should be organised in each district as alternative forms of such service for those students for whom no other programmes of social service have been organised in their own institutions.

Promoting National Consciousness

India is a land of different castes, peoples, communities, languages, religions and cultures. The main role of our schools, colleges and universities should, therefore, be to enable our students to discover 'unity in diversity' and in this way, foster a sense of national solidarity and national consciousness among them. This can be done by—

The Promotion of Understanding and Re-evaluation of Our Cultural Heritage. This can be achieved by the well-organised teaching of language and literature, philosophy, religion and history of India and by introducing the students to Indian architecture, sculpture, painting, music, dance and drama. Holiday camps and summer schools on inter-state basis, can also be organised fruitfully, for breaking down regional and linguistic barriers.

Creation of a strong faith in the future towards would involve an attempt to bring home to the students, the principles of the constitution, the great human values, referred to in its preamble, the nature of the democratic and socialistic society.

Education for International Understanding. There is no contradiction between national consciousness and developing international understanding. Schools should promote international outlook through the study of humanities and social sciences, simultaneously with developing national consciousness.

Democratic Values. The educational programme in schools and colleges should be designed to inculcate democratic values, such as scientific temper of mind, tolerance, respect for the culture of other national groups etc. This will enable our young citizens to adopt democracy not only as a form of government but also as a way of life.

Education for Modernisation

In a modern society stock of knowledge is far greater, the pace of its growth is infinitely quicker and social change is very rapid. This needs a radical change in the educational system. Education in a modern society is no longer concerned mainly with the imparting of knowledge or the preparation of a finished product but with the awakening of curiosity, the development of proper interests, attitudes and values and the building up of such essential skills as independent study and capacity to think and judge for oneself, without which it is not possible to become a responsible member of a democratic society. Therefore the process of modernisation will be directly related to the pace of educational advance. Education brings modernisation in following ways:

(a) The way to modernise quickly is to spread education.

(b) By producing educated and skilled citizens.

(c) By training an adequate and competent intelligentsia.

(d) By bringing a radical change in the method of teaching and in the training of teachers.

Education for Social, Moral and Spiritual Values

The expanding knowledge and the growing power which it places at the disposal of modern society must be combined with the strengthening and deepening of the sense of social responsibility and a keener appreciation of moral and spiritual values. For this purpose, active measures should be adpoted to give a value-orientation to education. These measures are:

(a) The Central and State governments should introduce education in moral, social and spiritual values in all institutions.

(b) The privately managed institutions should also follow the same steps.

(c) Some periods should be set apart in the time table for this purpose.

(d) University department should undertake preparation of special literature for this purpose by students and teachers.

(e) For this purpose, a syllabus giving well chosen information about each of the major religions, should be included as a part of the course in citizenship or general education to be introduced in schools and colleges.

We may say that education is the most vital force which can help in the realisation of national objectives. While keeping in view the best features of the modern European culture and civilisation, the Commission did not ignore the essential characteristics of our ancient culture and civilisation as well as the needs and aspirations of our present day society. It is for the first time that we have been given an integrated picture of Indian education in all its wide and diverse dimensions.

EDUCATIONAL THOUGHT OF ROUSSEAU'S

In modern times, we make use of a number of progressive methods of teaching and a variety of audio-visual aids, to make classroom teaching effective and attractive. But upto the seventeenth century, there was no systematic organisation or arrangement for imparting education to children. Schools in those days were very few and those that existed, were the terror of pupils and the slaughter-houses of mind. They followed no methods and used no aids. Every teacher had his own methods to follow. Severe punishments were given to pupils and all types of rods, canes and sticks were used for this purpose. The early educators, if any, "had confined their education to the training of the governing classes of the community and until the time of Comenius, it was only idealistic. There were many who could hazard the suggestion that all in their childhood be instructed in learning, in their own native tongue." During the seventeenth, eighteenth and the nineteenth centuries a number of educationists were born who, in fact, revolutionised education, Rousseau, Froebel, Montessori and Dewey are the most prominent among these.

Rousseau (1712-1778), was the great educator of the 18th century and one who belonged to the new school of education. Rousseau's life was greatly influenced by the prevailing atmosphere of society in France, his native country. In the beginning of the 18th century, the privileged classes in France, flourished at the cost of the poor and the helpless. Hypocrisy, artificiality, cruelty and despotism of the privileged classes, led to discontentment among the common people. However, in the later half of the 18th century a new era of 'Equality, Liberty, and Fraternity,' began in France which revolutionised the entire French society. Rousseau and Voltaire were the pioneers of this new era. It was a result of these new ideas that in the sphere of education also many new changes found their way. Children began to be treated well, properly understood and humanly educated.

1. Rousseau's Philosophy and Concept of Education. Rousseau's philosophy goes by the name of "Naturalism". The keynote of his philosophy was to have a "Natural State, a Natural Man and a Natural Civilisation". He felt that all ills and miseries in the Modern world were due to a departure from the previous "State of Nature". He declared, "Everything is good as it comes from the hands of the Author of Nature (the Creator), but everything degenerates in the hands of man." He believed that child was essentially good but was made bad when he came in contact with society and its environment. He contended that "man in society is born, lives and dies in a state of slavery. He is fettered by our institution, which drags him away from his good nature." So Rousseau pleaded, "Leave the child alone. Let him be a natural man rather than a civilised man. Let him have a state of nature rather than artificial surroundings that stunt his proper growth and arrest his natural development." Thus Rousseau preached for a life according to nature—which was simple and real and free from all customs, traditions and conventions. He, in fact, wanted to educate the child for manhood and not for citizenship.

It should, however, be clearly understood that by Natural State and Natural Man, Rousseau did not mean the primitive social order and the savage man. He believed that human institutions were one mass of folly and contradictions. To regain the old vitality and happiness, human society should give up the present artificial modes of life and revert to the natural state. He favoured natural civilisation, free from all artificial and rigid barriers that pollute the goodness of our nature. The Natural Man of Rousseau's conception was a fully developed Man enjoying social life, without being carried away by the passions and prejudices of society. Reason was the only guiding force in producing natural Civilisation and Natural Man by Natural State also he meant 'a simple farming community or state, without the evils of large cities, corrupt rulers, social classes and luxury. His Natural Man is a true man, who is 'governed and directed by the laws of his own nature rather than those of social institutions. Natural powers, emotions and reactions are most trustworthy as basis for action, rather than reflections or experiences that come from association with society.' The catch-words of Rousseau's 'Naturalism' were freedom, growth, interest and activity. And all these words are the life and soul of modern progressive education.

2. Three-fold Meaning of Nature. Rousseau made use of the word 'Nature' in a very wide sense. He gave three-fold meaning to it, namely:

(a) ***Isolation from Society.*** Rousseau advocated that children should be saved from the evil influence of society. They should be isolated from society and brought up in contact with the beauties and wonders of nature. This, however, does not mean no-education. It simply signifies a non-social education *i.e.* an education which is not based on meaningless traditions and formalities of society. For Rousseau, society was not natural, but an artificial product, the outcome of a contract and evil. Nature and society, thus, become opposed to each other. Nature is accordingly, defined 'negatively to society'. It is a preventive education saving the child from the evil influences of society.

(b) ***Instinctive Make-up of the Child.*** Instinctive make-up means the native instincts, tendencies and capacities of the child. Rousseau believed that learning takes place when the child is free to develop and grow according to his natural impulses. So education must start from the child's instinctive tendencies and should be based on the same because these tendencies are more reliable bases of education than experiences, gained from society. According to Rousseau, "Education is no longer a procedure, artificial, harsh, dull, unsympathetic and repressive of all natural inclinations. It is, on the other hand, an organic growth. It is a development from withim."

(c) ***Contact with Natural Phenomena.*** Education according to child's nature, must be provided in natural environment. Rousseau himself was a great lover of nature, mountains, streams, sun-rise, sun-set, solitude and country life. He, therefore, recommends contact with hills, streams, plants, trees, animals, birds and physical forces of all kinds. One who is brought up and taught in natural environments

automatically becomes a 'natural man' He follows nature and obeys, the voice of his own conscience.

3. Three Source of Education. At the outset of his book "*Emile*" Rousseau states that education comes from nature, from men and from things. In other words, the problem of education is the relationship of man to his physical and social environment. Explaining these sources of education, he says, "The internal development of our organs and faculties is the education of nature; the use we are taught to make of that development, is the education given by men; and the acquisition made by our own experience on the objects that surround us, is our education from things." In other words, by education from nature, he meant development according to the child's natural endowments and capacities. By education from men, he emphasised the importance of social environment, teaching how to make use of that development. By education from things, he understood physical environment, helping to gain experience by ourselves. He says that the harmonious development of these three factors constituted an ideal scheme of education.

Such harmony in education is possible by subordinating the education of men and things to that of nature because we have no control over nature. We must, therefore, direct the other two, to ensure cooperation of these three factors for imparting ideal education.

4. Rousseau's Aims of Education. Before Rousseau's time, the aim of education was either spiritual or social or vocational, Efforts were made to mould the child into the artificial forms of conduct, satisfactory to the judgement of adults in society. The child was trained to speak, think, act as a miniature adult without any consideration of his natural instincts and interests. Rousseau revolted against this wrong concept of education. He believed that education was a life-long process, which began from birth and ended only with the end of life. It was development from within and not an imposition from without.

So Rousseau's aim of education was the attainment of fullest natural growth of the individual leading to balanced, harmonious, useful and natural life. The real aim of education is to help the child to live his life. He says, "To live is not merely to breathe. It is to act, to make us of our organs, senses, our faculties and of all those parts of ourselves, which give us the feeling of our existence."

This general aim of education was split up by Rousseau, according to the nature, at different stages of human development.

(i) In infancy *i.e.* from birth to the age of five years, the aim of education is to develop a well-regulated freedom. For realisation of this aim, he recommends purely physical education in an atmosphere of perfect liberty.

(ii) In childhood *i.e.* between the age of five and twelve, the main aim of education is to provide the child with the strength which he needs for the attainment of well-regualated freedom. So at this stage also no formal education is recommended, but the continuance of the same physical care and natural education, Rousseau's advice for this period is, "Exercise the body, the organs, the senses and powers and keep the soul lying fallow, as long as you can."

(iii) In boyhood or pre-adolescent period *i.e.*, from twelve years to fifteen years, the aim of education is "to acquire such knowledge which may satisfy the wants of the child and must be functionally useful". This is the period for intellectual education—the period of instruction, labour and study.

(iv) In adolescent period *i.e.* from 15 to 20 years, the aim of education is the training of heart, to make the child loving and tender-hearted so that he may live peacefully in social relationship. In this period religious, moral and social education is recommended. In the previous periods, the child has already developed physically and intellectually. He must now grow emotionally, aesthetically, socially and morally. The sex instinct, which is suficiently

developed by this time, is to be sublimated by re-directing it to the love of some noble idea and by keeping the young person occupied in work and activity.

5. Role of the Teacher. Rousseau assigns a very minor place to the teacher in the educative process. He is not called an instructor but only a guide. His main responsibility is to motivate the child to learn. This he can achieve by exploiting the innate tendencies of the child. He must possess a profound understanding of the child's nature and be able to control his emotional reactions. He is not to impose any rules of control upon the child. He is to allow him perfect feedom and guide him properly.

6. Rousseau's Theory of Negative Education. As we have already stated, Rousseau believed that everything is good as it comes from the Author of Nature. Everything degenerates in the hands of man. By saying so, he meant that child is good; but it is society that makes him bad. So he advocated that first education should be purely negative. The child should not be taught the principles of truth and virtue but guarded against vice and error. In his own words, "I call a positive education one that tends to form the mind prematurely and to instruct the child in the duties that belong to man. I call a negative education on that tends to perfect the organs that are the instruments of knowledge and endeavours to protect the way for reason, by the proper exercise of the senses."

The following are the chief characteristics of his theory of Negative Education:

(a) No Time Saving. According to Rousseau, in childhood no time should be saved. It should rather be lost. Let the child run, jump and play all day long. In all these activities he will have a continuous reconstruction of experience which is nothing but education, pure and simple. Time lost on play and recreational activities in childhood, is not lost but profitably gained. Childhood is not the time for intellectual pursuits.

(b) No Book Learning. Rousseau says, "I hate books because they are a curse to children. They teach us to talk only that which we do not know. Instead of making the child stick to his books, I keep him busy in the workshop; his hands will work to the profit of his mind." Rousseau felt that ready-made material found in books, was of little advantage. Let children gain knowledge by their own efforts and through different types of experience.

(c) No Social Education. In Rousseau's time, society was corrupt to the core. So he wanted children to be isolated from such a society and to educate them in the midst of nature till their power of reasoning and judgement is perfected, with which they are in a position to protect themselves from the evils of society.

(d) No Habit Formation. In his own words, "The only habit which the child should be allowed to form is to contract no habit at all." Young children should not be made slaves of rigid habits. They should be left free in all their activities. If any habits are to be formed in childhood, let them form natural habits.

(e) No Formal Discipline. Rousseau is in favour of free and positive discipline for children. Let the children suffer natural consequences of their own actions without the intervention of humam beings to protect or punish and in this way they will set themselves right. If a child breaks a window pane, let him sit in the cold wind that gushes in, as a result of his folly. If he climbs a tree, let him fall down and learn not to do so again.

(f) No Direct Moral Education. Rousseau is not in favour of direct teaching of morals. Let the child be left free to act and learn what is right and wrong, by the consequences of his own actions. He says, "Much more harm than good is done by your ceaseless preaching and moralising." He further says, "Inflict on the child no sort of punishment and never make him ask your pardon. As there is no moral quality in his actions, he can do nothing wrong.

(g) No Sticking to Traditional Precedure of Education. Rousseau was greatly disgusted with the prevailing social, political, economic, religious and educational conditions in his country. So he said, "Follow the reverse of the current practice and you will almost do right." He challenged the traditional procedure of education saying,

"Give me a child of twelve who knows nothing at all. At fifteen I will restore him to you, knowing as much as those who have been under instruction from infancy, with the difference that your scholar only knows things by hearts, while mine knows how to use his knowledge.

It will, thus, be clear from his theory of Negative Education that many of its principles have been accepted by the modern educators. No doubt, at times, Rousseau went to the extreme. But it was natural and he had to eradicate wrong social practices like a reformer by focusing public attention to those practices. His play-and-activity principles in a child's education, his free and positive discipline, his advice against formal book-learning and his principle of no direct moral instructions of children, have all been incorporated in modern educational theory and practice. However, it is his theory of natural consequences which is not acceptable and dependable at all times.

JOHN DEWEY'S VIEWS OF AN IDEAL SCHOOL

John Dewey (1819-1952) was a famous American philosopher, psychologist and educator. Being brought up in rural environments, he realised from the very beginning that traditional methods of instruction were not at all effective and that social contacts of everyday life provided effective, dynamic and unlimited learning situations. These very ideas formed the foundation of the educational theory, formulated later by him. His outlook on education reflected the Industrial Revolution and the Development of Democracy. He believed in the dynamic nature of things and values. So he changed with the change in ideas, as a result of experience and experimentation, and finally emerged out as a Pragmatist. Today, he stands in the front rank of the world educators. His works on education are a great source of inspiration and hope and help in developing our experimental and scientific attitude of mind. Perhaps no other educator has written so much on educational problems as John Dewey.

1. Dewey's Philosophy—Pragmatism. Dewey's philosophy represents a happy blend of naturalism and idealism because it is based on the evolutionary concept soft Darwin and Pragmatism of

William James. Like Darwin he believes that world is still in the process of making and that life in this world is an every-changing and self-renewing process. Like William James, he believes that whatever useful is good and whatever good, is useful. Truth is also that which works, which fulfils our purposes and satisfies our desires.

For John Dewey there are no eternal and absolute values. All values change with time and space. Man is the creator of his own values. What is true today may cease to be true tommorrow. Man's life is a series of experiments and purposeful action. "Everything is provisional, nothing ultimate. Knowledge is always a means, never an end itself." It is purely instrumental. Hence the title of Dewey's philosophy is "Instrumentalism".

Then Dewey believes that knowledge and thinking are closely associated with action. They are tentative plans of action. They have to be tested by action and by knowing the result of their being acted upon. He affirms, "The essence of pragmatic instrumentalism is to conceive of both knowledge and practice as means of making good. It does not imply that action is higher and better than knowledge and practice inherently superior to thought. Constant and effective interaction of knowledge and practice is something quite different from an exaltation of activity, for its own sake. Action, when directed by knowledge, is method and means, not an end. The aim and end is the securer, freerer end more widely shared embodiment of values in experience, by means of that active control of objects which knowledge alone makes possible."

Further more, he is convinced of the organic relationship between the individual and the society, to which he belongs. He is conscious of both the physical and the social environment. Self can neither grow in solitude nor in natural surroundings. For his proper growth an individual must live both in natural (or physical) environment and (human or social) environment. Man is not a solitary self but an individual, who lives with the rest of mankind. "He is a citizen, growing and thinking in a vast complex of interactions and relationships."

Lastly, Dewey holds that barriers of creed, religion, language, nationality and colour have divided humanity and separated man from man. These barriers must be broken to establish harmony between individuals and groups, and ensure the process of human growth. To him, growth stands for the "being process" and not for the "done product". Not perfection as a final goal, but the ever enduring process of perfecting, maturing and refining, is the aim of living. He further declares, "The bad man is one, who is beginning to deteriorate, to grow less good. And the good man is one, who is moving to become better." This is the function of education to break the barriers of separation and bring men and nations together for establishing a happier and nobler world.

2. Dewey's Educational Theory and Aims. About the importance of education, John Dewey writes, "What nutrition and reproduction are to physiological life, education is to social life. Education is a social necessity. It is a means of social continuity of life. It is a means by which a person is helped to have useful and helpful experience." All this he said in the light of the rapid changes in social and economic life of his own time.

Defining education, Dewey says, "Education is development of all those capacities in the individual which will enable him to control his environment and fulfil his responsibilities." It means that education extends the limits of human possibilities. It is progressive both for the individual and the society. Thus education, to John Dewey, is a bipolar process. It has two sides, the psychological and the sociological; neither of the two can be subordinated or neglected. The psychological side is the study of the child, with all his inclinations, instincts, endowments and interests. It forms the very basis of education. The sociological side is the social environment in which the child is born, lives and grows for society. On a further analysis of his educational theory, we find the following four fundamentals:

*(i) **Education as Growth.*** Growth is the real function of education. It, therefore, must lead to growth. But growth is not directed towards any pre-determined goal or end. The end of growth is more growth and so the end of

education, more education. An individual is a changing and growing personality and education is to facilitate that growth. It is, therefore, the duty of the teacher to provide opportunities for proper growth by arousing the instincts and capacities of children and by providing to them the solution of those problems which make the children think.

(ii) ***Education as Life.*** Dewey believes that education is not a preparation for life. It is life itself. "Life is a by-product of activities and education is born out of these activities." School is now taken as a miniature society which faces problems, similar to those faced in life outside. For education, pupils should be made active participants in the social and community life of the school and thus trained in co-operative and mutually helpful living. They should be encouraged to face actual life problems in the school and gain varied experiences. As our children are required to live in a democratic society when adults, they must experience same life in the school.

(iii) ***Education as Social Efficiency.*** Man is a social animal who continuously draws energy, strength, knowledge, experience and attitudes in a social medium. As a social being, he is a citizen, growing and thinking in a vast complex of interactions and relations." He owns character and mind, habits and manners, language and vocabulary, good taste and aesthetic appreciation, to his interaction with the social consciousness of his community. When as an individual he shares such rich resources of a good society, he should also be ready to give back to that society and thus help other members to develop. It is the function of education to teach him this give-and-take process and make him aware of his social obligations. Education must transform the immature child into a social human being. It is in this sense that education becomes a social process and social efficiency becomes the aim of all education.

(iv) ***No Fixed Aims of Education.*** However, being a pragmatic education, John Dewey has no fixed aims of education. He believes that since physical and social environments are always changing, aims of education must also change. They cannot be fixed for all times to come. Thus, he revolted against the traditional aims of education—namely: the moral aim, the disciplinary aim and the knowledge aim etc. of the nineteenth century. He rejected the very idea of education as preparation for future life and said that education must cater to the present needs of the child rather than the future because the child is not interested in the unknown future. He therefore, said that educational aims must be restated and re-formulated in the light of the rapid social and economic changes in present day life.

(v) ***Education as Reconstruction of Experiences.*** According to John Dewey, experience is the only source of true knowledge. One experience leads to further experiences and each new experience calls for the revision, modification or rejection of the previous experiences. In this way the old pattern yields place to a new pattern. Dewey says, "We should so regulate the learning and experiencing activities of the young, that a newer and better society will arise in the end." Therefore, there is a need of continuity of experiences, helping man to grow physically, mentally, socially and morally. Education must create environments for the promotion of continuity of experiences. Dewey, therefore, conceived of education as a process, involving continuous reconstruction and reorganisation of experience. He says that education is by experience, for experience and of experience.

3. Dewey's Ideal School. Dewey was dissatisfied with the existing system of education. In his opinion, the Industrial Revolution, the development means of communication and transport, various discoveries and inventions of science and ideals of democracy, had brought about extraordinary changes in social life. As such, an ordinary school had not been able to keep pace with these changes. It could not give the present day child an exact idea of the social, political and economic life of the community around him. It is, therefore, that social education is not connected with his daily life. John Dewey wanted to bridge this gulf between school life and home or social life, outside the school.

4. His Concept of an Ideal School. Dewey considered ideal school as an enlarged ideal home. In this home, the child learns to subordinate his interests to the general interest of the household. Here he learns the habits of obedience, regularity, hardwork, cooperation, sacrifice, fellow-feeling, patience, and discipline. In the ideal school, teachers play the same part as parents at home. Being better equipped than home, the school must provide ideals, high and noble, and worthy of being pursued and lived upon. These ideals are quite in conformity with the ideals of society which the school is required to serve.

Then the ideal school of Dewey's concept, is a society in miniature in which real life experiences of the community are provided on smaller scale. It is an activity school, wherein ample opportunities are provided to the child to construct his experiences, under the scientific guidance of teachers. In this ideal school, the child learns by doing and by actual participation in purposeful and intelligent activities. These activities include cooking, sewing, wood-work, weaving as well as other occupations and violations. Thus the schools provide various types of social, economic and moral experiences of practical utility.

5. Scheme of Education. Dewey outlined a definite scheme of education, according to the stages of mental development of the child. These stages were:

(a) Play period from 4 to 8 years of age

(b) Period of spontaneous attention from 8 to 12

(c) Period of reflective attention from 12 onwards.

In the Play period, the child studies the life and occupations of the home. Then he studies larger social and community activities on which his home-life depends. Finally, he learns about the development and significance of other occupations and inventions. In the last year of this period, he also learns reading, writing and geography.

In the period of spontaneous attention, the child understands the difference between means and ends. He is able to act for the solution of practical problems of life. At this stage he is also taught social studies with a view to make him understand how man achieved his purposes under various conditions in different periods of history.

In the period of reflective attention, the child is grown-up enough to raise new problems and find out their solutions. At this stage he acquires definite skills and arts so that after leaving the school, he should adjust himself as a useful and efficient member of society.

6. Curriculum. Dewey's curriculum is not a mere scheme of studies. Nor is it a list of subjects. It is an entire range of activities and experiences, because to him subjects are only summaries and recapitulation of human activities. Dewey does not recommend any ready made curriculum. He rather wants the curriculum to grow out of the pupils own impulses, interest and experiences. It consists of activities and projects, leading to reconstruction and re-organisation of experience. Thus he makes occupational activities or crafts, the core of school curriculum. He also includes moral, aesthetic and religious education in the curriculum. But this education is also imparted through parctical experiences and not through "chalk and talk lessons," in the classroom. In his opinion, "Purposeful activity and a curriculum comprising standard factors of social life, would give the children more interest and insight, through the functioning of intelligence and will, in the achievement of self-control and the appreciation of social values."

7. Dewey's Contributions and Influence. John Dewey is, by far the most original thinker in the field of educational philosophy. He stands in the front rank of the educators of the world. It is under his influence that today we find freedom, happiness and friendliness in schools. Dewey is a philosopher of the present dynamic age, which is dominated by the forces of science, technology, industrialism and democracy. He has made an original approach to the problems, confronting man to-day and has offered sound solutions for them. To educators, he has given a new progressive outlook and called it life itself. He has also given new aim of education, new curricula, new methods of teaching, new role of the teacher and new concept of discipline. In fact, he glorified every aspect of education that he touched. His watch-word, "Progress more and more progress; growth, unlimited and illimitable," has given a new impetus of education.

Rousseau glorified the individual at the cost of society. This was not a balanced approach. Dewey fused both the psychological and the psychological aspects of education. He said that education is impossible without social medium. Education must proceed by the participation of the individual in social relationship, with other persons. Children should, therefore, be acquainted with social institutions and industrial processes by creating the same environment in the school and by actual living and working.

Another great contribution of John Dewey is democracy in education. Democracy stands for providing equal educational opportunities to all. It thus, stands for free universal education. It emphasises education through cooperative and shared efforts, in a social medium, to secure the best for the individual and the society. It also emphasises the breaking down of social, national, religious and economic barriers between man and man, group and group, and nation and nation. So John Dewey says that it is the school which can contribute a lot in this direction by training young children in experimental thinking and democratic cooperation.

Then, his Project Method is the practical outcome of his philosophy. It is based on "learning by doing and experiencing". This method encourages pupils to learn through self-effort and creative activity in real life situations. It is based on the fact that different branches of knowledge are not separate. They are studied separately for the sake of convenience alone. It incorporates integration and correlation of activities and subjects. It upholds the dignity of labour, favours social discipline and stresses problem solving, in place of cramming and memorisation.

Let us conculde with the words of R.R. Rusk:

"In education we cannot but be grateful to John Dewey for his great services in challenging the old static cold-storage ideal of knowledge and in bringing education more into accord with the actualities of present day life. The general principle, underlying the developments in his philosophy and his application of these in education. Appears to be that both philosophy and education should reflect the main currents of contemporary thought and incorporate the techniques that have so signally contributed to modern material and social progress."

❐

2

Philosophy of Education

The traditional view of philosophy is that its business or aim in knowledge of Being or Reality, which is more comprehensive, fundamental and ultimate than the knowledge which can be provided by the organs and methods at the disposal of the special science, for according to this view, with the possible exception of matter; Science deal with what is temporal, changing and contingent while philosophy aims at knowledge of that which is eternal and inherently necessary. Its (Philosophy) knowings are so primary and final that it alone can give sure support to the claims of truth put forward by the lesser form of knowledge.

Since the business of philosophy is with ultimate reality behind and beyond the phenomenal world, the possibility of knowledge, the conditions of knowing before knowing, takes place, becomes the chief problems of philosophy.

Dewey's conception of philosophy widely differs from this. He does not believe in two levels of beings: the phenomenal level and the ultimate level, 'Dewey is out to abolish all dualism in ontology, and epistemology, science and philosophy.

Dewey's conception is that philosophy is not outside of and above all other human pursuits, cultivating in secrecy and silence a remote, stacked-off pressure of its own. Philosophy is and works within the open and public domain of all human activities, one among others, differentiated by its scope and function, but in no way set apart.

The scope of subject-matter of Philosophy, as described by Dewey can be represented in the form of three concentric circles. The first area, bounded by the innermost circle, is occupied by reflective thought, by logic or what logic or Dewey now calls Inquiry. In the second area are the typical modes of human experience, such as the practical or utilitarian, the aesthetic, religious, socioethical, scientific. Philosophic inquiry here concerns itself with analysing what these modes of experience are and particularly, with discovering their inter-relations, how the practical or utilitarian developes with scientific, the scientific into aesthetic and vice versa. The third area is that of the socio-cultural world. The social world raises such questions as "the value of research for social progress: the bearing of psychology upon educational procedures: the mutual relation of fine and industrial arts; the adjustment of religious aspirations to scientific statements, the relation of organisation to individuality."

The significance of Dewey: conception is not, to be found in the mere extension of the range, significant as that is. It is to be found in the inter-relations of the three areas, that they are functional distinctions, discriminable divisions within one inclusive field of experience, the boundary lines being neither fixed nor impermeable, marking off, but not insulating any one from any of the rest.

Philosophy is an enterprise of reflective thought and can only deal with problems in a reflective or intellectual way. But when each bundle of actualised problems labelled with its own bag of epistemology, ethics, logic, aesthetics, social philosophy, are treated as if each constituted a separate and distinct substantive realm, as being the original and primary subject-matter of inquiry, philosophy instead of prospering as a reflective enterprise, degenerate into a mere process of untying each bundle in some way and tying it again in another.

Reflective inquiry, philosophic or otherwise can handle and actual condition that is a problem only transforming it into an intellectual form. An architect engaged on the problem of remodelling a house uses a blue print. The blue print is an intellectualised form of the actual house. An architect does not substitute his blue print for the house; he does not consider the blue print as constituting the original and primary subject-matter of his inquiry and he does not think that he changes the house when he changes the blue print although changing the blue print may be all that he professionally contributes towards the consummation of that final end.

In philosophy blue prints have taken the place of the actual house. This substitutions in philosophy has resulted in vain disputes and arid verbal jugglery. It has led to a diseased formulation of philosophic problems. Dewey distinguishes between problems in 'General' and the 'General Problem'. The problem of *e.g.* knowledge in General, *i.e.* 'Is knowledge prossible'? is a disceased formulation of the problem of developing a general theory of knowledge. It is just as intelligent for a philosopher ask 'Is knowledge possible' as it would be for a scientist to ask 'Is motion possible'. There are specific cases of motion and scientific inquiry experiments with these specific cases. There is no 'motion in general' and hence no 'problem in general'. But there is a general problem of theory of motion, which for the scientist consists in Central laws of motion. The general laws are not proved valid by evaporating out of scientific existence, specific cases of motion, but their validity rests on their ability to explain or account for the specific cases. Similarly there are specific cases of knowing. There is no knoweldge in general and hence no problems of knowledge in general. But there is the general problem of knowledge, which consists in finding general conditions in knowledge.

Thus a philosophic generalisation must satisfy the same requirements as a scientific generalisation. The philosophic task is to reach generalisations that meet specific conditions. It is true that generalisation of the nature of the reflections process certainly involves elimination of much of the specific material and contents of the thought situations of daily life and of critical science. Quite compatible with this, however, is the notion that it seizes upon certain specific conditions and factors, and aims to bring them to clear consciousness not to abolish them while eliminating the particular materials of particular practical and scientific pursuits, *(i)* it may strive to hit upon the common denominator in the various situations which are antecendent or primary to thought and which evoke, *(ii)* It may attempt to show how typical features in the specific antecedents of thought call out diverse typical modes of thought-reaction; It may attempt to state the nature of the specific consequences in which thought fulfils it careers.

There is thus no conflict between the philosophic concern with the general or generic and interest in the specific. Where philosophic activity eliminates the specific entirely, it gets into insoluable problems.

Philosophy if it is to escape being confined to the futile world of blue prints must adopt empirical method so that its activity is in continuous functional connection with socio-cultural and scientific world. All philosophic problems have empirical fathers who can be empirically traced, located and identified. An insoluable problem in philosophy is an intellectual disease which can be caused by tracing back the problem as it appears in philosophy backs to its origins in the primary subject method of experience and finding out how, in the course of its intellectual genetic history, it got that way. Again the prevention against a insoluable problem and futile and frustrated philosophic activity consists in working back and forth between the narrow and large fields of the technical study of the intellectualised problems in philosophy and the socio-cultural, and scientific world that generate those problems. A working back and forward between the three areas of problems called by Dewey 'double movements'. This "double movements" is both corrective and cummulative. It tests the increment in our field by transferring into method of work in another field. Again it functions to uncover new clues for different fields.

To sum up Philosophy has at various times been set up as a separate and peculiar science, sin genesis. This according to Dewey, is not true. Philosophic problems arise out of the common matrix of experience. For philosophy to solve its own intellectualised problem it must move into the common field of problematic situations. The solution of problems in philosophy can be reached only by working back and forth between the technical or private domain of philosophy and the final or public domain of socio-cultural experience.

RELATIONSHIP OF PHILOSOPHY AND EDUCATION

Philosophy as a field of knowledge deals with three things *(i)* reality (metaphysics), *(ii)* knowledge (epistemology) and *(iii)* problems related to values (axiology). What is reality? What is the purpose of creation? What are time and space? These are some of the questions that are answered by metaphysics. It is the main branch of philosophy. It discusses three aspects of reality *e.g.*, the world, the self and the God. Epistemology examines different methods to achieve different types of knowledge. Axiology is mainly concerned with value. It is a science of value. It concerns itself with problems such as what is value, what is good, what are fundamental values? and so on.

Reality, knowledge and values are very much the concern of education. All problems of education, finally get concerned with these. What knowledge should be imparted to pupils, what values should be learnt by them, exactly is the reality to which education should be made to conform are questions which can be answered in several ways depending upon the kind of philosophy one believes in. Different views about reality, knowledge values etc., have been expressed by different philosophers. There is no philosophy. There are several schools of philosophy. Within each school there are several philosophers who have contributed to the thoughts on that philosophy. These have influenced the theory and practice of education also.

1. **Philosophy of Education.** Education is said to be the dynamic side of philosophy. It means philosophy tells what education should be and what it should aim at, but education implements that or practices that. Education is the purposive influence to be brought upon the pupils. But what kind of influence this ought to be has to be decided prior to any atempt on making it real. Who should do this? How should it be done? Philosophy of education helps in solving these problems.

2. **Different Philosophy of Education** have described the content and methods of education in different ways. This is so because each one of them makes different assumptions about human nature, knowledge, ethics, morals and values. For example, idealists consider man a spiritual being, a supreme creation of God who is regarded by them as the source of all knowledge. So they consider values of life absolute and unchanging and recommend that education should make all-out effort on teaching these values. To the naturalists material world alone is real and so all values exist in nature, in living close to nature. So they recommend that goals of education and methods of education should be determined by the nature of the child. Like that other philosophies of education also differ in their philosophical views and corresponding aims and methods of education. Thus, philosophy of education means a specific point of view on aspects of education. Dewey, for that reason, said that "philosophy is the theory of education in its most general phases". It is philosophy applied to education. There are several aspects of education like the aims, the curriculum, the methods, the discipline, the values to be taught, etc. Philosophies of education present specific ideas about each of these. Thus, it may be said that they constitute different foundations on which the superstructures called education are raised.

3. Philosophy of education is a critical method of approaching education and its various elements. It is true that there are certain well-defined philosophies of education but apart from these views, underlying them is essentially a spirit or method of approach to education, the philosophical way of thinking and appraising educational matters. Thus, philosophy of education is a way of looking at various aspects of education. In other words it may be regarded as a general theory of criticism of education. It is a reflective approach to education leading to "wisdom".

4. The main problems of philosophy of education are aims and ideals of education, analysis of pupil's nature, relations of education and state, analysis of knowledge and curriculum, methods of teaching, place of the school in the society, relationship of education to social system, education of religions, etc. Critical evaluation of these from

philosophical point of view constitutes the subject-matter of philosophy of education.

5. Philosophy of education is a rational way to taking decisions in the field of education, a rational process to solving problems. Instead of taking decisions about what to teach, how to teach on *ad hoc* basis without any rationale underlying them, philosophy of education makes it possible to provide sound and reasonable basis.

Determination of educational values of largely, a function of philosophy of education.

How does it Influence the Field of Education

Philosophy of education influences almost all the aspects of a country's educational system. Particularly, it influences the following aspects:

1. Relationship between the State and Education. Depending upon the philosophy a country believes in there are rigidly controlled and free schools. In the totalitarian states the schools have to teach what the state wants with strict discipline and rigid schedule enforced in them. In democratic countries there is ample freedom for the schools.

2. Philosophy of Education Influences the Aims of Education. The aims and ideals of education, too, are determined by the philosophy of education a country believes in. Different philosophies of education have different views on education. A country that tends to believe in the philosophy of idealism will stress on creating a spiritual environment in the school as that pupils develop spiritual values and attain self-realisation. Naturalism will like to see that the child is made to learn from nature in a natural way and realises his potentialities. Pragmatism does not accept any universal or eternal and preconceived aim of education. Like that aims of education are necessarily influenced by the philosophy of education.

3. Philosophy of Education Influences Teaching Methods. Methods of teaching, too, are influenced by the philosophy of education a society adopts. A system of education based on naturalism stresses learning by doing, learning through experience and learning through observation. Societies which tend towards idealism prefer to have a system of education which prescribes rigid methods of teaching such as lecturing and prefer learning through imitation, memorisation and discussion. Pragmatism stresses problem solving and project methods of teaching.

4. Philosophy of Education Influences the Curriculum. What should be taught in the schools is also influenced by the kind of philosophy of education a society supports. Various philosophies of education advocate differing views on curriculum. Naturalism, for example, lays stress on subjects that help in self-expression and self-preservation. It advocates teaching of basic sciences, physical and health education. Idealism emphasises teaching of higher values through ethics, religion, art and subjects of humanities. Pragmatism focusses on child-centred curriculum consisting of activities and based on child's experience.

5. Philosophy of Education Influences Theory and Practice of Discipline Also. The concept of discipline and its practice also are influenced by the philosophy of education. To naturalists discipline is to be learnt by natural consequences. The child enjoys maximum freedom. Self-discipline is preferred to external control. The idealists on the other hand wish to enforce discipline through cultivation of higher values, moral and religious teachings and strict control over the child. In the scheme of the pragmatists, there is no place for punishment and discipline is learnt through moral training which is based child's experience gained through various kinds of school activities and programmes.

In the same way several other aspects such as the place of the child in education, the importance of the teacher, preparation of textbooks, etc., are influenced by the philosophy of education adopted by a system of education.

Influence of Philosophy on Different aspects of Education

1. *Philosophy and Aims of Education.* Every educational system must have some goals, aims or objectives. These act as guides for the educator in educating the child. In fact, we cannot think of any process of education without specific aims and objectives. Bode says, "Unless we have some guiding philosophy in the determination of objectives, we get nowhere at all." These aims of education, in different countries, are determined by the aims and ideals of life which the people of those countries have at that particular time. The aims and ideals of life, in their turn, are determined by the philosophy of the time. It is, therefore, that aims and ideals of education vary with the different philosophers. It is the philosophy of the time which determines whether the aim of education should be moral, vocational, intellectual, liberal or spiritual. In the words of Rusk, "Every system of education must have an aim and the aim of education is relative to the aim of life. Philosophy formulates what should be the end of life while education offers suggestions how this end is to be achieved." The philosopher struggles hard with the mysteries of life and arrives at their solution after mature reflection and thinking. He then suggests ways and means of dealing with them. Thus he lays down ultimate values and explains their significance to the community. In this way, he tries to convert people to his own beliefs and philosophy. These ultimate values, as formulated by the philosopher, become the aims of education for that community. The training of the younger generation, according to those aims and values, then lies on the shoulders of the educator in the field. He selects the material for instruction and determines the methods of procedure for the attainment of those aims. In this way, the entire educational programme proceeds with its foundations on sound philosophy.

2. ***Philosophy and Curriculum.*** Curriculum is the means through which we realise the aims of education. Naturally, therefore, our educational aims determine the curriculum of studies. But aims of education, in their own turn, are determined by philosophy, as we have noted above just now. So we can say that philosophy also determines the curriculum. As is the philosophy so will be the aims of all education and courses of study. Thus they are closely inter-related. It is philosophy and courses of study. Thus they are closely inter-related. It is philosophy which will decide why a particular subject should be included in the curriculum and what particular

discipline that subject will promote. Thus, as Briggs has put it, "It is here (in curriculum) that education seriously needs leaders—leaders who hold a sound comprehensive philosophy, of which they can convince others and who can direct its consistent application to the formulation of appropriate curricula."

It should be clearly noted that curriculum is not fixed for all times. It changes in accordance with the aims of education determined by philosophy. It is, therefore, that curriculum differs with different schools of philosophy, according to their own beliefs. The naturalists advocate the selection of subjects according to the present needs, interests and activities of the child. They insist that adult interference should be reduced to the minimum and that the child should grow up in a free atmosphere. They are, therefore, of the opinion that curriculum should include subjects which are useful for the present life situations, experience and interests of the child. Those subjects must, in no case, be included in which the child is not interested at all. The idealists, on the other hand, approach the problem of curriculum from the point of higher values in life rather than from that of the child or his present needs. Their emphasis is on the experience of human race as a whole. They, therefore, advocate that curriculum should be graded in such a way as may enable that child to march gradually towards self-realisation. The pragmatists emphasise the principle of utility in the choice of subjects. They are of the opinion that only such functional subjects should be included in the curriculum as are useful to the child in the present day world. The curriculum should give knowledge and skills which the child requires for his present as well as future life as an adult. Only that bookish knowledge which stuffs the mind with abstract ideas, is condemned as it does not equip children to face the real problems of life. Instead, curriculum should consist of subjects which may improve the health, vocational efficiency and social fitness of the child. Realists also put greater premium upon the vocational education.

Thus, we conclude that philosophy not only influences the curriculum, it also determines the subjects of study that meet its requirements.

3. ***Philosophy and Text-books.*** Text-books are important instruments, through which the aims of education are realised. In the selection of text-books, therefore, there is as much need of ideals and principles as in the choice of subjects. Those who select text-books, must have a standard of judgement, which should enable them to select the right type of books. This standard is supplied by philosophy.

Again, a good text-book must reflect the prevailing values of life, fixed by philosophy. If it does not, it is out-of-date and inappropriate. An appropriate text-book, therefore, must be according to the accepted ideals of the society as a whole. Then and only then it will be able to serve its desired purpose.

In the case of text-books also, there is difference of opinion among the different schools of philosophy. While the naturalists are in favour of illustrations, pictures and diagrams for capturing the interest of children, the pragmatists are satisfied only with the objective statement of generalisation in a logical order. The idealists, on the other hand with the text-books should reflect the individuality of the author. They are in favour of the subjective presentation of the subject-matter so that there may be interaction of the prosonalities of the author and the reader.

4. ***Philosophy and Methods.*** Method is the procedure through which the aims of education are realised. And as we have already noted, aims of education are subject to the philosophy of life. It is, therefore, that there is close relationship between philosophy and methodology of teaching.

Every philosopher formulates his own methods of teaching, according to his own philosophy. It is, therefore, that different schools of philosophy have laid down their own methods of teaching. The naturalists emphasise the child-centred methods of teaching. They recommend proper motivation and effective use of illustrative aids to capture and maintain the child's interest in the lesson. The idealists believe that teaching is essentially an impact of the teacher's personality on that of the pupil. They recommend discussion method, rote-learning and a meditation in a cordial atmosphere. The pupil is expected to obey his teacher and have full faith in him. The pragmatists advocate that teaching is possible only in a social medium. So they recommend project and problem methods of teaching in which the pupils are engaged in a useful activity of their own choice and interest. Thus, we can say that all the methods of education that have come into vogue, have been the result of one philosophy or the other.

5. *Philosophy and Discipline.* Like curriculum, text-books and methods, discipline, too, reflects the philosophy of life, accepted at a particular time. It is mainly governed by the aim of education. In ancient India when salvation was the chief aim of education, stress was laid on a strict type of discipline. The student was required to lead a life of austerity and self-denial. In medieval ages when despotic system of government was established, a very harsh and strict discipline was advocated and practised. "Spare the rod and spoil the child" was the maxim for the guidance of teachers. In the present age of democracy, however, the concept of discipline is totally different. Whereas in the past, perfect order and silence prevailed in the educational institutions, now we insist on self-government of students and free discipline.

Different schools of philosophy also differ in their concept of discipline. While the idealists are in favour of punishment for maintaining order in the class, the naturalists advocate perfect freedom to the child. They believe in discipline by natural consequences. The pragmatists, on the other hand, emphasise social discipline, which is maintained by the proper direction of the pupil's natural impulses through cooperative activities.

6. *Philosophy and Teacher.* Teacher is the back-bone of the entire process of education. It is, therefore, essential that the teacher's philosophy of life should be in perfect consonance with the philosophy on which the educational system is based. To be a successful teacher, he must know his subject, his pupil, the society and the philosophy of education. A teacher in a Basic school, who has no faith in and no regard for the Gandhian way of life, will never prove to be a successful teacher.

The naturalists insist that the teacher should never interfere with the free activities of children. He is simply to set the educational environment and that is all he is expected to do. Then his role is a negative one. The idealists advocate that the teacher's role should be that of the head of a family. Pupils should be inspired by his personality and develop full faith in him. According to pragmatists, the teacher is not to impose anything on the pupil. He is simply to provide opportunity to his pupils for activity and learning.

7. *Philosophy and Evaluation.* Evaluation is the pivot of educational system. Goals or aims are only cherished desires which decorate the reports of education commission. Curriculum also remain confined to booklets on syllabus. It is evaluation alone which gives an exact idea of what has actually been achieved at the end of a particular period or stage as a result of the teaching-learning experiences, provided in the classroom. Evaluation is also the process of determining the extent to which the aims and objectives are being attained. Again, the maintenance of good educational programmes and the improvement of techniques and procedures of education also require good evaluation. It is, therefore, that there is a close relationship between objectives, learning experiences and evaluation. Object-ship between objectives, learning experiences and evaluation. It is, therefore, legitimate to ascertain how far our evaluation programme is in conformity with the philosophy that has determined the aims and objectives of education, its curriculum and its methodology. It was this judgement that led the educationists in many progressive countries to search for the philosophical analysis which proved very helpful in thrashing out the issue and in overhauling the entire system of examination. The term 'examination' which was mainly based on essay and which measured only the factual knowledge retained by the pupils, was replaced by the new term 'evaluation' which takes into account the growth of the child as a whole individual and in his total environment. It is also this philosophical analysis which is responsible for the movement of objectivity in the field of relationship between philosophy and valuation.

8. *General Impact of Modern Philosophies on Education.* The nineteenth and the twentieth centuries have witnessed a radical change in the educational practices as a result of some common elements in all the modern philosophies. Firstly, education has been psychologised. Instructions have become paedo-centric or child-centred rather than book-centred. Individual differences have been recognised. Secondly, the principles of activity has gained ground. Learning by doing has been the common watch-word. Thirdly, the social discipline has been recognised as a potent factor of educational development. The child is to be trained for community life. Fourthly, democracy has been recognised in most of the developed or developing countries as the guiding factor of educational practices. Fifthly, there has been a metamorphis in the social structure of each country. There is shift of emphasis from rural to urban, joint family to individualism, capitalism to socialism and spiritualism to materialism. New concepts of citizenship, social life and political life have emerged. Westernisation has taken place rapidly, and there is a scientific outlook on all matters of life. There are new business and professional practices. Hence there is need for a new type of education which can meet the existing demands of life. Man is a socialised being, and so the current social philosophies have their bearing or education. To cite one example, the restless adolescents of today cannot be treated in the same nanner as they were treated during the last century. The concept of discipline in education has undergone a radical change.

We can now conclude by saying that philosophy, life and education are intimately linked with one another. For the successful harnessing of education, for the good of life, for the good of individual and for the good of society, it stands in need of direction. This direction is provided exclusively by philosophy, which is the mother of all sciences and to which education is very intimately related. In fact, philosophy and education are two sides of the same coin. While philosophy is the contemplative side, education represents the dynamic side. In the words of Rusk, "From every angle comes a demand for a philosophic basis of education. There is no escape from a philosophy of life and philosophy of education." Education, therefore, is the dynamic side of philosophy. It is an active aspect of philosophical beliefs and a practical means of realising the ideals of life. Without wisdom and philosophy, education is irrelevant. In the words of Whitehead, "Wisdom is the fruit of balanced development. It is this balanced growth of individuality which should be the aim of education to secure....when you understand all about the sun and all about the atmosphere and all about the rotation of the earth, you may still miss the radiance of the sunset."

REALISM IN EDUCATION

Realism was born as a reaction to excessive idealism.

Characteristics of Realistic Education

The chief characteristics of realistic education are given below:

1. ***Emphasis on Present Life of Child.*** The second characteristic of realistic education is to make the present life of child as the focal point of educational system. As we know the fact that Realism was born as a reaction to excessively Idealism, it opposed the academic education of mere ideals and values and emphasized the immediate real and practical problems of day to day living which only can promote individual goods and welfare.

2. ***Based on Science.*** The supporters of Realism emphasised the importance of useful and purposive education. They advocated the inclusion of scientific subjects in the curriculum and in place of academic and artificial education, they laid stress on the natural education which gave birth to Naturalism. Thus, the emphasis on scientific education is the first characteristics of realistic education.

3. ***Emphasis on Experiment and Applied Life.*** The third characteristic of racialistic education is emphasis on experiments, experiences and application of knowledge learnt. It lays great stress on learning by doing, by developing creativity and urge of political work in children so that they are able to solve their immediate practical problems and lead a real successful life.

4. ***Opposition of Bookish Knowledge.*** Realists decry mere academic, theoretical and bookish knowledge which develops only rote memory and encourages cramming. It does not enable the child to understand the realities of external things and natural phenomena. According to Realists, education should inculcate in the child an understanding of both the thing and the environment. Thus, the slogan of realistic education is 'Not words but things'. Such type of education promotes intelligence and a sense of judgement which the bookish education does not do.

5. *Emphasis on Training of Senses.* The sixth characteristic of realistic education is to train and develop the senses of child. Unlike Idealists who impose knowledge from above, Realists advocate self-learning through senses which ought to be trained. These senses are the gateways of knowledge and develop by use and experience.

6. *Limited Freedom of Child.* Realistic education realises the prime importance of child. Hence, according to Realists the child should be given full freedom to develop his self according to his innate tendencies. But this freedom should promote self-discipline and self-control. In other words, the child should proceed from ignorance to knowledge slowly but surely through his own efforts and self-discipline.

7. *Equal Importance of Individuality and Sociability.* The seventh characteristic of realistic education is to emphasize equally the individuality and sociability of the child. Thus, the aim of realistic education is to develop both the individual self and the society of which he is an integral part. Bacon clearly asserts that realistic education develops the individual on the one hand and on the other hand tries to develop society through the development of social consciousness and sense of service of the individual.

Aims of Education

The following are the aims of realistic education:

1. *Preparing the Child for a Happy and Successful Life.* The first aim of realistic education is to prepare the child to lead a successful and happy life. Thus, education should be such that the child is able to love his problems of life successfully and lead a happy life promoting the welfare of society as well.

2. *Preparing the Child for a Real Life.* The second aim of realistic education is to prepare the child for a real and practical life. Realists believe in the reality of knowledge of external material world gained through senses. Thus, they wish to prepare the child for the real life of material world.

3. *Developing the Physical and Mental Powers of Child.* According to Realism, mind as well as the physical organs together constitute an organism composed of matter. Hence, according to this ideology, the third aim of education is to develop the physical and mental powers of the child so that with the help of his developed intelligence, discrimination and judgement, he is able to solve all the problems of life successfully.

4. *Imparting Vocational Education.* According to Realism, education should be of practical utility of child. Since the problem of livelihood is main problem of life these days, so according to this ideology, the sixth aim of education is to provide vocational education to the child.

5. *Developing and Training of Senses.* Resists believe that unless the senses of the child are developed fully well, he will not be able to have full knowledge about the external world. Thus, the fourth aim of realistic education is to develop and train the senses of the child through varied experiences.

6. *Acquainting the Child with Nature and Social Environment.* According to Realism, a child is related both to the external Nature and the social environment. Hence, the aim of education is to provide the child full knowledge of both the society and the external Nature so that he is able to strike a balance between the two.

Curriculum

Realists insisted that only those subjects and activities should be included in the curriculum which prepare children for actual day to day living. Accordingly, considering the real situations, conditions and circumstances of the present day life of human beings, realists emphasised to give prime place to Nature, Science and vocational subjects whereas secondary place to Arts, Literature and Languages. It is to be noted that Realists have recommended about thirty subjects for the curriculum. They have also advocated free choosing by the children from among these subjects. At the same time they have made clear that teaching of mother-tongue is the foundation of all development and vocational subjects which are essential for livelihood. Hence, the essential subjects in the curriculum should be language and vocational subjects.

Methods of Teaching

Traditional system of education gave to the child only bookish knowledge which was purely academic and wordy. Hence, it failed to prepare the child for real life. Realists changed that system of teaching to gaining knowledge through senses according to the child's nature and capacity by way of observation and experience. Emphasising that objects are real, the Realists insisted to impart knowledge of objects and external phenomena through senses. In their opinion, objects should be first shown and allowed to be handled if need be arise and then only they be interpreted and explained to the child.

Bacon, the famous Realist introduced the inductive method in the process of education. According to this method the object is shown to the child first and then its interpretation is done. In addition to this, the child does his own observation, experimentation and derives conclusions. In short, the child does self-learning to a great extent by employing inductive method.

Milton advocated learning by travelling. John Locke also spoke of tours, observation and learning by experience as powerful means of education. Some Realists also propounded many maxims of teaching which discourage rote memorisation and prescribed instead learning by observation and experience.

Role of Teacher

The role of teacher according to Realists is neither as high and important as the Idealists advocate nor so negligible as the Naturalists speak out, it is fairly important. The teacher, according to Realists, is expected to have full knowledge of the content and the needs of children. Not only this, he must also be capable to present before children the content in a clear and intelligible way by employing psychological and scientific methods. It is the duty of teacher to tell children about scientific discoveries, researches and inventions by others in various fields of knowledge. He himself should also be engaged in some research work on experimentation. At the same time he must inspire children to undertake wide and close observation and experimentation themselves so that they are able to find out new facts. Not only this, the teacher must understand well the amount of knowledge to be provided to each child at a specific time.

Discipline

Realists emphasise moral and religious education of the child. For this type of education, discipline is essential and a pre-requisite condition. But what type of discipline? The upholders of this ideology decry repressibilities discipline. They advocate self-discipline to effect smooth adjustment of the child with external environment, the teacher only inspiring and encouraging sympathetically. According to Coummnis the school should be like the lap of mother full of affection, love and sympathy. In short, Realists advocate a synthetic form of impressionistic and emancipator forms of discipline.

School Management

Realists have different views about school. Some Realists do not feel any need of school at all. They prescribe wide travelling, tours and teaching by private tutors as the best means of education. On the contrary, other Realists emphasise the importance of school and class teaching. They regard school as a mirror of society reflecting its true state of affairs. As such, the school should not only include, in its work, all the activities going on in society, but it should also be well-furnished and equipped with all the necessary aids and device for effective observation and experimentations by children. According to them, the school is an agency which meets the needs of the child and the demands of society as well. Insert, it is school only which provides for the fullest development of the child according to his nature and needs.

PRINCIPLES OF REALISM

The principles of realism are as follows:

Material World is True. This philosophy considers materialistic world as true which we see directly. Moor has said, "Existence is perceiving." This world is a combination of matters. Matter is true. It is real. Therefore this world is also real. Spiritual world is thought-oriented, thus it is unreal. Soul and God is a figment of imagination and mind is just a thing of the world.

Man is Supreme. Realism considers man as the supreme creature of the material world. The ultimate aim of life is to live a peaceful life after acquiring the knowledge of things.

Universe is not External. Realists believe that universe is not external. There is law that governs the universe and the law is supreme since it is through this law and order that cohesion prevails.

Emphasis on Present Life. Realism lays emphasis on the present life and behavioural (practical) aspect of man. It opposes the ideals. It has no concern with the ideals and rules of past and future.

Senses are the Gateway of Knowledge. According to realism whatever sensation we get while coming in contact with objects through our senses is the only reality. This philosophy considers senses as the gateway of knowledge. We receive knowledge by seeing, smelling, touching and tasting. This knowledge is real.

Realism and Philosophy

Metaphysics. This world is made of many materials. Material world is true and real. It is directly visible to us. Whatever is beyond this is unreal. Soul and God is a figment of imagination. Matter is dynamic. Mind is matter-oriented.

Axiology. Realism believes in the material-oriented world. Realists search for beauty in the natural beauty. They have no faith on eternal values, because they consider spiritual world as a figment of imagination. They believe that beauty is the reflection of nature. They stress on the practical aspect of the present. Man is the maker of his destiny. It does not believe in the pre-determined values.

Epistemology. Realists consider senses as the gateway of knowledge. This material world is real because it has existence, this existence is felt through senses. Therefore, it is real and true.

Realism and Aims of Education

Realism recommends the following aims of Education:

Preparation for Real Life. The aim of realistic education should be such that the child is able to solve his problems of life successfully and lead a happy life. Realists believe in the reality of knowledge of external material world gained through senses. They want to prepare the child for the real life of material world. Spencer recommends, 'complete living' as the aim of education.

Training of Senses. The aim of education is to develop and train the senses of the child through varied experiences. Realists believe that unless the senses of the child are developed fully well, he will not be able to have full knowledge about the external world.

Physical and Mental Development. Aim of education is to develop the physical and mental powers of the child so that with the help of his developed intelligence, discrimination and judgement, he is able to solve all the problems of life successfully.

Social Development. To ralism, a child is related both to the external nature and social environment. The aim of education is to provide the child full knowledge of both the society and the external nature so that he is able to keep a balance between the two. Aim of education is the social development of the child.

Scientific Outlook. Realism considers the 'development of scientific attitude' as an important aim of education. It aims at the development of the habit of reasoning, independent thinking and judgement among the pupils.

Vocational Development. Realism lays emphasis on material comforts and facilities. Attainment of material happiness is possible through a vocation. Therefore, we must make a child self-sufficient by developing vocational skills in him so that he may live a happy life by fulfilling his needs.

Realism and Curriculum

Curriculum is a means of realising the aims of education. Realists insisted that only those subjects and activities should be included in the curriculum which prepare children for actual day to day living. Accordingly, considering the real situations, conditions and circumstances of the present day life of human beings, realists emphasised to give prime place to Nature, Science and vocational subjects whereas secondary place to Arts, Literature and Languages. Knowledge must be given through the medium of mother tongue so that the child is in a position to solve his daily life problems and make his life happy. Hence the essential subjects in the curriculum should be language and vocational subjects.

Realism and Teacher

Realism recognises the teacher but does not attach much importance to the personality of the teacher like Idealism. The teacher is supposed to put the facts as they are in their real form. He should present the knowledge in an effective and intelligible way. He should create opportunities for observation and experimentation. He should be well versed in the psychological methods, techinques and skills of teaching. Realists insist upon the training of teachers before they engage themselves in the teaching work in an effective way.

Realism and Methods of Teaching

The realism is opposed to the traditional methods of teaching. Realists stress the use of objective and scientific techniques. They support inductive-deductive experimentation, tours, self-experiences, use of audio-visual aids and other methods of teaching. In their opinion objects should be first shown and allowed to be handled if need be and then only they be interpreted and explained to the child.

This encouraged the use of audio-visual aids in education. They are the supporters of correlation method.

Realism and Discipline

Realism emphasises moral and religious education of the child. For this type of education, discipline is essential condition. Realists advocate self-discipline to effect smooth adjustment of the child with external environment with the teacher only inspiring and encouraging sympathetically. To Comenius the school should be like the lap of mother full of affection, love and sympathy. They advocate a synthetic form of impressionistic and emancipatory discipline.

Realism and School

According to Comenius, 'schools are true foregoing places of men'. Realists emphasise the importance of school and class teaching. They regard school as a mirror of society reflecting its true state of affairs. School should also be well furnished and equipped with all the necessary aids and devices for effective observation and experimentations by children. According to them, the school is an agency which meets the needs to the child and the demand of society. It is school only which provides for the fullest development of the child according to his nature and needs. Not only this, school is the only agency to provide vocational education to prepare the child for some livelihood.

Contribution of Realism in Education

Aims. Vocational efficiency is an important aim of realism which is relevant even to-day.

Curriculum. Realism gave a comprehensive curriculum and attached great importance to science which is approriate in the present age.

Method. Realists emphasised inductive method. They advocate the principle of correlation between various subjects.

Discipline. They advocate a synthetic form of impressionistic and emancipatory forms of dicipline.

Student. They give important place to student.

School. They accept the necessity of school.

Teacher. Teacher should have full knowledge of the content and the needs of children.

Evaluation of Realism

- Realism accepts the real needs and real feeling only. It does not believe in imagination, intense emotion and sentiments. These also are the realities and genuine needs of the individuals.
- Realism emphasises scientific subjects to the neglect of arts and literature. This is creating imbalance in the total curriculum.
- It gives undue importance to the need of material world and neglects spiritual world.
- Realism emphasises exclusively on facts and realities of life. It does not give any importance to ideals and values. Denial of ideals and values often creates helplessness and pessimism which retard growth and development of the individual.

CONTRIBUTIONS OF NATURALISM IN MODERN EDUCATIONAL THOUGHT

Although no system of education in the world may be found such as wholly operating according to the tenets of the philosophy of Naturalism, yet education in general throughout the world has been greatly influenced by it. In a sense the contributions made by naturalism to education are many. Some of the most important of these are as follows:

1. Paidocentric Movement. A natural consequence of the philosophy was that education was made paidocentric, *i.e.*, child-centred. It constantly emphasised the nature of the child as the focal point of all aspects of education. The child was put in the forefront and all other things such as the educator, the books, the curriculum, the school, etc. were thrown into the background. This tendency was called by John Adams as the paidocentric tendency in education. This conception emphasised that education is not preparation for life but life itself. Children should live like children and enjoy life. Education should be guided by the nature of the child. They take it for granted that the child is basically good. Rousseau himself said, "Eveything is good as it comes from the hands of the Author of Nature, but everything degenerates in the hands of men." The child is good, but he should be protected from a degrading environment. The child is desirable for his won sake. He should not be burdened with restrictions and made miserable. Allow him to develop naturally. These views constitute an important contribution of naturalism to education.

2. Education was Psychologised. This was another contribution made by the naturalists to education. When the naturalists stressed the nature and the natural development of the child, they immediately entered into the arena of psychology as it raised the question 'what is child's nature, what is natural development, and so on'. Thus, a psychological tendency was developed in education which forced educators to view every aspect of education from psyschological point of view. It was emphasised that education must study the nature of the child and should adapt itself to this nature. Rousseau may be considered the pioneer for introducing the psychological tendency in education. He was the first person among the naturalists to say that education should follow the child's nature. Rousseau's ideas were, then, put into practice by Pestalozzi, Herbert, Froebel and several other educators. This emphasis in education generated a lot of new ideas and approaches in the field of education. Research in child psychology gained momentum. Educational psychology assumed greater importance. Methods of teaching and curriculum construction began to be considered from psychological point of view. McDougall made valuable contributions to child psychology. Psychology of individual differences came into prominence. It was considered desirable to make education flexible in view of specific differences in the nature of children. Psychoanalysis assumed still greater importance by bringing unconscious nature of the child into the picture.

3. Playway Method of Teaching. Naturalism made a very great contribution to teaching method at the early stages of education. Playway method was exclusively the contribution of naturalism. Even this method is considered important by educationists. The psychology of playway method was made explicit by Rousseau and several other naturalists. It was emphasised that all learning should take place in the spirit and by the method of play. Play reveals the child's nature most clearly. It is considered nature's mode of education. To James S. Ross "Playway in its manifold forms in the outstanding general method of creative education and it is essentially naturalistic." It is a method of teaching which includes all methods of learning which foster the spirit of joyous spontaneous creative activity. Playway method has become the ideal of all infant schools. Montessori, Froebel and A.S. Neill developed methods of educating children which prominently use playway method of teaching-learning. In fact invention of playway method was a great contribution of naturalists to education.

4. Principle of Self-Education. This was another contribution to education made by naturalism. Rousseau's negative education was another name for child's self-education. He emphasised that it is child's natural development which should form the basis of child's education. For natural development self-education was the only means. The naturalistic educator should leave the child to himself. He should be there to only observe the child, not to give him knowledge or information. He should only provide an environment in which the child undergoes certain experiences and learns through them on his own.

5. Principle of Direct Experience of Things. Learning by doing or learning one's own experience is considered important even today. This was first emphasised by the naturalist philosophers. Rousseau said, "Give your scholar no verbal lesson; he should be taught by experience alone." Direct observation of things around and direct contact with the persons of object were considered important for this reason. It was stressed that science, instead of being taught through lectures, should be taught through experimentation in the laboratory; Geometry by actual measurement of the places around and geography by taking the pupils to various parts of the country. Similarly, the child should be taught concepts of responsibilities, duties and obligations by direct experience of social life. For this reason it was insisted that the schools should have practice of self-government in which students can participate and learn through their own experience, self-discipline, self-control and self-regulation.

In this way the naturalists were responsible for most of the revolutionary ideas in the field of education that are accepted widely even today.

"NATURALISM" AS A PHILOSOPHY OF EDUCATION

Naturalism has been described to have three forms *(a)* Naturalism of physical science which has little to contribute to education, *(b)* Mechanical naturalism which regards man as a machine and has given us the behaviourist psychology, and *(c)* Biological naturalism which is founded on the notion of evolution and is most important of all forms of naturalism. The materialistic explanation of the word was the ground of naturalism in education. According to naturalism the ultimate reality is nature which is material. The naturalists are empiricists and believe that all knowledge is acquired through sense organs. They believe in living according to nature. "Follow nature" is their slogan. Be natural is their motto. They hold that nature has made all persons different. The most important modern naturalist thinkers are Rousseau, Bacon, Hobbes and Herbert Spencer.

1. Naturalists View on Aims of Education. According to Rousseau education means "natural development of organs and powers of the child". He said child's first education should be negative which means avoiding teaching of virtue or truth to him. He was against imparting any education to the child in early years of life. Development of body, development and strengthening of every part of the body and making the child grow healthy and strong was considered the most important aim of education during infancy. Then, developing child's sense organs and personality were considered important during childhood and adolescence. Development of emotions and sentiments leading to development of moral and social qualities including religious sentiment was emphasised at the level of the youth between 15 to 20 years. Thus the aim of education according to Rousseau was bodily, sensory, mental, social and moral development of the individual. Herbert Spencer (1820-1903) another modern naturalist, in his book '*Education*' enumerated the following aims of education:

1. Self-preservation which means growth and development of both the body and the mind.
2. Earning a living.
3. Upbringing of children which means making the students successful parents in future.
4. Development of citizenship through scientific study of history.
5. Teaching the individuals how to utilise their leisure time by teaching them painting, music, sculpture, poetry, recreation.

And all these subsidiary aims must ultimately aim at "preparing the child for complete living".

2. Views on Curriculum. Rousseau was against any kind of curricular teaching or learning upto twelfth year of life. He was against any kind of verbal lesson on history, geography, or even language. He was also against teaching of morality. This was his concept of negative education which suggested that child's mind should not be stuffed with information of different kinds. So he objected to the use of any text-books for education of the young child. Giving to the child a chance to learn everything through direct experience and observation is what was stressed by him by way of child's curriculum. Even morality was to be learnt by the child through natural consequences of his own action. Thus, upto the childhood stage no curriculum of any kind was needed. Formal curriculum consisting of education in natural science, language, mathematics, woodwork, music, painting, social life, and some kind of professional training was suggested to be introduced at the adolescence stage. Rousseau, however, said that books do not give knowledge, they only train one to talk. So he emphasised that curriculum for adolescence should be based on active work than on books. The youth should, however, by taught history, mythological stories and religious stories with stress on moral and religious education. Spencer also, like Rousseau prescribed the formula of returning to nature as the basis of all learning. Providing an environment, to him, was enough of the curriculum. Learning by consequences was considered enough, although he said that in case of dangerous consequences the child should be fore warned. In order to realise the aim of complete living Herbert Spencer prescribed physical education which was considered necessary for good health. In the words of Monroe Rousseau was the first person who proclaimed that "education finds its purpose, its process, its means wholly within the child life and the child experiences".

3. Views on Method of Teaching. Rousseau was against the oral and theoretical methods of teaching which was pursued in his time. Instead he recommended playway method of teaching learning. Real education to him was self-education acquired through experience and observation. Two great principles of teaching which he stressed were *(i)* learning through self-experience and *(ii)* learning by doing. Naturalism, thus, stands for a kind of teaching which is not dependent so much on schools and books, as on the "manipulation of the actual life of the educaned". Its watchword is "Back to Nature". Herbert Spencer was the naturalist who enunciated several principles of teaching such as:

(i) Proceeding from easy to difficult situations and experiences.

(ii) Proceeding from indefinite (vague) to definite (clear) meaning; thereby that the teacher should make child's knowledge which is vague, clear and definite.

(iii) Proceeding from known to unknown which means the new experience to be given should follow the one which the child has already undergone.

(iv) Conforming to the stages of development which means that the method of teaching should be suitable from the point of view of the characteristics of child's development. For very young children playway is the most suitable method.

(v) Proceeding from concrete to abstract which means concrete things and experiences should be presented first and abstract ones after them.

(vi) Proceeding from experimental to rational knowledge. It means that the child should, first, be allowed to experiment with things around. This will prepare him to acquire and retain rational knowledge given in books.

(vii) Create interest in learning by using audio-visual aids, charts, diagrams etc., in order to concretise knowledge.

Thus, playway, experience and experimentation are the most desirable characteristics of teaching method according to naturalists.

4. Views on the Place of the Child in Education. In Naturalist child is the measure of all things, the centre around which revolves every aspect of education. Naturalists' view of the child is very close to that of Wordsworth who said 'child comes from heaven trailing clouds of glory'. They are interested in the child as he is rather than as he will be. To them adult standards of behaviour are not at all important for being followed by the child. They conceive of childhood as something desirable for its own sake and expect children to be children before they become men and women. Hence, they abhor all kinds of restrictions to be imposed on children in schools. They recommend that the natural powers and inclinations of the child should be allowed to develop freely with a minimum of guidance. The naturalistic educators allow the child to follow the lines of his natural interests and to have free choice of activities with no interference or thwarting. No knowledge, no development of any kind (social, moral or religious) should be forced on the child. "These the child will forgo for himself. He knows better what he should learn, when and how he should learn it" (James S. Ross). Rousseau's negative education advised to leave the child largely to himself.

5. Views on Discipline. Discipline, according to Rousseau, is learnt by the child as a consequence of his actions. It cannot be imposed on him by the teacher. Naturalists did not support the idea of punishing the child for ensuring discipline. Rousseau said that consequence of child's action was enough and natural punishment. Oral teaching of morality through lectures and preachings was against the naturalistic philosophy. Left to himself the child will learn better discipline. This was their belief. Rousseau and Spencer both had the same views. In fact Rousseau's conception of education was it is "the process of development into an enjoyable, rational, harmoniously balanced, useful and hence natural life".

IDEALISM AND ITS CONTRIBUTIONS

Man has two facts—Spiritual and Material. When the emphasis is on the realisation of spiritual life, it is called idealism.

Idealism is the oldest theory of philosophy. It reflects in the complete history of philosophy. It is born out of Plato's 'Theory of Ideas'. According to this, the ultimate supermacy is of ideas. The word idealism has been derived from the word idea. It should be taken as that of ideas and not to be confused with philosophy of ideals. Plato and other idealism philosophers believed that only ideas are permanent. Idealism holds that the essential nature of man is spiritual which is revealed in mental, religious and aesthetic areas. To them spiritual world is more important than material world. This spiritual world is a world of ideas and feelings. To idealists 'Mind and Soul' are more important rather than Matter and Body. These ideas are eternal and unchanging.

The important definitions regarding idealism are as follows:

According to **Dutta,** "Idealism holds that ultimate reality is spiritualism."

According to **Ross,** "To Idealistic Philosophy spirit is the essential world stuff and true reality is of a mental character."

Supporters of Idealism. Protagonists of idealism are Plato, Socrates, Kant, Hegal, Green, Gentile, Vivekanand, Mahatma Gandhi and Dayanand.

Idealism and Philosophy

Metaphysics. Idealism is concerned with the Natue of Reality. For Idealist Ultimate Reality is of the Nature of Mind. Universe is the idea of the division of reality. The visible universe does not exist of itself, its existence depends upon the real world of mind or spirit. Spiritual world is the reality and true. Man is different from other creatures due to his spiritual power. Man is the grandest creation of God.

Epistemology. For Idealists truth can exist only in the 'Real world of Ideas'. To arrive at truth man uses the methods of reasoning and intuition and through his mind trascends his physical impressions and gets some insight into the real world. Through logic and reason man discovers the pre-existent truths of the physical world and gains some insight into the ultimate truths of the world of ideas.

Axiology. Idealism believes in Truth, Goodness and Beauty. These values are eternal and permanent. To this philosophy God is truth, beautiful and good. It emphasises faith in God, character building, social responsibilities and other values.

Fundamental Principles of Idealism

Fundamental Principles of Idealism are as follows:

- Idealists believe that spiritual world is real and the ultimate truth whereas the material world is transitory and mortal.
- They hold that the order of the world is due to the manifestation in space and time of an eternal and spiritual reality.
- To them, ideas are the ultimate reality. They are eternal and unchanging.

- To idealists man is more important than material nature. It is because man can think and experience about meterial objects.
- The spiritual or cultural environment is an environment of man's own making. It is a product of man's creative activity.
- Idealism believes in spiritual values. They are Truth, Beauty and Goodness. The realisation of these values is the realisation of God.
- Idealists give full support to the principle of unity in diversity.
- To them God is the Supreme Force which is omnipotent and omnipresent.
- Idealists insist upon the fullest development of the personality of an individual. Human personality is of supreme value and constitutes the noblest work of God.

Idealism and Aims of Education

The following are the aims of education according to the philosophy of Idealism:

Self-realisation. Idealism considers self-realization as an important aim of education. Self-realisation involves full knowledge of the self. The aim of education is to enable man to become his truest self. Human personality is of supreme value and constitutes the noblest work of God. Every individual life has got the possibility of becoming a perfect pattern after his own self.

According to **Ross,** "The aim of education is the exhaltation of personality or self-realisation, the making actual or real the highest potentialities of the self."

Spiritual Development. To idealism the aim of education is to develop the child mentally, morally and spiritually, Teacher should so organise education as to develop the child spiritually. To them truth, beauty and goodness should be encouraged more and more. The more an individual realises these ideals the more spiritually enlightened he will be.

Character Formation. To develop morality in man is an important aim of education. Man is essentially a moral being. Idealism emphasises character building and character formation. The process of education must lead to the deepest spiritual insight to the highest moral and spiritual conduct.

Preservation and Enrichment of Cultural Heritage. To idealists the aim of education is to acquaint the child with the cultural heritage so that he conserves, promotes and tansmits it to the next generation. Our cultural heritage is of great value and worth. This cultural treasure belongs to the whole humanity and it is the purpose of education to preserve, develop and transmit it in all corners of the world.

Preparation for Holy Life. To Froeblel "The object of education is the realisation of a faithful, pure and holy life." Idealists uphold that education should create such conditions and provide an environment which are conducive to the development of spiritual values in a child. Good ideals will lead a child towards self-realisation and prepare him for a holy life.

Intellectual and Physical Development. The aim of education is to ensure the intellectual development and rationality of the child so that he may develop his innate and creative powers and thereby achieve his goal and seek adjustment with the environment. The aim of education is to ensure physical development of the child also. Sound mind lives in a sound body. Physically developed students can easily achieve their goals of life.

To Develop the Feeling of Integrity. Idealists give full support to the principle of unity in diversity. They believe that implicit in all the diversities is an essential unity. This implicit unifying factor is of spiritual nature. The underlying divine force is God which is omnipotent and omnipresent. On the basis of caste, sex, colour and religion there are differences in the society, but God is present in all humanity. Feeling of unity is developed among the students through education.

Universalisation of Education. Idealism is in favour of universalisation is of education so that an ideal society may be established. Every child must have an access to education. In idealistic society, no exception should be made in the education of children. It should be universal because all human beings are equally the children of God.

Development of Moral Values. The aim of education is to develop morality in students. Education should develop the will power of the child so that he may be able to follow the good and avoid evil. This power can be developed by the correct appreciation of truth, goodness and beauty which are the highest moral values.

Idealism and Curriculum

Idealistic curriculum is thought-oriented and it stresses on those subjects which are related to the spiritual world. It provides for the training and cultivation of moral, intellectual and aesthetic activities.

For the asethetic and moral development Herbart gave prime importance to subjects like history, fine-art, music, poetry, ethics and religion.

For intellectual development of the child literature, language, science, social studies and mathematics are included in the curriculum.

Ross holds the view that man can develop spiritually only when he is physically fit and healthy. This philosophy insists on a sound mind in a sound body. It is essential to keep the body in a proper working order through physical activities. Hence this philosophy insists subjects related to care of body and skills, intellectual, moral, aesthetic and religious activities in the curriculum.

B.B. Bogoslovasky in his 'Ideal School' has given the new scheme of Idealistic curriculum construction as follows:

The first is the universe division an enlarged science department in which students study the inanimate forces of nature, the origin of our solar system, the development of life and the entire background of human drama, the second section deals with the civilisation division which offers an inclusive study of social sciences. By civilisation means all the activities, achievements and institutions of humanity which control our environment, and provide the necessities of life. Security and comfort, food, clothing, shelter, technology, communication and government are all within the field of civilisation. 'Culture Division' includes philosophy, art, literature, religion etc. The fourth is the 'personality division' which offers study of physical, physiological, emotional, and intellectual factors that shape and determine the human personality.

Nature of Idealistic Curriculum is cleared through the following Chart:

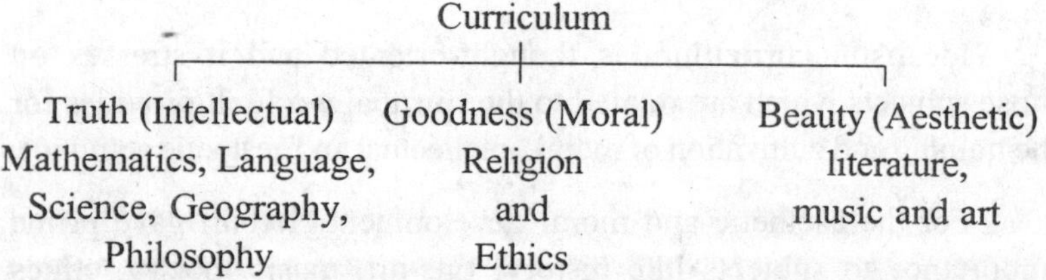

In nut shell we can say that idealistic curriculum insists on values and ideals.

(a) It gives more importance to religion, ethics music and art.

(b) This curriculum is thoughtful-centred curriculum. In this only those subjects have been emphasised which are helpful in the personality development.

(c) This curriculum lays more importance to those subjects which reflect the achievements of human culture and civilisation.

(d) It includes the subjects relating to social, spiritual, intellectual, moral, religious and aesthetic activities.

(e) According to Horne "Information will become knowledge, books will become tools and best ideas will become ideals."

Idealism and Methods of Teaching

The ultimate goal of the teacher is the attainment of the aim(s) of education for his pupils. Therefore, whichever method is appropriate should be practised. After all, method is a means and not the end. Teaching methods should be chosen according to the nature of ends and means. The teachers have also to put their maximum efforts in formulating the aims. They should select any method keeping in view the content or nature of learner, or the educational objectives.

Idealists consider themselves creators and determinators of method, not devoters of someone method. An idealist has adopted different methods according to the needs such as Socrates followed Question method, Plato developed Dialectic method, Aristotle initiated Deductive-Inductive method, Hegel followed Instruction method and so on.

Most of the idealists considered Lecture, Discussion and Questioning as the best methods of teaching.

Froebel developed the methodology of play which is known as kindergarten. He regards the school as garden and the teacher as a gardener, whose main function is to tend the little human plants under his charge, very carefully, and thus help them to grow to beauty and perfection.

There is a regulated and directed freedom for teachers in Idealistic methods of teaching. A teacher remains active, in teaching. To Butler, "An Idealist teacher is the creator and determinator of independent teaching method. He is not slave of any method." Idealism has advised the teacher to follow the method of teaching according to his convenience. To Horn, "The aim of teacher is to develop the personality of the child. For fulfilling this aim, the teacher should select the teaching method." Teaching methods followed by Idealistic philosophy are as follows:

Question Method. Socrates followed Question method. In this method effort is made to draw out right answer from the students by putting questions.

Dialectic Method. Plato developed dialectic method to develop the knowledge of the students.

Deductive and Inductive Method. Aristotle initiated inductive and deductive method. Today this method occupies an important place in teaching learning.

Lecture Method. This method is followed to enrich the knowledge of the students.

Kindergarten Method. Froebel developed this method. It is used for small children. It is known as Play Method. It is essential for the physical and spiritual development of the child.

Text-Book Method. In this method more emphasis is given on the reading of text-books.

Instruction Method. Hegel followed this method wherein teacher gives instructions to the students.

Discussion Method. Teacher and students discover the truth through discussion method.

Imitation Method. This method is followed in Gurukul. In case of imitation the teacher sets before students some models and directs them to observe and try to reproduce them. The pupils are expected to follow the examples of great personalities and imbibe some of their good qualities.

Drill and Repetition Method. Pestalozzi advocated practice and repetition method in order to evaluate the knowledge of the students.

Idealism and Discipline

Idealism believe that there can be no spiritual development of the child without discipline. They give importance to impressionistic discipline in comparison to repressionistic discipline. They assert that the teacher should gain respect from the child by his affectionate and sympathetic behaviour and then motivate him by his praiseworthy ideals. Idealist believe in guided freedom and strict discipline. Children must endure a restraint on freedom. Self insight and self analysis are the main disciplinary factors. Teacher's guidance is essential. The discipline is not to be imposed on pupils. The teacher has only to help them to develop self-discipline through that self-knowledge. To them freedom is not means but it is an end. Idealists are the supporters of self-discipline. They are not in favour of militant discipline. They want to combine humility, courtesy, obedience and subordination in discipline. This approach signifies effective discipline.

Idealism and Student

Idealists have imagined an ideal student. To Bogoslovasky, "The student is a finite person, growing, when properly educated into the image of an infinite person." Idealists give more importance to thoughts and secondary place to student in the educational process. They consider a child under the control of the teacher. Teacher is the maker of his destiny. A student must obey his teacher. The order of his teacher is supreme for him and he must follow it. Other directions may be ignored. A student must have qualities like respect towards his teacher. The relationship between teacher and taught must be positive and congenial.

Idealism and Teacher

According to **Gentile,** 'Teacher is a spiritual symbol of right conduct'. Teacher leads a child toward absolute perfection. That is why he is considered as pilot of God in perfecting man. He provides to the child the knowledge of his cultural heritage. He is the priest of man's spiritual heritage. He tells the child the way to reach God. He is a living ideal. Children imitate him. His personality therefore must be ideal. He acts as a friend, philosopher and guide.

According to **Aurobindo,** "The first principle of true teaching is that nothing can be taught. The teacher is not instructor or task master; he is helper and guide. His business is to suggest and guide and not to impose. He does not impart knowledge to him; he shows him how to acquire knowledge for himself. In idealistic philosophy the teacher has a very important role to play in education as he has to lead the pupil from darkness to light and he has to help him in development of his personality.

Idealism and School

School is a place where the capacities of logical thinking, reasoning and evaluating of the child are progressively sublimated and developed by the teacher. According to Idealism spiritual ideals and values are achieved through proper guidance of teacher given in school.

- Idealists lay more emphasis on the inner aspect of the school and less on its building.
- Such schools are based on ideal principles.
- Idealism incorporates the principle of simple living and high thinking.
- Idealism has imagined such an ideal school where a child is equipped with spiritual and human qualities.

They want to develop in child love for the nation, humanism, love of God and religion through school.

Contribution of Idealism to Education

Idealism has contributed to education in the following ways:

(a) Aims. Idealism emphasises individual and social aims of education. It gives importance to the aim of self-realisation which leads the child towards perfection and enables him to realise the self.

(b) Teacher. Idealism has emphasised the position of teacher as Guru. The teacher has been described as a living ideal and co-worker with God. He humanises the child and develops high ideals and values in him.

(c) Child. Idealists want to develop eternal values in the child so that he may become an ideal human being.

(d) Curriculum. Idealism paves the way for the construction of a systematic curriculum.

(e) Discipline. Idealism stresses on self-discipline. Idealists want to develop child's personality through discipline.

HUMANISM

Humanism implies both a human and a humane approach to educational problems, human in the sense that human nature (including likes, dislikes, interests, aptitudes etc.) should not be suppressed by religion in favour of an ascetic ideal and a narrow dogmatic interpretation of the world; humane in the sense that the nature of the child and its growing mind should not be suppressed by cruel discipline, teachers and rigid methods of teaching.

Humanism is a revolt against theology, society and dogma.

In simpler words we can say that when human world and human being become the concern of philosophy the result is humanism.

It also means studies of humanities.

It also means reasonable balance of life.

It is a philosophy, the centre of whose study is man. Man is the measure of everything.

Implications in Education

The aims of humanistic education are:

(i) ***Broadly Educated Man.*** To produce a broadly educated man possessing a well rounded personality who could assume leadership in society and state.

(ii) ***Accomplishments.*** To produce men who should have a wide range of accomplishments. They should be able to express themselves in poetry, song, dance etc. All men should be physically and mentally healthy.

Jacks says that according to Humanists human perfection must be final objective.

Curriculum

The main tenet of humanism, *i.e.,* education for all and child is the centre of all education and the broad aims of education reflect on the type of curriculum. Hans says that the humanistic curriculum had in it the 'real' studies so that those could light the minds of children since it was the pupil who came first or got priority—method and theory later.

(i) Accordingly, curriculum included the study of old classics of Greeks and Romans since early humanists considered these to possessing profundity of content, literary style etc. and they believed that all the values such as wide leraning, all round development, life of action, qualities of artistic enjoyment could be achieved by teaching Greek and Roman literature. In comparison with literature and classics, they gave slight attention to mathematics, natural history, music etc. and much less attention was given by them to the vernaculars in their curriculum. They believed that if history and ethics is to be studied—we should study those as a part of the work of the old classical writers.

(ii) Training for Good Manners such as modesty was also stressed.

(iii) Physical Education was also included in their curriculum and there was due place for it. It aimed at producing a new brave class of people.

Academician J.B. Florin and his Humanistic Curriculum. In the 18th century Florin asserted, "Philosophy and the sciences ought to be made the principal study of young persons." He classified all subjects of instruction into three groups: *(i)* Relation of man to nature, *(ii)* Relation of man to himself, and *(iii)* Relation of man to other men.

He advised a ten years course for the ages seven to seventeen presuming that the boys would enter his academy with a fair knowledge of writing and reading. The subjects included all branches of mathematics, history, applied sciences for the first group; Latin, French, Italian, Grammar, Rhetoric, poetry, drawing, music and exercise for the second group; History, politics, economics and biography for the third group.

Method of Teaching

(i) It was Erasmus who had left in writing about the method. He had tried the old methods in teaching literature and he told us, "Do not give the personal account of the author—rather appreciate the work of the author." We should talk about his style, about his vocabulary etc. rather become personal with him.

(ii) Talking about difficulties in the way of learning, humanists say that the teacher should give few simple directions to overcome difficulties. Do not hurry because learning comes easily when the proper stage is reached. Avoid difficulty which can be easily ignored. Postpone things.

(iii) Next item in the method of humanistic education was to set exercises for the matter taught. It should not be literal reproduction. The subject should be reproduced. He did not favour taking notes. He would encourage memorisation, understanding and reproduction. The substance be memorised. Let the child understand critically and then reproduce. The maxim was:—Understand—Arrange—Repeat.

(iv) For mature students, early humanists recommended lectures and debates. Independence and individuality were introduced in learning of lessons. It was a protest aganist verbalism and cram work.

Other Features

(a) Discipline. Humanists believed in discipline in the schools. It was a discipline of kindness than of vindictiveness. There was an appeal to pride and ambition in the child rather than to rigours of punishment.

(b) Role of Teacher. It is the teacher who is the chief agent in this enterprise of sensible integration and success or failure depends upon his outlook and methods. If he lives a unified life himself, he will help his pupils to find a unity in the multiplicity of their experience, but if he is to do all this, he will require different type of training.

PRAGMATISM

Pragmatism is midway between Idealism and Naturalism. It is an American philosophy typical in nature and practical in approach. The term pragmatism is derived from the Greek word 'Pragma' which means activity or the work done. Pragmatism is also known as Experimentalism because pragmatists believe experiment as the only criterion of Truth. It is noted that the fundamental start of Pragmatism is change. In this sense, no truth is permanent. It is always changing from time to time, from place to place. To them only those ideals and values are true which result in some utility to mankind in a certain set of circumstances, place or time. It is intimately connected with human life and human welfare, that is why, it is called as a humanistic philosophy of life.

Idealism is psycho-centric, Naturalism is neutro-centric and Pragmatism is anthropo-centric, according to which, man's own experiences are the centres of reality and truth. Idealist looks before and after and pines for what is not, naturalists look to present needs and problems and have no concern for future, Pragmatist looks here and now.

Idealist constructs a transcendental ideal which is beyond man's realisation. Naturalists follow the principle of struggle for existence and survival of the fittest. Pragmatists are practical people believing in finishing the book here, solving the problem now, making the social contact immediately, striking the business deal at once. Whatever they wish to do, they examine its utility and do it immediately.

Idealists live in the world of ideals. Naturalists live in the lap of nature. Pragmatists live in the world of facts. Pragmatism makes 'activity', 'engagement', 'commitment', and 'encounter' its central theme.

Different philosophers and educationists have defined pragmatism as follows:

According to **Prett,** "Pragmatism offers a theory of knowledge, a theory of truth and a theory of reality."

According to **William James,** "Pragmatism is a temper of mind, an attitude, it is also a theory of the nature of ideas and truth, and finally it is a theory of reality."

According to **Ross,** "Pragmatism is essentially a humanistic philosophy maintaining that man creates his own values in course of activity, that reality is still in making and awaits its part of completion from that future."

According to **Dr. Prem Nath,** "The nature of Pragmatism is naturalistic, its duration is scientific and practicable and its aim is social and humanistic."

Pragmatism is definitely a foreign ideology. In modern times, the introduction of pragmatism to human life was first done by American philosopher G.S. Pearce in 1878 A.D. He asserted, "our beliefs are really the rules for action". Due to inhuman cruelties in England, thousands of the oppressed people migrated from their native countries in Europe to America. The new way of thinking led them to new types of activities and new ways of learning by doing and by consequences and experiences.

Forms of Pragmatism

There are different types of Pragmatism which are as follows:

Biological Pragmatism. According to this the capacity of a human being is valuable and important which enables him to adjust with the environment or which makes him able to change his environment according to his needs and requirements.

Humanistic Pragmatism. According to this 'whatever fulfils one's purpose, satisfies one's desire, develops one's life, is true.' It maintains what satisfies the human nature is only true and real.

Nominalistic Pragmatism. It emphasises on the concreteness of an idea. When we do an experiment we come across future solutions. Its basis is concrete. It results in some visual solutions.

Experimental Pragmatism. According to this whatever can be experimentally verified is true. That principle is true which can be verified as true by experiment.

Supporters. Perce, William James, Kil Patrick and John Dewey were the supporters of Pragmatism.

Characteristics of Pragmatism

Characteristics of Pragmatism are as follows:

Faith in Democracy. This philosophy believes in humanism which is in accordance with democracy. Pragmatism shows its deep faith in democracy, as democracy is a way of life and a spirit of sharing experiences.

It does not believe in eternal values. Man makes his own values. Values change according to the change of time. They are relative. There is nothing in the name of eternal values. Truth is that which works, which serves some purpose and is useful to a man. Truth is man-made and the values of life and truth always change.

It is a Revolt against Traditionalism. This philosophy is a midway between Naturalism and Idealism. It neither believes in the established beliefs nor in the objective interpretation of naturalism. It lays emphasis on the practicability of thing and activity.

Principle of utility. Pragmatism believes in the principle of utility. Utility is the measure of a view point. The thing which gives satisfaction is useful. According to this only those ideas and things are true which have a utility for man.

Thought in Subordinate to Action. Pragmatism sees thought as intrinsically connected with action. It gives supreme position to action.

Pragmatism and Philosophy

Metaphysics. Pragmatism regards the material world as true. It regards human being as the supreme person. He is a social being and his development is possible only in the society. To it this world is the combination of different elements. It considers truth as changeable. Truth is man-made. There is a change in its form and concept. Pragmatism believes in the power of God if the existence of God is helpful in the growth of human being otherwise not. It lays stress on action and its consequences. It considers reality as a process of the completion of a task.

Axiology. Pragmatism does not believe in eternal values. Man himself creates values. Values are not predetermined. Pragmatists consider consequences as the basis of selection of all types of values. If the values are useful their selection is appropriate otherwise not. In the context of religion, Dewey has said, 'God is active relation between Ideal and Reality, They consider the use of intelligence in the solution of problems.

Epistemology. Pragmatism considers experience as the source of attaining knowledge. Human being receives knowledge through experience based activity and ideas by acting and reacting with human environment. Pragmatists consider experimental methods as the best means of attaining knowledge. To them problem, selection of problem, data collection, hypothesis and experimentation are the steps of experimental method. Truth is the outcome of expected consequences through this method.

Principles of Pragmatism

Principles of Pragmatism are as follows:

Pragmatism believes in the power of God if the existence of God is helpful in the growth of human beings otherwise not. It recognises the importance of human power. The essence of human life is humanity. The world is like a laboratory where man solves his problems. In it means are more important than ends.

Stress on Social Values. Pragmatists uphold social and democratic attitudes and values. Pragmatism holds that man is a social being. He is born in society and all his development takes place in and through society.

Principle of Utility. Pragmatism is a utilitarian ideology which holds that the reality of a principle lies in its utility. Any idea or thing which is useful to us, is proper and right. In case it is of no use, it is improper, wrong and untrue.

God is not Absolute. To the Pragmatists God is not infinite, absolute and immortal entity as the idealists proclaim. To them, God and Soul are not immortal and infinite. These entities as well as the religion are useful to human beings only when they serve usefully to develop human personalities, otherwise Pragmatism shows an attitude of indifference towards moral and spiritual ideals and values.

Emphasis on Activity. The greatest contribution of Pragmatism to education is the principle of learning by doing. It lays great emphasis on activity rather than on ideas. It holds the view that ideas are born out of activities. Man is active by nature. He learns by his activities.

Problems are Motivating Force. According to Pragmatism, human life is like a laboratory wherein each individual undertakes various experiments to solve the problems which confront him in course of his growth and development. The success of the experiment is a search of truth. Hence problems are the motivating force for the search of truth.

Past is Dead. According to Pragmatism past is dead and gone. It is of no use to think and talk about what is dead and gone. To it each individual has to solve the problems of his present and future life. Hence present and immediate future are of great value to an individual.

Importance to Human Intelligence. Pragmatism gives more importance to human intelligence and mental capacity which brings about harmonious and progressive adjustment with environment which results in human welfare and happiness. It is against old customs and traditions. It believes in realities of life.

Faith in Pluralism. This philosophy is pluralistic. It takes "life" from naturalism and 'Psyche' from mentalism and evaluates and explains God, nature and man. It is just in the middle of naturalism and idealism.

Pragmatism and Aims of Education

All Round Development. Education ensures all round development of the child. The child must develop physically, mentally, socially, morally, and aesthetically. The aim of education is for development. To Dewey, "Education has no aims, only persons have aims." Therefore the aims of pragmatic education are changeable".

According to **Ross,** "The general educational aim of the pragmatists is just the creation of new values. So the main task of the educator is to put the educand into a position of developing values for himself."

Adjustment. Pragmatic education is flexible. Therefore it wants to develop a child as a dynamic and flexible intellectual so that he may adjust with the changing environment and ensure his progress by controlling it. It wants to enable a child adjust mentally for the present and future by making him as the centre of education. The aim of education is 'to direct the impulses, interests and abilities towards the satisfaction of the left needs of the child, in the environment.

Social Efficiency. Pragmatism wants to develop social efficiency in the child through education. Education wants a child to stand on his feet by providing him vocational efficiency so that he may fulfil the needs of his family and society besides his personal needs. Thus, social efficiency tries to enable him to adjust with the society.

Reconstruction of Experience. As every individual is required to solve many diverse problems in his life, the aim of education should also be the formulation and cultivation of a dynamic, adoptable, resourceful and enterprising mind. It is with such a mind that original and creative thinking is possible which will enable a person to cope successfully with the varied situations of life.

Pragmatism and Curriculum

Pragmatists want to construct such a flexible, dynamic and integrated curriculum which helps in the development of the child. According to pragmatism only those subjects, activities and experiences should be included in the curriculum which are useful to the present needs of the child and meet the future expectations of adult life as well. Knowledge, of languages, hygiene, physical training, history, geography, mathematics, science, agriculture and professional subjects is compulsory. The main purpose is to help the child more and more in his development in all the fields of human activity. Only those activities and experiences in which the child takes interest should be included in the curriculum. The curriculum should consist of such varieties of learning experiences which promote original thinking and freedom to develop social and purposeful attitudes.

According to Pragmatism knowledge is one unit. It cannot be divided into water tight compartments of separate subjects. Teaching of various units should be closely inter-linked and co-related so as to form right concept and proper understanding in the children.

Pragmatism and Methods of Teaching

Pragmatism is opposed to the traditional methods of teaching. It favours child-centred, scientific and psychological and active methods of teaching. Pragmatism has contributed significantly to the methods of teaching. Pragmatists laid stress on learning through activities and the real life situations. Their main methods are Project method and Problem-solving method. Through these methods a child attains knowledge by solving his practical problems. These methods are experimental and creative.

These methods lay emphasis on learning by doing and learning through experience. Both the teacher and taught remain active. Pragmatism does not merely insist upon practical activities but tries to provide real life experiences and real life situations so that the child gains the required insight and capacities to face and solve the problems and challenges of life successfully. To it only that method is most effective which employs correlation and integration of all subjects, activities and experiences.

Pragmatism and Discipline

To Dewey discipline is a sort of mental state in the formation of which social conditions play a major role. Pragmatism condemns enforced discipline and advocates social discipline based on child's interests, activities and a sense of social responsibility.

Pragmatism advocates the merging of play with work. This merging of play and work will develop interest and a sense of purpose in the child to do his work with joy and eagerness without interfering with the work of others. This mental condition will infuse in him seriousness, sincerity and consideration for others. He will develop self-confidence, self-reliance, co-operation, sacrifice, sympathy and fellow-feeling for others. With the development of these social qualities he will develop a sense of social discipline and moral obligation towards self and others.

Hence according to pragmatism, the school should provide purposeful and conducive experiences to the child in a free and congenial atmosphere, which helps him becoming a true citizen in the real sense. Such activities create in children virtues like mutual respect, toleration, self-control and originality. This helps him in the training of character formation and establishment of self-discipline.

Pragmatism and Student

Pragmatism gives an important place to the child. The aim of education should be to prepare the child for the society so that he can become responsible citizen and succeed in life. This philosophy stresses child-centred education. There are three aspects of child's personality—Biological, Psychological and Social. Pragmatism lays emphasis on social aspect. This philosophy considers a child as an important part of educative process. It does not want to impose external ideas upon the child. It is in favour of giving him academic freedom. It wants to educate the child in social envionment.

Pragmatism and Teacher

According to pragmatism teacher is a friend, guide and philosopher to the child. He must educate the child in social environment so that he may attain social efficiency. There must be positive relationship between teacher and taught. His behaviour towards children must be sympathetic. His attitude should be democratic and child must have academic freedom. His function is to suggest problems to his pupils and to stimulate them to find for themselves solutions which will work. His emphasis is not on the knowledge as arranged and systematised in the text-books. He wants the children to do one experiment or to have a particular experience. 'Doing' is more important than knowing. Like Socrates the Pragmatist teacher wants "his pupils to think and act for themselves, to do rather than to know, to originate rather than to repeat."

Pragmatism and School

John Dewey maintains that school is a 'Miniature Society' here a child gets real experiences to act and behave according to his interests, aptitudes and capacities. Pragmatists regard school as a social institution where the child gains real experiences of actual life which develop in him social sense and a sense of duty towards society and the nation. Group games, working in laboratories and studying in libraries with others are the various activities and experiences which inculcate in children social qualities, social attitudes together with a spirit of mutual help and cooperative activities. In this way, according to Pragmatism the school is not a centre of education alone but it is also a community centre of various activities and experiences.

Contribution of Pragmatism in Education

Aims. It lays more stress on social and vocational efficiency.

Teacher. It gives important place to teacher.

Student. It stresses on child-centred education.

Teaching Method. New teaching methods is the contribution of pragmatism.

Curriculum. It lays more stress on experience and learning by doing.

Evaluation of Pragmatism

Opposition of Pre-determined Ideas. Pragmatism opposes pre-determined ideals and values. They are man-made and change according to the changes in circumstances, time and place.

Opposition of Eternal Truth. Pragmatism does not have any faith in eternal truth. Pragmatists believe that if the result of an activity is satisfactory then it is true otherwise not.

No Fix System of Education. Pragmatism provides academic freedom to every institution which leads them no where. Pragmatism gives no fixed ideal to education. Such an education is bound to be fruitless.

Emphasis on Material and Negation of Spiritual Values. There is no room for spiritual values in pragmatism. It gives more weightage to material values. Without spiritual values, we cannot achieve happiness, contentment and peace of mind and can go astray.

Laxity in Discipline. Pragmatism allows full freedom to the child which is not proper at the school stage and it leads to serious chaos and confusion.

Condemnation of Formal Education. Pragmatism advocates that all knowledge should be acquired through direct personal experiences. But knowledge is so vast and the span of life so short, that it is quite impossible to receive all knowledge through direct experiences. Hence acquiring all knowledge needs personal experiences and formal education both.

Negation of the Past. Pragmatism gives undue importance to the present. It ignores both past and future. The study of past is important to understand the present. Also there is need to link the present with future.

Pragmatism is a Method Only. Pragmatism is not a philosophy of life but only a method of education, growth and development. In the words of **William James**. "There is absolutely nothing new in the pragmatic method. It is just empirical attitude. It has no dogmas and no doctrines save its methods."

Pragmatism believe in Pluralism which is not proper.

Merits of Pragmatism

Project Method. Project method is a gift of pragmatism. Through this method child attains knowledge by solving his practical problems. He performs the problematic acts in natural conditions. This method lays emphasis on learning through experiences.

Importance of Child. Opposing bookish knowledge and formal education, pragmatism lays great stress upon the development of child's individuality by his own efforts. This makes education child-centred.

Emphasis on Activity. The principle of learning by doing is the main contribution of pragmatism. Children are active by nature. It emphasises on the activity of the child. It prepares the child for future life in a very effective manner.

Revolutionised the Process of Education. This philosophy has infused life and zest in contribution. The concepts of 'New Education', 'Progressive Education' and Activity-centred curriculum which have changed the education outlook are the contribution of pragmatism.

Social and Democratic Education. Pragmatism infuses in a child a spirit of freedom, initiative, equality and also a sense of responsibility in relation to rights and duties of a citizen. This develops in the child love for democratic values and social efficiency which bring harmonious adjustment and development of personality.

Progressive Attitude. Pragmatism emphasises the qualities of freedom initiative, expression, conducive experiences, congenial environment, purposeful creativity and development of human values for the welfare of whole mankind.

In the words of Rusk. "It is merely a stage in the development of a new Idealism that will do full justice to reality, reconcile the practical and spiritual values and result in a culture which is the flower of efficiency."

Pragmatism is an attitude and a way of living which, opposing the old doctrines of Idealism and Naturalism, inspires the individual to look ahead and create new values for an unknown future so that he leads a better, happier and a richer life.

Educational Philosophy of Gandhiji

His Life and Work. Gandhiji, the Father of the Indian Nation, the apostle of Truth and Non-violence, was born on the 2nd of October, 1869 at Porbandar in Kathiawar. Gandhiji's mother was a saintly woman. She had a strong influence on his life. After studying Law in England, he started practice in Bombay, but he could not earn sufficient to live on. He went to South Africa. His experiences in England, India, and South Africa made him bitter against the British Rule. What he did for the liberation of the country is known to all of us. At present we are concerned with his Educational Philosophy.

Background of His Educational Philosophy

There are three important elements in the background of his educational philosophy:

1. His philosophy of life.
2. His dissatisfaction with the British System of Education.
3. His educational experiments at Tolstoy Farm, Sabarmati and Sewagram Ashrams.

1. ***His Philosophy of Life.*** He had Faith in God. All things move due to God. To him God is every thing—"Life Truth, Light and Love". Other important principles of his life were Faith in Truth, Ahimsa—Creed of Non-violence, and Dignity of Labour.

2. ***His Dissatisfaction with the British System of Education.*** British System of Education did not suit to the Indian Socio-Economic conditions. Teeming millions of Indian were wrought in ignorance, superstition, inertia and illiteracy. This education is not related to life. It makes the Indians foreigners in their own homes.

3. *His Educational Experiments at Tolstoy Farm, Sabarmati and Sewagram Ashrams.* In these Ashrams, the inmates, living and working together, adopted certain codes. All the inmates were to work with their hands. There was no servant. Every job was performed by the inmates. Gandhiji found that manual work has great virtues in its trail. One can learn and can also be self-sufficient. These experiments encouraged him to put forward important principle of the education philosophy *i.e.,* earn while you learn.

His Educational Philosophy. There is a general tendency among educationists and laymen to identify Gandhiji's educational philosophy with Basic Education or Wardha Scheme of Education. Basic Education is, no doubt, an integral part of Gandhiji's educational philosophy but it is a scheme or programme of education not synonymous with Gandhiji's philosophy of education, which aims at bringing about a revolution in the hearts and minds of men all over the world. Basic Scheme is primarily meant for children between 7 and 14 years of age.

Concept of Education. According to Gandhiji, "By education, I mean an all-round drawing out of the best in child and man—body, mind and spirit." The aim of education is not literacy. Gandhiji laid emphasis on the development of the whole personality. Education which draws out the best or Truth consists in the development of the mind and body with a corresponding awakening of the soul. "True Education", says Gandhiji, "is that which draws out and stimulates the spiritual, intellectual and physical faculties of the children."

Aims of Education. Aims of education are implied in the very meanings of education. He has given two sets of aims—*viz.* immediate and ultimate aims of education.

(a) *Ultimate Aim.* Ultimate aim of education is identical with the goal of life, which is 'Self-realisation'. Self-realisation is the realisation of the self proper. True education should result not in the material gains but in spiritual uplift.

Gandhiji laid great stress on religious education which teaches fundamental virtues of truth, love, justice and non-violence. According to Gandhiji, "Like without religion is life without principles." Gandhiji is also of the opinion that God could be achieved not by returning into jungles but by living in a society and serving it. He preferred to call a student "Brahmachari", a searcher after God.

Selfe-realisation can take place through self-control, character and abstinence.

(b) *Immediate Aims*. Immediate aims, include 'bread and butter aim', the cultural aim, the harmonious development of all powers, the moral or character development aim, and sociological aim.

1. Bread and Butter Aims. This is also called utilitarian aim. It is due to this aim that he gave the principle of 'self-supporting education'. The educand should not only be made capable of earning his own livelihood in later life after school but also during the schooling. The child must be an earning unit who must be self-sufficient right from the beginning of the education of the child. This aim is really an important aim of even modern education.

2. Cultural Aim. Cultural aim refers to the refinement of the personality. Mere knowledge is not enough. Education should lead to that quality of mind which may be reflected in daily conduct. Speech, behaviour and manner must be refined. Culture brings in humility and frankness. Education should not take Indian children away from its own culture. There is a need of synthesising cultures so that one could inherit world cultures. This aim enables the students to assimiliate and appreciate other cultures.

3. Harmonious Development Aim. Harmonious development or perfection of nature is another aim that Gandhiji advocates. Harmoniously developed person is that who adjusts to his life and environment. He laid greater emphasis on the development of 3 H's *i.e.,* Head, Heart and Hand than on 3 R's *i.e.,* reading, writing and arithmetic. Present system of education leads to unbalanced development.

4. The Moral or Character Building Aim. It is the chief aim of education. The central purpose of education is to build character. If choice is to be made between character and other things in life, then every thing else can be subordinated to the former.

Man must be a man of word. He must be ready to do something for the humanity at the first call to his conscience.

5. Sociological Aim or Training for Citizenship. Gandhiji reconciled the individual and social aims of education. In democracy the first slogan is 'Educate your Masters'. Thus Gandhiji advocated 'Universal education'. Every member of this Samaj should be educated so that he could uplift it. He must have qualities of a good citizen. Essential qualities are—spirit of courage, self-sacrifice and industry.

Curriculum. Gandhian curriculum includes following subjects:

1. Basic craft which may be agriculture or spinning and weaving or card-board work and mental work.
2. Mother tongue both as a language and as medium of instructions.
3. Arithmetic/Mathematics: More emphasis is to be laid on numerical and geometrical problems connected with craft and community life.
4. Drawing, Painting and Music.
5. Domestic science for girls at higher stages. At lower stages same for boys and girls.
6. Social Studies.
7. General Science.

Methods. Gandhiji framed teaching through physical and mental activities. Activity is the starting point of his teaching. Gandhiji advocated teaching through a method.

Craft. Correlated knowledge should be given through a craft.

Discipline. The spirit of non-violence should prevail in the school. Love and truth should be the basis between the teacher and the taught. Self-discipline is the only discipline worth the name.

Basic Education. Gandhiji's philosophy is reflected in Basic education. The four features are:

1. Education should be free and compulsory for all children between the age group 7-14 years.
2. Mother tongue should be the medium of instruction.
3. Education should be craft-centred.
4. Education should be self-sufficient.

❑

3

Educational Psychology

Educational psychology is an applied branch of psychology. It is made up of two words education and psychology. Education is the change in behaviour or modification in behaviour. Psychology is the scientific study of behaviour. Thus education and psychology are closely related.

Educational psychology is the application of psychological findings in the field of education. Educational psychology is the systematic study of the development of the individual within the educational setting. It helps the teacher to foster harmonious development of the student into a responsible and participating citizen, a sensitive and reflective human being, a productive and creative person.

Educational psychology is an applied discipline which combines the two different fields of education and psychology. It is the scientific study of human behaviour by which it can be understood, predicted and directed by education to achieve goals of life.

It is concerned primarily with learners and how they respond to various conditions they meet in school and life situations. It selects from the total field of psychology those facts and principles that have direct bearing upon the growth, learning and adjustment of children. More specifically, educational psychology is a study of human behaviour as it bears upon learning and teaching activities. It is an application of principles of general psychology to the problems of education.

In a layman's view, educational psychology is that branch of psychology which deals with the problems of education.

According to **Skinner**, educational psychology is that branch of science which deals with teaching and learning. According to **Crow and Crow**, educational psychology describes and explains the learning experiences of an individual from birth to old age. According to ***Judd,*** educational psychology is the science which describes and explains the changes that take place in individuals as they pass through stages of development from birth to maturity.

According to **C.V.Good,** "Educational Psychology is the investigation of psychological problems involved in education together with the practical application of psychological principles to education."

According to ***Trow,*** "Educational psychology is the study of the psychological aspects of educational situations."

It is concerned primarily with the study of human behaviour as it is directed under the social process of education.

On the basis of above definitions it can be concluded that educational psychology is an applied science which employs the principles and findings of psychology in the field of education.

The word Psychology is derived from two Greek words, 'Psyche' and 'Logos', "Psyche' means soul and 'Logos' means science. Hence the original or etymological meaning of Psychology is the science of soul. In due course the meanings of psychology have undergone many changes. From Science of Soul, it became 'Science of Mind', 'Science of Consciousness' and 'Science of Behaviour' which is its modern concept.

1. Psychology as a Science of Mind. Philosophers in the middle ages considered psychology as the science of mind. They used to distinguish between the mental and spiritual life of the individual. These philosophers, however, failed to give the exact nature and, force of the mind of the individual. Hence psychology the science of mind could not progress.

2. Psychology as a Science of Soul. The earliest definition of psychology was 'a Science of Soul'. Philosophers like Plato, Aristotle and Descartes interpreted psychology, according to this concept. In 16th century this meaning of psychology was rejected.

3. Psychology as a Science of Consciousness. In the 19th century psychologists like William James, William Wondt and others considered psychology as a science of consciousness. By consciousness the psychologists meant awareness or wakefulness. They, however, had different interpretations of the term wakefulness. As this definition of psychology had a very limited approach, it was not universally accepted.

4. Psychology as a Science of Behaviour. The latest and modern concept of Psychology is in times of behaviour. Behaviour is the resultant manifestation of both conscious and unconscious urges. Behaviour can be observed objectively and is a more suitable method of studying Psychology.

Modern Definitions of Psychology. Let us now acquaint ourselves with some of the definitions of Psychology:

1. 'Psychology is the study of human nature'. (Boring Lang Feld).
2. 'Psychology is the science of behaviour and experience'. (Skinner).
3. 'Psychology is the study of human behaviour and human relationships'. (Crow and Crow).
4. Psychology undertakes to make a scientific study of the individual considered as a unit as he really is in his dealings with other individuals and with the world.' (Woodworth).

The most acceptable Meaning and Definition of Psychology. It is in terms of behaviour. A lot of work has been done by psychologists in this field. Detailed experiments have been conducted on human behaviour. William Wondt established the first Psychological Laboratory at Leipzig in 1879.

Human behaviour is highly complex. All human beings do not behave in the same manner. They differ in abilities, likes-dislikes, interests, attitudes, emotions and sentiments. Why is it so? The science that answers such questions and studies human behaviour is called Psychology:

Classification of Psychology. Psychology can be divided into eleven branches:

1. *General Psychology.* It studies the behaviour of human organism in general. Its scope is very large but generally it studies normal organisms. It is the mother of all other branches of Psychology.

2. *Abnormal Psychology.* The scope of Abnormal Psychology is limited to the study of abnormal individual only.

3. *Child Psychology.* It deals with the development of behaviour of the child. The child is an adult in the making. He differs from the adults very much. "His life urges, his emotions, his sentiments, his intelligence and his aspirations all differ from those of the adult individuals. Therefore, Child Psychology is a fullfledged science in itself.

4. *Adult Psychology.* It studies the behaviour of adult humans. An adult is a mature person and his emotional, social and intellectual behaviour is not like the behaviour of a child. So it is totally a separate branch of Psychology.

5. *Individual Psychology.* It deals with the variation in human beings. No two persons are alike. They always differ in their behaviour according to their intelligence, race and sex. They also differ in behaviour in other factors such as interest, philosophy and education.

6. *Social or Group Psychology.* This branch of Psychology deals with the behaviour of individual as member of a group or mob does not act in the same way as a majority of the individual members would act individually.

7. *Educational Psychology.* It is the most important branch of applied Psychology. It is the study of the psychological aspects of educational situations. It is study of educational problems with reference to psychological facts. Psychology is science of behaviour and Education aims at modifying the behaviour in the most desirable way. But modification of behaviour depends on some fundamental psychological laws and limitations. Educational Psychology studies those facts and limitations. It covers the development of the child from early childhood to maturity, general facts of Psychology which may have any relation with the modification of the behaviour of the child, psychologised methods of learning, measurement of capacities, attitudes and interests and other problems of applied Psychology related to education.

8. *Industrial Psychology.* This is also a branch of applied Psychology. It is in fact Social Psychology with reference to work, individual as well as collective. Industrial work may be made more attractive and interesting and output of industry may be increased and improved if we exploit the finding of Industrial Psychology.

9. *Para-Psychology.* This is the latest development in the field of psychology. It deals with the problems of what happens to an individual after death.

10. *Experimental Psychology.* It studies mental processes and behaviour in laboratories with the help of experiments.

11. *Comparative Psychology.* It may be named as Animal Psychology also as it is a comparative study of the behaviour of man and various animals. Animals cannot express themselves. Therefore, we can study their behaviour with the help of experiments only. It is very difficult to do some experiments on human beings. Therefore, some of the experiments are first tried on animals and then the results are applied to human beings. The laws of learning, now applied with much success to pupils in schools, were discovered in this way.

NATURE OF EDUCATIONAL PSYCHOLOGY

Nature of educational psychology is scientific, as it uses scientific methods. Following are the essential elements of science:

1. **Scientific Method.** A science makes use of the scientific method.

2. **Factuality.** Science is the study of facts, the search for true facts.

3. **Universality.** Scientific laws are universal.

4. **Validity.** Scientific laws are also valid. They are valid at all times and in all places. They are found to be invariably true. They are open to examination at all times.

5. **Discovery of Cause and Effect Relationship.** Science studies cause and effect relationship, it searches for cause and effect relationship in its material. On the basis of such relationships it creates universal and valid laws.

6. **Prediction.** Science makes predictions.

On the basis of above criteria of science we find that educational psychology is a science as it possesses all the characteristics of being a science.

The nature of educational psychology is scientific as it employs scientific method in the study of behaviour of the learner in an educational environment. Educational psychology makes use of scientific techniques such as observation, experimentation, case history, interview and projective techniques. Thus, educational psychology as a science is systematic as its procedures are orderly.

Educational Psychology is Empirical and Factual

— It is a body of facts or information that has resulted from observations and investigations. Its conclusions are objective and unperjudiced.

— It is one of the applied branches of psychology. It studies the behaviour of the learner in relation to learning situation.

— It has developed a methodology by which investigations are made, information is discovered hypothesis tested and theories are derived.

— It defines cause and effect relationship and on the basis of this knowledge it analyses behaviour of the learner.

— It is a positive science of human behaviour. Its function is to describe, control and predict human behaviour. Human behaviour is quite dynamic and unpredictable.

— After establishing cause and effect relationships concerning the behaviour of learners it becomes possible for the educational psychologist to predict the behaviour of other learners. He can predict the development of learners in future.

It is clear that educational psychology is an applied and positive science of behaviour of the learner. Its subject matter is subtle, complex and varied. As the human behaviour is unpredictable, more variable and less reliable, viewing this concept, we can say that educational psychology is not a perfect science. Educational Psychology cannot claim the same degree of validity, accuracy, objectivity and exactness as claimed by natural science.

Aims of Educational Psychology

Aims of educational psychology are parallel with aims of education. Various views have been expressed by different thinkers about these aims as given below:

According to **Kuppuswamy,** "The aim of educational psychology is to use psychological principles for good teaching and learning."

According to **Garrison,** "The aim of educational psychology is to know the behaviour of the child and to predict and control it."

According to **W.A. Kelly,** the following are the aims often subject to:

(1) To give an insight with teacher about the nature of child.

(2) Enlightening the teacher with the growth and development of the child.

(3) Imparting knowledge about the principle and methods of learning.

(4) Helping the teacher in finding out ways and means of social adjustment for the child.

(5) Giving knowledge about the character formation of the child.

(6) Studying about the control of emotions and their educational importance.

(7) A study of the techniques of evaluation of various school subjects.

(8) A study of the psychological methods of investigation used in the field of educational psychology.

Charles Skinner has classified the aims of educational psychology as general and particular:

The gerneral aim is to provide a body of organised facts and generalisations that will enable the teacher to realise increasingly both cultural and professional objective:

The particular aims are as follows:

(1) Creating confidence in the teacher to plan harmonious development of the child.

(2) Approaching the problems of children in a sympathetic and impartial manner.

(3) Understanding the social problems of children and planning for their total social adjustment.

(4) Planning education of children according to their age, ability and aptitude.

(5) Imparting knowledge to the teacher about the latest developments in the field of child psychology and various methods of teaching.

(6) Enabling the teacher to evaluate himself and his methods of teaching.

(7) Helping the teacher in solving the problems that may arise in the classroom.

(8) Helping the teacher to understand and analyse the behaviour of children.

In other words we can say that the general aim of educational psychology is to provide a body of facts and principles which will enable the teacher to enhance and enrich his own life and which will help him to bring about improvement in the quality of instruction, thus, equipping him adequately, both culturally and professionally and the specific aims are following:

(a) To explain the nature and characteristics of the learner.

(b) To describe the nature of learning processes.

(c) To explain the manner in which these processes may be facilitated by the teacher, and in the light of these, to explain, how he or she should teach.

(d) "To assist in defining and setting up educational objectives and standards in terms of desirable behaviour (conduct, attitudes etc.) that ought to be the goals of all teaching efforts. If the teacher knows what the desired outcomes should be, he can set-up appropriate situations (curricular materials, teaching procedures etc.) for bringing about the wanted changes." (Skinner)

(e) To assist the teacher in the better adjustment of children and in the prevention of maladjustments.

(f) To help the teacher in defining and planning suitable guidance programmes, and functional forms of organisation and administration.

(g) To aid in developing a scientific problem solving attitude toward the problems of learning and teaching.

(h) To help in the evaluation of the outcome of the educational process.

Relation Between Psychology and Education

(1) Education determines aims and ideals, and psychology decides which aims can be attained.

(2) Psychology deals with facts as they are. Education determines the standards to be achieved. Psychology tells the way of attaining these standards.

(3) Psychology helps the teacher to know the child and plan for the maximum development of the child, which is the ultimate goal of education.

Importance of Educational Psychology to the Teachers

1. ***Psychology Helps the Teacher in the Realisation of the Aims of Education.*** The main aim of education is the harmonious and all-round development of the educand. Development comes from within and the inner potentialities must be understood and approached for the desired modification in the development of the child. The knowledge of Psychology helps the teacher to understand the inner potentialities which underlie the behaviour of the child. He can direct and modify the development of the educand quite efficiently if he knows Psychology.

2. ***Character Development.*** Educational Psychology helps a lot to the formation and development of character. The teacher comes to know the methods he should adopt in inculcating character traits, and moral principles among the children.

3. ***Educational Psychology Proves Useful in the Methods of Teaching.*** Psychology has discovered many secrets about mental forces. Recent researches made in the field of psychology gives us valuable suggestions for the better methods of teaching and memorizing, for making desirable habits and eradicating anti-social tendencies. Psychology tells us how significant play and recreation are for the children and how play-way-methods turn the work of learning into an interesting play.

4. *The Knowledge about the Child is as Necessary as that of the Subject.* The educator will have to consider the mental processes of the child and not only the quality of knowledge which he is going to be put into the living mind. Psychology helps him in understanding 'John'. The teacher may be a great scholar but he will not succeed in teaching if he has no knowledge of the mental forces of the child.

5. *Educational Psychology can Change the Outlook and Attitude of the Teacher towards his Pupils.* The knowledge of psychology will change the outlook and attitude of the teacher towards children. He will no more denounce his pupils on account of their undesirable behaviour. He will not hate the juvenile delinquent. Instead of being fed-up with the backward child the teacher will be more interested in him. The problem child will no more be a problem for him but he will be simply a child with problems and the teacher will be ever-ready to help him in the solution of his problems.

6. *Educational Psychology Helps the Teacher in His own Mental Adjustment.* A maladjusted personality can never be a good model for hundreds of developing personalities. He cannot solve his own problems and therefore he cannot help the children in this aspect. The study of psychology may help the teacher to readjust himself. He will know his own weaknesses and merits and will overcome his complexes.

7. *Psychological Measurements are Very Useful for the Teacher.* Psychology has developed many reliable tests and instruments of mental measurement. These are providing to be extremely useful in the field of education. We can quite easily measure mental capacities, basic intelligence, temperamental attitudes and special inclinations of children and base their educational programmes on these findings. These measurements show that all the children differ in their eventual capacities and that every child is a unique being. The teacher can know that children with I.Q. below 90 cannot do well in medical, engineering, administrative or other similar vocations. But he knows that such young ones are not doomed if they cannot do well in intellectual callings. He can easily explore some other fields where such children can also flourish.

8. *Knowledge of Educational Psychology will Give a Scientific Attitude to the Teachers.* The knowledge of psychology will make an educator more scientific in his educational practices and consequently he will be more and more objective and methodical in his work.

9. *Educational Psychology and Process of Learning.* Teaching and learning go side by side. All education depends upon the learning of new responses and the capacity of a human child to learn new responses. Educational Psychology discusses the nature of learning theories and types of learning for different age levels and situations. It tells that learning is not possible if the child does not cooperate in the learning process. Therefore, knowledge of Psychology becomes essential to a teacher to study all these problems.

10. *Educational Psychology and Nervous System.* The entire education depends on the function of the brain and nervous system. It becomes essential to teacher to study the nervous system which controls human behaviour. He must have the knowledge of sensory organs which are the gates of knowledge.

11. *Educational Psychology and Play.* Play is a natural tendency having great educational quality. Psychology helps in playgrounds also. Child finds outlet for pent-up feelings and energy through play. It also gives joy and pleasure to the pupils. Hence there is a great importance of play-way in education.

12. *Individual Differences.* No two persons are exactly alike. There is individual difference. Pupils always differ in their level of intelligence, aptitudes, likes and dislikes and in other propensities and potentialities. Different minds are to be trained by the teacher. There are gifted, backward, retarded, talented and handicapped children. All of them should not be treated in the same manner. So, the teacher should know their Psychology to satisfy them.

Educational Psychology and the Parents

1. Educational Psychology enables the parents to understand the process of development and growth of their children.

2. Educational Psychology acquaints the parents with the emotional, mental and physical needs of the children.

3. Educational Psychology impresses upon the parents for the necessity of providing wholesome environment to the children so that they lead a happy life and are free from anxiety.

4. Educational Psychology enables the parents to know that they should not take recourse to repression and punishment which adversely affect the mental health of children.

5. Educational Psychology enables the parents to observe keenly the behaviour of children. It enables them to control their habits.

6. The knowledge of Educational Psychology points out to the parents that they should show love and affection to their children. They should bear in mind the maxim, "Love the child and the child will love you. Hate the child and he will hate you."

To sum-up, Educational Psychology has revolutionised education. It has made education child-centred. It is only with the knowledge of Educational Psychology that it is possible for the teachers to render proper guidance, arrange the learning situations and plan the instructional programmes and other activities for the all-round development of children.

PSYCHOLOGY ITS RELATIONSHIP WITH EDUCATION

Psychology has assumed an extraordinary importance in the life of an individual. Infact, every action of life, may it be home, school, neighbourhood or social gathering, is influenced by it. All communications between the teacher and students are based on the knowledge of psychology. Theories of intelligence, creativity and personality have been responsible for shaping and designing the educational system according to individual needs.

Psychology is the Science of Soul. The word 'psychology' comes from Greek words 'Psyche' and 'logos' where psyche means soul and logos means science. Thus, literally psychology means a science of soul. But this is not acceptable because of following criticisms:

(i) Nature, origin and place of soul is not known. It has no physical existence. It cannot be seen and heard. It has no weight and volume. It is a metaphysical cancept.

(ii) It makes psychology more of religion than of science because it is a theological concept and implies certain theories of religion and relationship to God.

(iii) Soul makes science speculative as it is not open to observation and experimentation and therefore not given to verification. So this definition of psychology is unscientific and hence this is discarded.

Psychology is Science of Mind. Alternatively philosophers evolved another definition of psychology as science of mind. Mind is a combination of sum total of mental processes and it stands for personal internal experiences of man, *e.g.*, pleasures and pains, hopes and wishes, dreams and desires. But this is also criticised on following grounds:

(i) It is subjective. We can know our own mind and not the mind of others. So it is half true.

(ii) Mind implies continuity and unity but it is lacking in abnormals, insanes and animals etc.

Psychology as a Science of Consciousness. Failing to define the nature of soul and mind, the psychologists defined psychology as a science of consciousness. The definition was considered too narrow as this did not include the unconscious and preconscious activities of mind. Freud in his psycho analytical theory described that mind consists of 3 states—preconscious, unconscious and conscious. About 9/10th part of behaviour is determined by unconscious and preconscious mind whereas only 1/10th part is determined by conscious mind. But in Freud's terminology, unconscious mind plays a major role in the development of personality of an individual. This definition was also discarded.

Psychology as a Science of Behaviour. Psychology was finally defined as the science of behaviour where the term behaviour carries a very wide meaning. According to **Woodworth,** "Any manifestation of life is activity" and behaviour is a collective name of all such activities. It includes all types of activities such as cognitive, affective and conative. So behaviour refers to entire life activities and experiences of all living organisms.

According to **Watson,** "Psychology is the positive science of behaviour."

According to **Skinner,** "Psychology deals with responses to any and every kind of situation that life presents by adjustment activities."

According to **Bernard,** "Behaviour is an attempt of the organism to adjust to the multiple stimuli which impinge on it." Behaviour is classified in three categories according to its content:

(a) Cognitive Behaviour where it is dominantly knowing or thinking, *e.g.*, solving questions.

(b) Effective Behaviour where the dominance is of feeling, *e.g.*, the emotional experience of anger, fear, jealousy etc.

(c) Conative Behaviour where the dominance is of motor activity, *e.g.*, cycling, playing hockey etc.

According to **Crow and Crow,** "Psychology is the study of human behaviour and human relationship."

According to **Munns,** "Psychology today concerns itself with the scientific investigation of behaviour."

According to **Garrison,** "Psychology is concerned with observable human behaviour."

Thus, it can be concluded that psychology is a behavioural science which helps us to describe, understand, predict and control behaviour.

PROBLEMS OF EDUCATIONAL PSYCHOLOGY

1. Development of a Balanced Personality. The main problem that engages the attention of educational psychology is the development of a balanced personality in the child. And, generally speaking, a balanced personality is one in whom the intellectual, emotional, ethical and moral aspects are properly blended and synthesised, functioning properly.

2. Motivation. Often enough, the problems that are at the root of various adjustment defects are problems of motivation.

3. Increase in Understanding and Meaning. Another factor at the root of the motivation problem is sometimes a deficient understanding and an inability to comprehend the implications of the problems existing. It is to this end that the material chosen in teaching nowadays is such as is drawn from an environment with which the child is reasonably familiar and with which he is conversant enough not to be embarrassed by it. A simple example would be the creation of a model government within the class in order to explain the working of the actual government of the country to the student. In democratic societies the students usually understand the functioning of a democratic system in their student groups.

4. Individual Importance of Heredity and Environment in Individual Differences. The aim of education is the development of the child. Hence, one of the important problems facing the educational psychologist is the determination of the relative importance of heredity and environment in the child's development and in causing individual differences among children. Can education change the inherited qualities? Can children reach an adequate stage of development on their inherited qualities alone if they are placed in a common environment? Is it possible to make a child into anything on the basis of education irrespective of his heredity? These are questions of this nature that encourage and inspire the educational psychologist to make a comparative study of hereditary and environmental factors. For example, one important question is the extent to which intelligence can be developed through education regarding which educational psychologists have discovered numerous facts after much investigation.

5. Methods for Maximum Progress in Learning. Fundamentally, the process of education advances with learning. The most prominent question that interests the educational psychologist in this regard in what methods of learning can most facilitate learning and achieve the maximum progress? One such question could be—is there any conflict between imitation and creation? Should education pay more attention to the collection of factual details or concentrate on creative activities? Psychology has made considerable experiments with such methods as imitation, conditioned response, trail and error and insight, and has tried to discover the conditions that are best attened to the application of these methods, the coordination between the condition and method being productive of the best results.

6. Measurement and Development of Intelligence and Attainment. Education develops intelligence and attainment. Educational psychologists search for and discover methods and measures whereby one can know how this development can be achieved and once it has been achieved, to know how much development in the child has taken place.

7. Education of Emotions. The proper and adequate development of personality demands the proper and complete development of emotions. An absence of such education of emotions results in many mental diseases such as indiscipline, split personality, etc.

8. Individual Differences. Practical psychology is based on the fact of individual differences. Educational psychology, a knowledge that makes practical use of psychology in the field of education, finds out why and in what respects individual beings differ from each other. These differences are so obtrusive and well defined that the skilled teacher cannot function properly unless he can understand them. For example, the mental level of some individuals is so low that they can be taught even fundamental activities such as wearing clothes and eating only with the greatest of difficulty, while some children, precocious ones, are so intelligent and quick-minded that the normal teaching and study level of the class is not enough to occupy them so that they soon tire of it. Hence, the educational psychologist attempts to discover the limits, if any, of these individual differences, and even evolves methods for their measurement in exceptional children. The modern teacher discovers these individual differences and then makes efforts to help the children progress individually.

9. Problems Relating to Learning. Many of the problems of educational psychology are concerned with learning. The main among them are:

(a) nature of the process of learning,

(b) relation between level of maturity and learning,

(c) importance of individual differences to the speed of learning and limits of learning,

(d) modes of evaluating the progress of learning,

(e) relative importance of the formal and informal methods of the education or learning,

(f) psychological effect of social conditions upon the learner.

(g) internal changes taking place within the process of learning,

(h) relation between the methods of teaching and the results of learning.

10. Practical Problems. Educational psychology is no less a practical science than it is a theroretical one. Hence, in it one comes across many problems that arise before the teacher when he is teaching normally. Such problems would be:

(i) knowledge of the nature of every student and of the possibilities of his development,

(ii) individual and social adaptation necessary for adjustment in modern culture,

(iii) search for the fundamental psychological causes at the root of the processes of the learning and teaching.

As Educational Psychology progresses, it comes face to face with newer problems. In modern democratic societies, educational psychology is engaged in adapting education to democracy. And it has the services of psychology on the one hand and many other social sciences on the other at its disposal in the solving of any problems that it come across in such an effort. And it is on the solution of these problems that the future of democratic societies depends.

SCOPE OF EDUCATIONAL PSYCHOLOGY

Scope refers to the fields of operations, applications, topics, and subject matter with which it deals. Since educational psychology is an emerging and growing subject, its scope has never been fixed or static. It has always been changing its boundaries. As a result of new findings in the field, educational psychology has always been adding new dimensions to its areas of activity.

According to **Crow and Crow,** "Educational psychology is concerned with the conditions that affect learning."

According to **Douglas and Holland,** "The subject-matter of educational psychology is the nature, mental life, and the behaviour of the individual undergoing the process of education."

It has been correctly said by **Garrison** and others that "The subject matter of educational psychology is designed to enhance and enrich the lives of the learners and to furnish teachers with the knowledge and understanding that will help them to bring improvements in the quality of instruction.

The following areas can be included in the scope of educational psychology:

Study of Stages of Child Development. Educational psychology studies the nature of growth and development and general characteristics of physical, mental, emotional and social development at the various stages, *i.e.*, at the stage of infancy, late childhood and adolescence.

Study of Heredity and Environment. Educational psychology studies the impact of heredity and environment on the student.

Study of Development of Various Aspects of Child. Educational psychology enquires how various modifications can be brought about in the behaviour of the child, how and when do physical, social, emotional and language development occur in children, and how do various instincts make their appearance.

Study of Psychological Basis of Behaviour. It studies the psychological as well as the physiological behaviour of the learner. Psychological basis of behaviour are instincts, emotions, sentiments, suggestion, sympathy, imitation and play etc. Physiological basis of behaviour are nervous system and glands etc.

Study of Learning Process. Educational psychology also studies nature and process of learning, laws and methods of learning as well as factors of learning. Interest, attention, motivation, memory, habits and transfer of training play very significant role in leraning.

Study of Motivation. Educational psychology studies the nature, principles and techniques of motivation in educational field.

Study of Individual Differences. Educational psychology studies individual differences and suggests ways and means to provide education to all types of pupils. No two individuals are alike. Individuals differ physically and psychologically. Individual differences are mainly caused by heredity and environment.

Study of Measurement and Evaluation. Educational psychology is helpful in giving newer and newer techniques and tests for measuring intelligence, personality, aptitudes, interests and achievements etc. It is educational statistics which helps us in measurement and evaluation.

Study of Intelligence and Personality. Educational psychology also studies nature, development and assessment of personality and intelligence.

Study of Exceptional Children. Educational psychology studies about exceptional children. It studies about backward, retarded, gifted and creative children and their adjustment problems with home, family and school.

Study of Group Dynamics. Educational psychology studies group dynamics and group behaviour in classroom teaching and learning. It studies importance and effect of group on the individual. It also considers how an individual can modify the group life. It emphasises the role of groups in the education of children.

Study of Guidance and Counselling. Child is like a book whose every page has to be studied by the teacher. The teacher has to guide and counsel the students at every stage. Educational psychology studies the nature and process of guidance and counselling.

Study of Statistics. Educational psychology studies mean, median, mode graph, rank difference and co-relation.

A careful analysis of the subject matter of educational psychology reveals that it has three important centres:

1. *The Learner.* In this area, educational psychology examines the following:

(a) The study of the child, his abilities, aptitudes and aspects of motivation.

(b) Individual differences among children.

(c) Various stages of growth and development.

(d) Influence of various social agencies like home, school, neighbourhood etc., on the child's presonality.

2. *The Learning Process.* In this area, the following aspects are examined:

(a) Nature of learning and how it takes place.

(b) Theories of learning and how maximum learning in the minimum time period can be achieved.

3. *The Learning Situation.* Under the aspect educational psychology examines the following:

(a) Nature of classroom management and discipline.

(b) Use of techniques and aids which facilitate learning.

(c) New techniques of evaluation and their effective use.

(d) Methods of teaching children with individual differences.

(e) Knowledge about educational and vocational guidance to be given by the teacher to the child.

Thus, it is evident that the subject-matter of educational psychology is designed to enhance and enrich the learners and to furnish teachers with the knowledge and understanding so as to help them bring improvements in their quality of instruction.

METHODS OF PSYCHOLOGY

Psychology is the science of behaviour. Mind as well as behaviour constitute the subject-matter of Psychology. Psychology like other sciences employs certain methods for establishing cause-effect relations. With the help of a planned procedure we try to discover the causes of phenomena that we observe and also we try to know the effects of those phenomena. Thus, methods employed in Psychology are attempts to find the responses of the given stimuli and stimuli of the given resonses. The methods of Psychology are—(1) Observation, (2) Experiment, (3) Introspection and (4) Psycho-analysis.

Observation

The main method of Psychology, as of all sciences, is observation. Observation is a regulated perception. To observe is to look at a thing closely and to take careful note of several parts and details. Observation of the behaviour of others is an important method of Psychological study. By observing their behaviour we know what is going on in their mind. We observe bodily behaviour—movement of the limbs, facial expression, heart-beat, breathing and the like. A man's anger is known from his clenched fist, loud voice, contoured face, gnashing teeth and quivering lips.

Advantages

1. We have to study mind in general and this we can do through observation. We study the mental processes of other human beings by observing their behaviour when they are angry or happy or sad or wonderstruck.

2. It is helpful in studying the mental life and behaviour of savages, children, animals, abnormal people, the people whose language we do not understand and illiterate people suitable words to convey an adequate idea of their mental processes.

Disadvantages

1. We do not observe impartially. We not only perceive but apperceive. We think that other people and animals think and feel in same way as we do. We look at the world through coloured glasses.

2. Observation without the help of instruments is no doubt subjective, because the observer may unconsciously neglect those factors of the situation which he does not expect. Moreover, the human senses have only limited powers. The teacher cannot observe the actions of all the students in a class of even twenty and even if he can observe he cannot record every item. This defect can be considerably reduced if instrumental aid is taken.

3. The mind does not always manifest itself in observable behaviour. Cognitive processes such as thinking, reasoning and imagining etc., have no counterparts in bodily behaviour.
4. The behaviour of a hypocrite defies all explanation. How would you explain crocodile tears of one who is out to deceive you.

EXPERIMENTAL METHOD

In every science, as far as possible, knowledge is obtained first hand. This knowledge is obtained systematised and organised. How is this knowledge obtained? It is done through observation and experiment. To observe is to find a fact; to experiment is to make a fact. Experiment is observation under known and pre-arranged conditions. Observation is the general thing of which experiment is the special form. When observation is controlled and ceases to be general, we have an experiment.

The tremendous growth of Psychology during the last fifty years is due mostly to experimental method. Until the late 19th century Psychology was not considered as a Science. It was regarded as a branch of Philosophy and the methods employed for Psychological investigations were those of Philosophy such as observation and introspection.

The first attempt of making experiments in Psychology was made by Wundt in 1879. He established the first laboratory at Leipzig in Germany. Experiments were made chiefly in the field of sensation, perception, association and memory. Later on, Germany and America took the lead and by 1894, a score of research laboratories started working. The last two decades have brought in important developments in technique, methods and trends in Psychology. In America and England there is a psychologist for every school. His task is to take care of the mental health of the children and this experiment is proving very successful.

It consists in the recognition of the inter-connection of the human organism and the external world. The essential principle of the method is to place a human individual in a certain situation and to note how he reacts therein. It is on the basis of his reaction in relation to the situation in which has been placed that the laws of objective Psychology have been derived. Woodworth expresses it as a stimulus-Response chain. (SR). 'S' is the stimulus presented to the individual or the situation in which he is placed and 'R' is the individual's reaction to the stimulus or the way in which he behaves in the situation. The essential task of Psychology is to take the course from 'S' to 'R' and to state the routes from 'S' to 'R' under various circumstances.

Experiment in Psychology is performed on a subject who is a living being. The living organism has got certain characteristics and the experimenter must take these into account both in the conduct of the experiment as well as in the interpretation of the results. The experimental psychologist has to depend on the co-operation of his subject, whether an adult or a child or an animal. He cannot lose sight of the time-honoured saying, "one man can take a horse to water but even twenty cannot make him drink", Woodworth has accordingly presented a modified formula in Experimental Psychology as follows:

S—stands for stimulus or situation.

I—stands for the individual (with his own initiative and urges).

R_1 R_2 R_3—stand for variety of responses.

STEPS IN THE PSYCHOLOGICAL EXPERIMENT

Broadly speaking the following steps are involved in a psychological experiment:

1. **Defining the Problem.** First of all the field of study is defined. The experimenter knows clearly which factors to control, which factors to change, what changes to observe and with the help of which material.

2. Selecting the subject or the individual on whom the experiment is to be performed.

3. Setting the material for observation.

4. Instructing the subject or telling him his functions during the experiment.

5. Observing the responses of the subject.

6. Getting introspective report of the subject. In psychological experiment we have to deal with living human beings and while stating the result of an experiment we must mention the reaction of the subject towards the experiment and his mental state during the experiment.

7. Anlaysis of the data obtained and interpretation of the data.

Problems Tackled. The following problems have been tackled in Experimental Psychology:

1. Sensation, sence training and preception.

2. Attention, its span and duration.

3. Memory and methods of memorising.

4. Laws of learning and transfer of training.

5. Habits.

6. Work and fatigue.

7. Imagery and association of ideas.

8. Thinking and reasoning.

9. Intelligence and its measurement.

Criticism. 1. Further, Experimental method has serious limitations when it is applied to Educational Psychology. While dealing with human beings it cannot be as objective as it is claimed by its advocates, because human behaviour cannot be controlled to that extent as is possible in the case of physical and chemical phenomena.

2. Secondly, human behaviour under controlled conditions is different from spontaneous behaviour. Therefore, the experimental findings should be cautiously applied to the spontaneous behaviour of human beings under normal and free conditions.

Concluding Remarks. It is not always possible for every teacher to experiment scientifically because of no special training in doing so and of lack of facilities for experimentation in schools. Yet he can adopt new teaching methods with better results.

1. New teaching methods suggested by Psychology should be tried.
2. Experimental Psychology helps the teacher in dealing satisfactorily with the backward, the deficient, the emotionally deranged and the delinquent child.
3. Experiments can also be carried on in the development of character and leadership. Schemes of self-government and of giving responsibility to students can be tactfully introduced in schools.

IMPORTANCE AND UTILITY OF EDUCATIONAL PSYCHOLOGY

The contribution of educational psychology to the theory and practice of education is rich and varied. The knowledge of educational psychology is important as it provides teachers with some basic skills and guidelines to solve the problems of teaching-learning process.

Teaching is not everybody's cup of tea *i.e.*, everyone cannot teach.

According to **John Adams,** "Teacher should know John as well as Latin". It means teacher should know child and subject-matter. A teacher should know the nature, capacities, likings and aptitudes and attitudes of the child. Child is like a book, teacher should know each and every page of it."

Skinner's view, "The teacher needs psychology to bridge the lives of the young and the aims of education in our democratic society."

Kuppuswamy's view, "Psychology contributes to the development of the teacher by providing him with a set of concepts and principles."

Teaching is an art. Knowledge of educational psychology is very useful and indispensable for the teacher because it gives knowledge to the teacher.

Knowledge of Behaviour. Educational psychology assists the teacher in knowing the behaviour of the child at different stages of development. It also helps the teacher in understanding the physiological and psychological basis of behaviour, *i.e.*, nervous system, glands, instincts, emotions, sentiments, motives, play, intelligence, heredity and environment etc.

Knowledge of Innate Nature. The child has got natural urges instincts, potentialities and propensities. These innate qualities are the "Prime movers" of his behaviour. The teacher who knows psychology can make his teaching very successful while keeping in view innate nature of the child.

Knowledge of Guidance. It helps the teacher in giving guidance to the pupils by having an understanding of interests, abilities, aptitudes, achievements, problems, educational and vocational plans of the pupils.

Knowledge of Unconscious Mind. It helps the teacher in knowing the unconscious mind of the students and plays very important role in the development of the personality of the individual.

Understand Development Characteristics. Children pass through different stages of development as infancy, childhood and adolescence. These developmental stages have their own characteristics. If the prospective teacher knows the characteristics emerging at different stages of development, he can utilise these characteristics in imparting instruction and moulding their behaviour according to the specified goals of education.

Knowledge about Himself. It helps the teacher to know about himself. He learns the psychology of being a teacher and acquaints himself with the traits of a successful teacher.

Understand the Individual Differences. No two individuals are alike. The teacher with the knowledge of the kind of individual differences may adjust his teaching to the needs and requirements of the class and thus may be helpful in creating conducive environment in the schools where the students can develop their inherent potentialities to the maximum.

Understand the Nature of Classroom Learning. The knowledge of educational psychology provides a teacher the knowledge of learning process in general and problems of classroom learning in particular. The teacher by the knowledge of educational psychology can understand the principles of learning and various approaches to learning process, problems of learning and their remedial measures and also about factors affecting and guidance for effective learning.

Understand the Problems of Childern. By studying educational psychology a teacher may understand the causes of the problems of the children which occur at different age levels and can successfully solve them.

Understand Effective Teaching Methods. Educational psychology gives us the knowledge of appropriate teaching methods. It helps in developing new strategies of teaching. It also provides us with the knowledge of different approaches evolved to tackle the problems of teaching at different age levels.

Knowledge of Mental Health. By studying educational psychology teacher can know various factors which are responsible for mental ill health and maladjustment and can successfully help in mental hygiene.

Measurement of Learning Outcome. Psychological tools help the teacher to assess the learning outcome of the students and also to evaluate his teaching methods for required modification.

Curriculum Construction. Psychological principles are also used in formulating curriculum for different stages. Needs of the students, their developmental characteristics, learning patterns and needs of the society all are to be included in curriculum construction.

Research. Eductional psychology helps in developing tools and devices for the measurment of various variables which influence the behaviour and performance of students.

Helps to Develop Positive Attitude. The teacher training programme aims to develop positive attitude towards teaching profession and provides the prospective teachers with the necessary competencies to meet the classroom challenges. Training colleges provide the knowledge of organising the subject matter in a sequential order to suit the needs of the class. The trainees are also aquainted with the techniques of motivating children for learning.

Understanding of Group Dynamics. Educational psychology helps the teacher to recognise the importance of social behaviour and group dynamics in classroom teaching learning.

Problem of Discipline. With the knowledge of educational psychology teacher utilises the importance of indirect discipline rather than corporal punishment. It tells the teacher that discipline should be self-discipline, dynamic, positive and constructive through participation in purposeful activity. Pleasure and pain, reward and punishment, praise etc., should be judiciously used. If the teacher is unaware of the principles of educational psychology he may be unable to solve the problems of his students and thereby fail to induce order and discipline among them.

School and Class Administration. Former autocratic method of administration in school and class has been charged by democratic way of life where in the teachers and administrators are more democratic, co-operative and sympathetic and problems of administration solved by mutual discussion.

Use of Audio-Visual Aids. Educational psychology has helped the teachers to make use of various types of audio-visual aids in classroom teaching so as to make the concept more clear, definite and learning to last longer.

Time-Table. The knowledge of psychology is helpful to the teacher in preparing time-table. He should keep in mind the relative importance and toughness of different subjects and level and index of fatigue of the students.

Co-curricular Activities. Activities like debate, drama, games are given due importance alongwith theoretical subjects for the harmonious development of the personality of children.

Use of Innovations. Activity-centred teaching, discussion method, micro-teaching etc., are some innovative ideas adpoted to improve the teaching learning process.

Production of Text-books. Educational psychology has helped in planning of text-books according to the intellectual development of children, their needs and interests at different age levels.

Undoubtedly the study of educational psychology may be very helpful to equip our prospective teachers with necessary skills to deal with classroom teaching learning problems.

REVOLUTION IN EDUCATION INDUCED BY PSYCHOLOGY

The extent to which psychology has produced into the field of teaching and learning education is so impressive that only the term revolution can be applied to it with any accuracy. In pointing to the changes in education caused by psychology. Ryan has written, "In many schools of today one finds an atmosphere of friendliness and happy activity. Much of the traditional formality, the forced silence, the tension, the marching is gone. Childern's voices are heard in the halls and classrooms. The younger children come gaily down the stairways, naturally and relatively unrestrained, the older boys and girls through the corridor or outside walk making their way to school rooms, shops, studios, libraries, laboratories and playing fields to tasks that mean something to them, that make demands upon their energies and their imagination, that often involve hard, difficult work, but work that they recognise as creative. Beauty of surroundings is considered a first, requirement in these schools—there are flowers about, brightly coloured murals painted by the children, attractive informal work rooms for the various groups....Art and music have begun to play the role that belongs to them as fundamental in education and life."

1. Child-Centred Education. In early times the teachers were mainly engaged in imparting various kinds of information to the children. In those times children were less the centre to attention, the school claimed more of their time. Today, it is the child who is the centre of attention in education. Every child is individually considered and treated. Efforts are always made to adapt the curriculum of study to the needs of the child with the result that the brilliant and dull witted children do not study the same subjects. Applied psychology has directed attention to the differing abilities and capacities of people. Such an attitude has made it possible for the teacher to gauge the special abilities of his wards and to make the best arrangements for the guidance of individual children. The teacher of today not only must be acquainted with teaching but also with his students since his profession is now centred about the child and not about the subject or teacher. The consequence of this kind of reasoning is that what matters isn't the beauty, knowledge or ability of the teacher but the extent to which he succeeds in developing the personality of his students.

2. Process of Education. Previously, education was believed to be a comprehensive process that trained the individual, provided him with a moral character and made him more cultured. In psychology as it is understood today, the conception of mind has completely changed. Analysis has led to the discovery that many kinds of forces and mental activities take place within the human being so that for the development of the child it is necessary to provide him with different kinds of programmes and subjects so that he may succeed in properly developing all his mental faculties and abilities. At present, variety is believed to be essential not only in education itself but it is equally held to be true that the education of one individual subject includes many different activities and functions. The teacher should be aware of all these functions. It is only than that he can understand the difficulties of the children in understanding the subject. If a child fails to memorise some one lesson, it can hardly be taken to indicate only a lack of effort on his part and no other cause. It is equally probable that he has a weak memory, or is not intelligent, or has no interest in the subject or that he is suffering from ill health. Learning is a complex activity and it is only through a complete knowledge of its various parts that one can diagnose the difficulty of a particular child in memorising or learning a lesson. The teacher has no alternative but to attend to the activity of learning.

3. Reform in Curriculum. Psychology has also managed to bring about important variations and reforms in educational curricula. Now it is the mental age and not the chronological age of the child that helps to determine the course of study to which he is to be subjected. Intelligence tests reveal the mental age of the child. Different courses are devised for brilliant and deficient children. After the eighth or delta class, the curriculum is sub-divided into various parts such as literary, scientific, agricultural or art class. The child then has the opportunity of selecting his subject according to his interest and aptitude. Various extra-curricular activities are organised for the emotional and sentimental development of the child. These include picnics, dramatic societies, etc. Other programmes are organised in order to develop the qualities of leadership, public speaking, etc., in the child. But no course of study or programme is foisted upon the child against his inclination. Inspiration is awakened in him according to his interests and his tastes. Education has now been made more interesting and appealing with the use of audio-visual aids such as television, film projection, etc. Many schools are also equipped with radio sets that provide both entertainment and information to the child. The use of analogies to penetrate the defences of the child is an inportant method in education. Childern who choose to study history are also taken to visit historical places. And even a glance at the curriculum of basic education makes clear the extent to which psychology has revolutionised education. And special curricula are also devised to meet the needs of adult education. They suit the psychology of adult individuals.

4. Discipline. Discipline has an important place in education. One of the aims of education is to instil respect for discipline in the child. But the recent discoveries of psychology have changed the ways and means in which discipline is taught. Previously physical punishment was one of the chief methods of teaching and imparting discipline in the children. The main motive behind the discipline was fear of physical violence and injury. But instead of injuring the body of the child it injured his personality by making it distorted. Psychologists attracted the attention of enlightened people to the injurious effects of physical punishment and also suggested alternative means of making children disciplined. One suggestive example is here described. The inmates of a hostel were given to indiscipline during lunch time. They threw morsels of food at each other and wasted much more. The warden made every effort to stop this nuisance used every means of arousing fear in the children but without success. He never discovered the name of the mischief makers and neither did the boys give up their behaviour. Some time later he was replaced by a new warden who resorted to psychological methods for solving this menace. He made an announcement to the effect that the best behaved table with the most seemly boys would win a flag that would entitle them to twice the normal ration of the most succulent food. The strategy took immediate effect and the indiscipline promptly ceased. The children seated at various tables were now busily engaged in trying to look more disciplined and seemly than all the others so that they now even prevented the more hardened and incorrigible boys among them from mischief. In this way, the warden took advantage of the psychology of children to effortlessly perform a task that had completely foiled all the efforts of the earlier warden with his shock and fear tactics. Nowadays it has become customary in schools to allow the children to adopt discipline rather than foist it upon them. At the college level it is from among the students that the prefects are chosen to create and maintain discipline among their fellow mates and to help the proctor in maintaining order within the college. Very recently there was a high level debate on the spreading indiscipline among university students in India and almost all speakers put forward psychological solutions because the problem of indiscipline is fundamentally and basically a psychological one. It need hardly be pointed out that the more a teacher knows of child psychology, the easier will it be for him to create discipline in the motley group with which he is faced in the class.

5. Education on Personality. The modern methods of education place great emphasis upon the education of personality. Education is now understood to mean something more than mere reading or writing, it is also understood to involve the development of personality. Many schools have resident psychologists who solve problems related to personality of the students and give advice to teachers and parents in this regard. At places there are also child guidance clinics, that make special efforts toward the correction and normal rehabilitation of problem children or juvenile delinquents. A study of psychology is an essential part of the curriculum of teacher's training. In addition to these individual efforts most states and districts have a bureau of psychology whose functions are to solve all problems of students relating to their personality, to give personal guidance and to give advice to their parents and teachers regarding them. The truth of the matter is that the psychologist has become a link for the child's adjustment between the home and the school since such an adjustment helps to improve his personality. In the role of specialist his contirbution to the school has become indispensable.

6. Individual Differences. In days gone by, the same curriculum was prescribed for all stduents in the class. The development of applied psychology led to the fact that different individuals differ from each other in respect of their interests, intelligence, ability, capabilities, etc. This knowledge of individual differences proved a variable source of revolution for education. Now-a-days the essential pre-requisite to guidance of an educational nature is a knowledge of the subject's ability and interests. Choice of his curriculum and other extra-curricular activities is definitely governed by these individual differences.

7. Teaching Method. In the manner already described psychology has changed teaching methods lock stock and barrel. All new research aims at evolving teaching methods that induce the child to learn for himself and thus himself achieve his development. The means of a changed teaching method are radio, çinema, cultural programmes, debates and other competitions, picnics, visits to historical places, games, election contests, students' unions, etc. It is psychology that has contributed the Kindergarden and Montessori methods of teaching. Speical learning and teaching methods have been evolved for the use of blind, dumb and deaf children and mentally backward or handicapped children.

8. Process of Learning. The experiments that psychology has carried on in connection with the process of learning have led to the discovery of many laws that economise of time and yet produce good results in terms of material learned. One example would be Thorndike's laws. It is the psychologist who has stressed the importance of reward and punishment in learning. Research in psychology has aimed at discovering the efficacy and inefficacy of the various methods of learning. The employment of the various methods of learning is improved and made more scientific by a knowledge of their qualities and drawbacks.

9. Mental Testing and Guidance. Mental testing and guidance are important factors in applied psychology. Psychologists have evolved scientific tests to measure intelligence and other abilities. Students can be guided in educational and vocational matters with the help of these tests. Now, education aims both at the complete development of the individual as well as his best possible adjustment to his vocation and of his vocation to his natural abilities. Teachers need the help of psychologists in either of these two matters. Psychologists solve the problems of students through personal guidance and inform them of the job they are best suited to through vocational guidance. In this way, the co-operation and co-ordination between the teacher and the psychologist in the field of education is on the increase.

10. Reform of Problem Children. One of the most notable contributions of psychology to education is the improvement and reform of juvenile delinquents, absconding children, morons, backward children, unsocial and problem children, and advice to their parents regarding them. To this end the state and district psychological bureau assist the educational institutions.

11. Extra-Curricular Activities. The aim of education is the complete development of the child so that mere book knowledge is insufficient to gain this end. In this connection many other programmes are included in the curriculum on the suggestion of psychologists apart from the normal theoretical knowledge.

In this manner, educational psychology provides the teacher with the means to attaining knowledge of the student's nature, capacity, characteristics, needs and motive. This knowledge is the equipment for him to modify his teaching methods sufficiently to attain the goal for education.

❐

4

Educational Thinkers

Education, to Gandhiji, was a means to achieve perfection of individuality on the one hand and an instrument of service to the nation on the other. Thus, individual and social both the aims of education were considered by him equally important. "By education I mean an all-round drawing out of the best in child and man—body, mind and spirit", he said. This in other words meant development of the whole child, the whole personality of the child. Harmonious development of all the aspects of human personality such as physical, intellectual and spiritual was emphasised by him as an individual aim of education. Emphasising the social aim of education he said that the individual has a responsibility to work for the welfare of the whole society. "Willing submission to social control and restrain for the sake of the well-being of the whole society" were considered by him important attitudes to be developed in the people through education. Good of the individual and good of the society were inter dependent. So education should be both for the child as well as for the state.

Education, to Gandhi, was something more than literacy. Though he did not belittle the importance of vocational aim of education, self-realisation and knowledge of the Ultimate, God were considered the ultimate aims of education. Emphasis on vocational aspect led him to say that education has to be self-supporting, a theory which culminated into his system of basic education.

Cultural refinement of human personality through education was also considered important by Gandhiji. But, it was Indian culture that was emphasised by him. Culture, according to him was in quality of the soul which was reflected in all aspects of human behaviour. For achieving this kind of cultural refinement he emphasised the study of the Geeta and the sacred books of all other religions.

Gandhi attached much importance to character education and moral development of the child through education. This would mean to him development of such qualities in the individual as purity of personal life, self-restraint, service of humanity, courage, strength of conviction, righteousness and sense of responsibility. The attitude of "Ahimsa", non-violence was the supreme value to be developed in the people through education.

The ulitimate aim of education according to Gandhiji is the Self-Realisation. All other aims are important as they lead to self-realisation. Self-realisation, to him, means realising that the ultimate reality, the Truth is the universal soul, some unknown supreme power and that the man is only a spark of that which fuses with that supreme ultimately.

The Curriculum. Gandhiji considered elementary education the most important phase of the educational system. He, therefore, expressed his views only about the curriculum of primary stage curriculum. About this stage he said that intellectual development alone should not be emphasised. The curriculum should be so designed that it caters to the development of all the aspects of child personality. Physical, social, moral and spiritual development, too, are important. Hence, there should be provision in the curriculum for activities, experiences and subjects of knowledge that can help achieve these developments also. He, then, suggested to make the curriculum activity centred by introducing teaching of some craft like spinning, weaving, handicraft, book craft, art, agriculture, pottery etc., whichever is close to the child's life in his environment. Besides, he recommended that mother tongue should be the medium of instruction at this stage. It was also suggested by him that mathematics, social studies, drawing and music should necessarily included in the curriculum. General science including biology, chemistry, physical science, hygiene, nature study, physical education and general knowledge of astronomy were also recommended to form the basis of the curriculum. He also suggested that upto class V boys and girls should be subjected to the same curriculum. But, after that girls should be taught home science instead of general science.

Method of Teaching. Gandhiji once wrote in *Young India* (1921) that "schools and colleges should become almost, if not wholly, self-supporting". He, then emphasised that teaching should be done through arts and crafts, work and play, voluntary activity and self-choosen activity.

Gandhiji said that the method of teaching should be such as it provides to the child freedom, a chance to come into closer contact with the teacher, a chance to be an active investigator, observer and experimenter.

Craft-centred teaching and correlation method may be said to be the most important ingredients of the educational method Gandhiji suggested. Correlation method would mean relating the knowledge, of each subject being taught to the craft on the one hand and to the child's life on the other. Gandhiji, emphatically, demanded that craft should be made the centre of all education, centre of the school life. The idea, afterwards, found an expression to the Basic Education System which was introduced in all the states of the country.

COMPARISON WITH NATURALISM, IDEALISM AND PRAGMATISM

Some writers have tried to put labels on Gandhiji as a naturalist, an idealist and a pragmatist. In fact we find elements of all these three philosophies in his views on education. But, basically, he was an idealist. His emphasis was on character formation and spiritual development of the child. He himself lived a spiritual life and stood for higher values throughout his life. The good of the society, according to him, was contingent upon the goodness of each individuals. The perfect and spiritually developed individuals alone could constitute an ideal society. So he emphasised that education should lead the individual to self-realisation, realisation of God and should develop in him attitudes of self-control, social service, ahimsa, sacrifice righteousness, brotherlihood. These are all higher values like the idealistic he also emphasised that education should be used to cultivate these moral and spiritual values in the people.

There are elements of naturalism and pragmatism too found in his educational philosophy. He considered the child an important element in the process of education and emphasised, like the naturalists, that education should conform to the nature of the child. The child should be allowed freedom. He should be taught in natural environment for "drawing out the best in the child". Like the naturalists, he also said that education should aim at the development of all aspects of child's personality. Activity, play, experimentation and own experience as the strategies of education were emphasised by Gandhiji also like, the naturalists. He also considered books as the means of imparting knowledge to young child unimportant. Thus, several ideas of naturalism are found expressed in Gandhiji's educational philosophy also. Yet, it cannot be said that he was a naturalist only.

Some elements of pragmatic philosophy may also be seen in Gandhiji's educational philosophy. His emphasis on making education self-supporting and preparing individuals for vocation, craft-centred education, activity centred, teaching, learning through child's own experience and experimentation, correlated teaching clearly brings him closer to the pragmatists.

VIVEKANANDA'S EDUCATIONAL PHILOSOPHY

Swami Vivekananda ranks among the greatest educationists of the world. Here in the following lines, we discuss the basic principles of his philosophy of education:

1. Only study of books is not education.
2. Knowledge lies hidden in the mind of man. He uncovers and develops it by his own efforts.
3. Concentration is the key of all knowledge. For this, practice of Brahamcharya is very essential.

4. Purity of thought, speech and deed is self-discipline.
5. Education should develop the child physically, mentally and spiritually.
6. Education should foster spiritual faith, devotion and self surrender in the individual and should full development through service and sacrifice.
7. Education should develop character, mental powers, intelligence and inculcate self-confidence together with self-reliance.
8. Religious education should be imparted through sweet impressions and fine conduct in preference to books.
9. Boys and girls should receive the same education.
10. Specially women should be imparted religious education.
11. Mass education schemes should be formulated and launched.
12. Provision for technical education should be made so that industrial growth leads to the economic prosperity of the nation.
13. Teacher is a friend, philosopher and guide. He should sympathetically bring out the latent knowledge in a child by inspiration and motivation.
14. There should be an intimate relationship between the teacher and the students.
15. All those subjects should be included in the curriculum which promote the material and spiritual advancement of a child.

Meaning of Education

Education is not the mass of informations which are inserted by force into the mind of a child. According to Swami Vivekananda if education meant information only, then, libraries could be the greatest saints of the world and Encyclopaedias had become seers and rishis. In his own words—"Education is the manifestation of perfection already reached in a man."

Aims of Education

According to Swami Vivekananda the following should be the main aims of education:

1. *The Aim of Reaching Perfection.* The prime aim of education is to achieve fullness of perfection already present in a child. According to Swamiji all material and spiritual knowledge is already present in man covered by a curtain of ignorance. Education should tear off that veil so that the knowledge shines forth as an illuminating torch to enliven all the corners by and by. This is meant by achieving fullness of the latent perfection.

2. *Physical and Mental Development Aim.* The second aim of education is the physical and mental development of the child so that the child of today, after studying *Geeta*, is able to promote national growth and advancement as a fearless and physically well developed citizen of tomorrow. Stressing the mental development of the child, Swamiji, wished education to enable the child to stand on his own legs economically rather than becoming a parasite on others.

3. *Moral and Spiritual Development.* According to Swami Vivekananda, a nation's greatness is not only measured by its parliamentary institutions and activities, but also by the greatness of its citizens. But the greatness of citizens is possible only through their moral and spiritual development which education should foster.

4. *Character Development Aim.* According to Swamiji character development is a very important aim of any education. For this, he emphasised the practice of Brahamcharya which fosters development of mental, moral and spiritual powers leading to purity of thoughts, words and deeds.

5. *The Aim of Development Faith in One's Ownself, Shraddha and a Spirit of Renunciation.* All through his life Swamiji exhorted the individuals to keep full confidence upon their powers. They should inculcate a spirit of self surrender, sacrifice and renunciation of material pleasures for the good of others. Education should fosts, all these qualities in the individual. He gave this call to his countrymen. "Arise, awake and stop not till the goal is achieved."

6. *The Aim of Searching Unity in Diversity.* The ture aim of education is to develop insight into the individuals so that they are able to search out and realise unity in diversity. Swami Vivekanandaji has further asserted that physical and spiritual worlds are one, their distinctness is an illusion (Maya). Education should develop this sense which finds unity in diversity.

7. *Religious Development Aim.* To Swamiji religious development is an essential aim of education. To him, each individual should be able to search out and develop the religious seed embedded in him and thus find the absolute truth or reality. Hence he advocated the training of feelings and emotions so that the whole life is purified and sublimated. Then only, the capacities of obedience, social service and submission to the teachings and preachings of great saints and saviours will develop in the individual. Education should foster this development.

Curriculum

According to Swami Vivekanand, the prime aim of education is spiritual growth and development. But this does not mean that he did not advocate material prosperity and physical well-being. He feelingly advocated the inclusion of all those subjects and activities, in the curriculum, which foster material welfare with spiritual advancement. For spiritual prefection Swamiji prescribed Religious, Philosophy, Puranic lore, Upnishads, Company of saints and their preachings and for material advancement and prosperity he recommended Languages, Geography, Science, Political Science, Economics, Psychology, Art, Agriculture, Industrial and Technical subjects together with Games, sports and other Physical exercises.

Methods of Teaching

Swamiji prescribed the same ancient spiritual methods of teaching wherein the Guru and his disciples lived in close association as in a family. The essential characteristics of those religious and spiritual methods were as under:

1. To control fleeting mental faculties by the practice of Yoga.
2. To develop the mind by concentration and deep meditation.
3. To gain knowledge through lectures, discussions, self-experience and creative activities.
4. To imitate the qualities and character of teacher intelligent and clear understanding.
5. To lead the child on the right path by means of individual guidance by the teacher.

Place of Child

Like Froebel, Vivekanand emphasised the education to be child centred. According to him the child is the store and repository of all learning material and spiritual. Like a plant a child grows by his own inner power naturally. Hence advising the child to grow naturally and spontaneously, Vivekanand asserted—"Go into your own and get the Upnishads out of your own self. You are the greatest book that ever was or will be. Until the inner teacher opens, all outside teaching is in vain."

Place of Teacher

Swamiji believed in self-education. According to him each of us is his own teacher. The external teacher only guides and inspires the inner teacher (soul) to rise up and start working to develop the child. Hence discussing the role of teacher Swami Vivekanand said—"Teacher is a philosopher, friend and guide helping the educand to go forward in this own way."

Education of Masses

In the times of Swami Vivekanand, education was not available to the common people. It was confined to the well-to-do persons only. The poor, the miserable and the lowly placed used to starve and die for hunger. Swamiji yearned to improve the condition of the masses and thus advocated mass education as the only way to achieve any improvement in individual as well as society. Swamiji exhorted his countrymen to know—"I consider that the great national sin is the neglect of the masses, and that is one of the causes of our downfall. No amount of politics would be of any avail until the masses of India are once more well educated, well fed and well cared for."

MEANING AND AIMS OF EDUCATION

To Vivekananda education was a man-making process which would mean arousing the people to an awareness of their own worth, dignity and responsibility, making them the source of all the strength and sustenance of society, creating a society which will provide a healthy milieu for the development of character and personality of all its children.

Educational philosophy of Vivekananda and the aims of education together with the concept of education are founded on Vedanta philosophy, particularly the Advaita philosophy which says that in the lowest worm as well as in the highest human being the same divine nature is present. "The whole object of Vedanta philosophy is, by constant struggle, to become perfect, to become divine, to reach God and see God". The belief of this philosophy is that every human being is spirit (Atma), the soul which is immortal, evolving up or reverting back from birth to birth and death to death. Swami Vivekananda only reinterpreted the basics of Vedic philosophy in the context of 20th century man and the society.

Swami Vivekananda had great faith in education to him, this was the basic means for achieving human excellence and solving national problems. He said there are no problems which cannot be solved by that magic word "education". He defined education as the "development of faculty, not an accumulation of words". To him education was meant for the training of individuals "to will rightly and efficiently". He further said that the education that does not help the common mass of people to equip themselves for the struggle for existence, which does not bring out strength of character, a spirit of philanthropy, and the courage of a lion is not worth the name. Real education, to him, means that which enables one to stand on his own leg.

Vivekananda stressed the need to educate the millions of our common people to revitalise Indian culture of the day. A nation is advanced in proportion as education and intelligence spread among the masses. National development rests upon the goodness and greatness of men; and goodness and greatness of men are determined largely by education.

Education for "total human development" was the vision of Vivekananda which, he believed, could be achieved by refining and processing of in eternal human energies through the science of man in depth (Adhyatma Vidya). Philosophy, the science, the art and studies of various other fields of knowledge could help nations in achieving this goal. Through education nations have to unfold the humanistic and divine possibilities lying hidden within their people and raise the levels from which their consciousness handles their external, natural and social environment. True education is that which does this.

Vivekananda was deeply spiritual and intensely human. His message is the message of humanism. But his humanism has a deeper content. He said that education which gives us intellectual energy must also give us humanistic impulse and its energy of character. If man's education combines these two energy sources he will become tremendously powerful, well educated, full of hope, endowed with a firm mind and will, and strength of muscle and nerve. Vivekananda said "We want our education to turn out millions of such young people enjoying that unit of human bliss."

Although Swami Vivekananda was an idealist and a spiritualist emphasising realisation of divinity in man, yet he was fully aware of the need for national development to be achieved through education.

He stressed education for democracy and said that strengthening of democracy was possible only through education. The strength of a democracy was seen to lie in its alert and patriotic citizens who could be produced and developed through education. All institutional education, socio-political education in a democracy, he held, should therefore be designed to produce citizens who are free, responsible, and politically aware, who feel to belong to the country in which they live, who are sensitive to what happens around them. Education should produce such enlightened democratic citizens. Thus, Vivekananda, emphasised education for democracy and citizenship. He, however, was in favour of creating an ethical basis of democratic politic through education. He stressed the need for developing democratic tolerance in the people and a sense of being truly free which could be fulfilled by properly organised and rightly conducted education.

Thus, Vivekananda's educational philosophy had two major components of aims—one the individual aims and second the social aims. Under individual aims of education he emphasised total human development including physical, mental, social, cultural and spiritual development of the child. He did not leave out even the vocational development aim. In a way he stood as the embodiment of man-making education. Under the social aims of education he stressed education for citizenship and democracy, education for national integration, education for the poor and education for women, education for strengthening the whole society. In a way he stood for nation-building education.

But, these two aspects were not considered by him as separate and independent. He brought a fine synthesis between the individual and the social aims of education when he said "they alone live who live for others; the rest are more dead than alive."

Approach to Curriculum

Vivekananda held that all knowledge secular or spiritual is in the human mind. Man only discovers it within himself. It is pre-existing and is manifested in man. Knowledge is eternal. Like fire being present in the wood, it is pre-existing in the human mind. It does not come from outside. It is all inside. Man only brings it out, discovers or unveils. Soul is reservoir of all knowledge. Man takes the cover of the soul and finds that all knowledge is there. "All knowledge that the world has ever received comes from mind, the infinite library of the universe is in your mind. The external world is only the suggestion, the occasion which sets you to study your own mind. The falling of an apple gave the suggestion to Newton and he studied his own mind. He rearranged all the previous links of thought in his mind and discovered a new link among them, which we call the law of gravitation. It was not in the apple nor in anything in the centre of the earth." Thus, Vivekananda considered the curriculum just as the massive suggestion, a series of stimulations only to bring out what is there in the mind of the child. All subjects, studies and activities should be treated as a series of stimuli. These, according to him may constitute his cultural heritage found in the form of history, art, poetry, paintings, Vedas,, Upnishadas, sacred books of all religions, language, stories about India's glorious past.

He was an idealist and a spiritualist and, hence, emphasised teaching-learning of such subjects which could be the powerful source of the development of higher values and child's character. But, on the other hand, being a staunch nationalist and an aspirant for nation's economic progress and prosperity emphasised teaching of science and its all branches. He was in favour of Western technology and engineering being taught in Indian institutions as it was necessary, through them to eradicate poverty from the society. He was of the opinion that the schools should produce self-reliant individuals who can earn their living after finishing their education. Hence, it seems, he suggested that vocational courses should also form a part of curriculum crafts may be taught along with other subjects. The curriculum for girls may include "needlecraft, cookery, child-rearing, and other uselful subjects.

Methods of Teaching

With regard to teaching methods Vivekananda was of the view that children should be made to learn themselves. As all knowledge is within them and learning is only a function of their mind, they should only be made active.

The teacher and the curricula should act only as stimuli. This shows that he was against child's cramming of pieces of information. The child should not be a passive recipient of knowledge.

Discussions with the teacher was considered most important a method of teaching-learning by him.

Meditation and concentration were also considered important by him as through them developed the mental powers of the child.

It was also emphasised by him that the teacher should encourage children and develop in them self-confidence for learning.

Thus, along with the teaching the teacher was advised to develop in children those qualities which are necessary for learning. The learner must be able to control the internal and external senses. He should control his lower nature and concentrate on learning.

CONTRIBUTION OF SRI AUROBINDO TO EDUCATIONAL PHILOSOPHY

Born in Kolkata and educated in England from the age of 7 years to 21 years Aurobindo was a top notch idealist, a unique philosopher who attempted to synthesise matter and spirit, science of the West and Vedanta of the East. To him the aim of life was to attain "Divinity" through "Integral Yoga" (development of inner self) and "Dharma" (perfection of Outer life). He said that every living being is a form, a part of the Universal Consciousness and one can come into contact with this "true" self through yoga and meditation. His assumption about life was that divinity in potential form is inherent in some amount in every individual. Realisation of that is the goal of life to which education should contribute. Following are said to be the contributions of Sri Aurobindo to educational philosopher:

1. Meaning and Aims of Education. Though not much is spoken about education by Sri Aurobindo, significant ideas may be inferred about education from his philosophy. Since he was a spiritualist who saw everything in the universe rooted in the soul. He wanted education also to be rooted in the soul and "founded on the rock of the Divine", aiming at the purity and spiritualisation of human life. Thus the aim of education according to Sri Aurobindo seems to be spiritual development of the individual and the society both. The spiritual aim "regards man not as a mind, a life, and a body, but as an soul seeking for divine fulfilment." Education, to him, must lead the individual to realise that "it is the some supreme force that is active in the universe."

Spiritual development of the individual was emphasised by Sri Aurobindo. Education could be a tool for this development. Knowledge was unavoidable in this context. But, all these could not be the end in themselves. Education, knowledge and its related aspects were considered only the means for the ultimate fulfilment of the individual. He said emphatically that the individual should learn not to multilate or destroy his "ego", but should learn to expand it out of its limitations and lose it in something greater. Thus, to Aurobindo education is not only for the individual and his developments. Individual development was, perhaps, seen by him as a means of the development of the total mankind. He said that the individual should "learn to fulfil himself in the fulfilment of mankind". He wanted that human society, human friendship, love, affection, fellow feeling all must have spiritual basis, a pure foundation instead of being founded on the ego. This requires, according to Sri Aurobindo, a "transmutation of the very substance of human nature." Education must play an effective role in this transmutation.

"The first natural aim of the individual must be his own inner growth and fullness and its expression in his outer life; but this he can only accomplish through his relations with other individuals" and the humanity at large. This view of Sri Aurobindo emphasised the ideal of human unity. It may be inferred from this that education should aim at the development of the total humanity by developing each individual separately. The individual and the whole mankind can never be separated for achieving this objective.

Sri Aurobindo emphasise five aspects of education each relating to a specific aspect or human personality. These are physical education, education of the vital, mental education psychic and spiritual education. They are complimentary to one another and should be taken up simultaneously. This is known as the principle of integral education.

2. Contribution to Human Development. Another contribution of Sri Aurobindo was in the field of human evolution, upward movement of man from matter to spirit. To grow is the inner urge of the Divined in every one. Sri Aurobindo firmly stood for the change in man from the vital and the mental to the spiritual order of life, transference of man's centre of living to a higher consciousness, so as to enable him "to become himself", "to exceed himself", to realise that he is divine potentially. The secret of this evolution is to Sri Aurobindo, is not the intellect and will; rather it is the spirit which is higher than the reason. He calls this development a form of free-self-rule, a development from within rather. Then a repression of his dynamic and vital being from without. Through "Yoga" (Integrated Yoga) of Sri Aurobindo this upward ascent of the individual may be possible. The law for the individual, according to Sri Aurobindo, is to perfect his individuality by free development from within. Education should be made an effective tool for promoting this process of human evolution.

3. Contributing to Principles of Teaching. Sri Aurobindo once said that nothing can be taught. This principle implies that learning and knowledge are a function of child's own will and effort. Nothing can be imposed on him from outside. Hence, instead of teaching, it should be child's own self-learning.

He again, suggested that teaching should mean only to provide the most relevant experiences and most conducive environment to the child which can cater to his physical, mental, social, moral and spiritual development.

Freedom to think for himself, freedom to realise what the reality is, freedom to experiment with the Truth should essentially be allowed to the child. This is the greatest principle of teaching-learning.

4. Contribution to Curriculum Development. Though specific suggestions about should be included in the curriculum have nowhere learn made by Sri Aurobindo inferences about this can be drawn from what is being followed at the Ashram School at Pondicherry. The curriculum includes physical and health education, teaching of academic subjects, vocational education, cultural activities, psychic and spiritual studies, education for international understanding. The emphasis, however, is on moral and spiritual development.

5. Views about the Teacher. About the teacher's place in child's education Sri Aurobindo's position was that of a pragmatist. He had to be there very much on the scene but only as a guide, a helper. He is not there to impart knowledge, but only to help the child know how he can perfect his instruments of knowledge. He helps the child in knowing what knowledge is and how he can acquire that.

To sum up, the whole purpose of his teachings was "that man can achieve an extension of consciousness beyond the mental principle he will continue to be trapped by the dilemmas which beset him." Education, to him, must prepare the individual for this transformation. "Integral Yoga" was suggested by him to be the most practical and effective way of child's education for this purpose. It is only in Yoga that the psychological knowledge essential for attaining extension of consciousness and divine life exists.

PHILOSOPHY OF RABINDRANATH TAGORE

Rabindranath Tagore was born on 7th May, 1861 at Kolkata. He was the fourteenth of the fifteen children of his parents.

He had unhappy schooling. He composed poems till his death on 7th August, 1941.

He own Nobel Prise in Poetry. He was a great thinker also.

His Philosophy

Tagore as an individualist, naturalist, Idealist, humanist—all these rolled into one. We shall presently examine his philosophy.

1. *Tagore as Individualist.* Tagore was out and out an individualist. He believed in the right and freedom of the individual to shape his life as the individual desired. Everyone knows that no two individuals are alike—so why bind all of them with the same rope? It was thus in the development of the individual that Tagore wanted the unity of the mankind. With the development of the individual the Creator will be realised by the individual. Some of us are likely to misunderstand Tagore. The development of individual is compatible with the growth of the social units! This is not to be forgotten.

2. *Tagore as Naturalist.* Tagore's naturalism is based on the Indian belief in fundamental unity of creation and man's kinship with nature. The essential fact is that this world has a vital meaning for us and we have to know it, was cannot ignore it, we have to establish a contact with it. This way, we shall be happy. When a man does not realise his kinship with the world, Tagore says, "he lives in a prison house whose walls are alien to him." He loved nature immensely—the moon, the stars, the hills. Nature had deeply moved him—had stirred the poet in him.

3. *Harmony with all Things.* The basic principle of the philosophy of Tagore is "harmony with all things," harmony with nature, harmony with human surroundings and harmony in international relations. The highest education is that which does not merely give us information but attains our life in harmony with all existence.

4. *Tagore as Spiritualist (Spiritualism of Tagore).* Tagore's naturalism as described above, paves the way for spiritualism. Music is an aid to the process. He started the Shantiniketan school to give spiritual culture to Indians. His belief was that every Indian should attain spiritual perfection.

5. *Tagore's Humanism.* According to Dr. R.L. Ahuja, the humanism of Tagore has two aspects: the actuality of individual joy and suffering, and the reality of a world—culture of humanity as its background. He worked unwearingly, to relieve the distress due to flood and famine in his own villages of Bengal. Equally untiringly did he endeavour to spread to the four corners of the world the message of the coming together of the races of mankind, of universal humanity.

(i) Tagore's Conception of God is also Human. To quote him, "He is there where the tiller is tilling the hard ground and where the pathmaker is breaking stone." This is the high point in Tagore's philosophy.

(ii) Tagore's Conception of Universe is Purely Human. All values have their origin in man. Truth is realised through man. Beauty is felt as such by man. He says, "Reality is human and even Truth is human.

6. *Tagore and Cultural Cosmopolitanism or Internationalism.* Rabindranath Tagore was an internationalist. He looked at the world as a whole. He was for unity of mankind and its brotherhood. He hated distinctions, made on caste, creed, sex. He was for the unity of soul between East and West. Thus in conformity with his culture and philosophy, he advocated a synthesis between East and West, so that the East should give its best to the West and in return assimilate the best that Western civilisation can give it. He faced the both—East and West. He was grateful to both—East and West. His University is "Visva Bharti". It is very much international.

7. He believed in spontaneous expression and creativity of the child. This again supports the first point in the philosophy—individualism.

8. Tagore believed in truth; beauty, peace and non-violence. He was also a lover of art, painting and music.

Educational Philosophy of Tagore

His educational philosophy sprang up from two sources:

(a) hatred towards school.

(b) love of nature.

To quote, "Tagore's philosophy of education is therefore, a result of the memory of his school days, when the school resembled an educational factory, lifeless, colourless, dissociated from the context of universe, within base white walls staring like the eye balls of the dead."

His contributors revolve round the two above.

Concept of Education. Education to be real must be of the whole man, of the emotions and the senses as much as of the intellect. Man in the fullness, said Tagore, is not limited by the individual but overflows in his community. And so in his school, alongwith training in individual initiative and self-reliance, equal emphasis was laid on community service.

Nor is education a plant that can be made to grow as an exotic variety in the hot house. If it does not strike roots in the soil and adapt itself to the natural environments, it has little value for the people as a whole.

In short, education according to Tagore meant development of the individual. It meant enrichment of personality and education should be Indian one and not borrowed from the West.

Aims of Education. The aims of education according to Tagore are:

1. ***Emancipation and Perfection of Man.*** About this Tagore says, "The highest education is that which does not merely give us information but makes our life in harmony with all existence." He aims at the emancipation of man from all kinds of bondages. He aims at a perfection not only of body or mind but also that of soul. It is the fullest growth and freedom of soul. In order to achieve that aim in his endeavours he makes education as broad based as possible.

2. ***Moral Development*** of the child is the second aim of education according to Tagore. Tagore attached for more significance to moral values in education than for mere results of science which produced a system and physical power.

3. *Unity of Truth.* Another object of education, according to Tagore, was that of giving man the unity of truth. He says that physical, intellectual and spiritual life are one and we must give this idea to the children. This way harmony will prevail and when we do not do this, there is a break between the intellectual, physical and spiritual life.

4. *Education should develop international outlook is another aim.*

5. *Education should be Creative.* Tagore does not want education to be mere informative but desires that it should be creative also. He says, "The great use of education is not merely to collect facts, but to know man and to make oneself known to man."

Of course, education is to develop one physically. It should be utilitarian too.

Curriculum. Tagore was a naturalist and also an idealist and he wants things of beauty and nice virtues to be taught in the curriculum. He lays stress on those subjects which make a child full and rich in knowledge. He also wants them to appreciate truth, beauty and goodness. This guides us towards the curriculum. Subjects recommended by him to be taught are: History, geography, nature study, language, science. Activities or finer subjects will include music, art, poetry, dancing, dramatics.

He was very particular about Music and Drama. Music is essence of life and drama releases the children's tensions and anxieties.

Methods of Teaching

Methodology. Rabindranath Tagore does not believe in routine methods of teaching. He broke new ground in the methodology of teaching. His belief is not in routine methods of teaching. Even at the outset, to quote Dr. R.S. Maini, when he opened his new school, he declared that the ordinary routine methods of teaching were not to be expected in his institution. To quote Tagore, "Those who still require an artificial method of feeding in their lessons, who need constant watching and goading from their teachers will find themselves out of place in Vishwa Bharti." He rejected mechanical methods of teaching. These methods were uninspiring. Tagore wanted the boys to progress at their own rate without being goaded by others. Tagore points out, "When I was young I gave up learning and ran away from my lessons. That saved me and I owe all that I possess today to that courageous step taken when I was young. I fled the classes which gave the instructions, but which did not inspire. One thing I have gained, a sensitivity to the touch of life and of nature who speak to me."

What then is his method?

It is clear that his method of teaching is method of freedom in teaching as well as learning and, therefore, does not like the lessons being forced upon the children.

Secondly, it is activity method. He wants teaching-learning to be a joyous adventure, full of thrills, wonders, surprises. It could be Heuristic approach. Let the child find out through activity. It is also sense training through and through. It is also naturalness in teaching. School is not to be a factory and learning has got to be enjoyable.

His approach is Gestalt approach. He believes that children learn their lessons with the aid of their whole body and mind, with all the senses fully active and eager. He thus believes whole methods of teaching rather than in part methods.

He also believers that child's mind is quite sensitive and it will pick up things of its own.

Discipline. Tagore does not want that we should be harsh to children. They should be treated with all symapthy and consideration. Discipline was never, in fact, a serious problem for Tagore.

Tagore says that if the atmosphere is good, discipline problems will not arise. It is only control that breeds in scandals and indiscipline. So where there is freedom—no question of indiscipline. He also believes in self-discipline. He wants children to experiment but not in indisciplined manner.

Tagore recognises that the boys are full of enthusiasm and when they find opportunities for self-expression, they may be little uncontrollable. He could rather enjoy the children expressing themselves freely in their outbursts of playful spirit which may seem uncontrollable, but not tolerate the repression of the child with no freedom to expand. Therefore, after analysing the psychological cause of indiscipline, he gave the children unrestricted freedom to do whatever they liked. This way, many psychological complexes are eliminated and "naughtiness" seldom occurs.

Further, man should be disciplined through art. Tagore discovered that the secret of maintaining discipline lies in the development of integrated personality. It is basically discipline of freedom.

Role of Teacher. Role of teacher is important. He is the Guru. He is to guide the students. He is to keep them on the track. He is also to keep in contact with them. Teacher is also to remain learner throughout his life. He who fails as a learner, fails as a teacher.

Vishwa Bharti University at Shantiniketan

To give his ideas and ideals a practical shape, Tagore founded what is now known as Vishwa Bharti University at Shantiniketan (Rly. Station Bolpar in West Bengal). It is an international university for Tagore believed in internationalism very much. Vishwa Bharti means a place where universal knowledge is given or gathered. In fact, Vishwa Bharti University has grown out of an ashram founded by father (Maharishi Debendranath Tagore of the Brahmo Samaj Fame) of Rabindranath Tagore in 1863. Since 1921, it is recognised as a university. It is said that India needs more such type of universities.

Why of Shantiniketan? The Vishwa-Bharti University at Shantiniketan was opened with the following aims:

(i) To bring learned people from East and West together.

(ii) To promote internationalism.

(iii) To help Indians create.

(iv) Lastly, to provide for the fullest development of man.

Tagore said that our knowledge was second-hand knowledge. There was nothing original in it. At Shantiniketan, all freedom will be given to create.

The Main Faculties of Vishwa-Bharti University

1. Vidya Bhawan: It is school of research. Here research is carried on in all languages and in Indian Philosophy.
2. Patha Bhawan (Just ordinary school).
3. Teacher's College.
4. Hindi Bhawan.
5. Industrial Training School.
6. Music and Drawing School (Kala Bhawan).

Other Features of Vishwa-Bharti

1. It is located in natural surroundings.
2. Classes are held in the open under the trees.
3. More stress is laid on teaching and learning of music, art, drama, poetry.
4. Unlike Gandhiji, Tagore did not lay much stress on manual work. He stressed on something fine and delicate. He did not reject manual work altogether.
5. Atmosphere is homely, prayers are sung and due stress and place is given to extra curricular activities.
6. Individual attention is paid to each and every student.
7. Students themselves make rules and run the university.

In fact, what Tagore said is fully practised here. Students work hard here.

FROEBEL'S EDUCATIONAL PHILOSOPHY

Froebel (1783–1852) was a great educator of Germany. He also had a neglected childhood and boyhood, and so he had to roam about from place to place, learning, studying and trying various professions. He also started his own schools in Switzerland and Germany but these could be flourish for want of proper finances and because of official restrictions. He, however, brought out his world famous books on education during this period which include "*The Education of Man*", "*Pedagogies of Kindergarten*", "*Mother Plays and Nursery Songs*" and "*Education by Development*". These books mainly deal with the education of children, below the age of seven years.

1. His Philosophy. Froebel's philosophy is of absolute idealism. He mainly pressed two great things, namely, his 'idea of unity in diversity' and his 'theory of development'.

With regard to the former, he viewed this whole universe as a unity from God—the Absolute. In his book, "*The Education of Man*", he remarked, "The whole world—the All, the Universe—is a single great organism in which an eternal uniformity manifests itself. This principle of uniformity expresses itself as much in external nature as in spirit. Life is the union of the spiritual with the material. Without mind of spirit, matter is lifeless, it remains formless, it is mere chaos. Only through the entrance of the spiritual into the material, does the cosmos originate....Every creature, object is matter, informed by spirit....God is the presupposition, the condition of their existence. Without God, they would not exist. God is the only ground of all things. God is the all-comprehending, the all-sustaining. God is the essential nature, the meaning of the world. He further says, "All things have come from the Divine Unity (God) and have their origin in the Divine Unity. The Divine affluence that lives in each thing is the essence of each thing."

With this belief Froebel formulated the principle that there is unity of man, nature and God. Men must be aware of this Absolute Unity of Universe. The real purpose of education was "to expand or develop the life of an individual until it comprehends this existence through participation in all-pervading spiritual activity."

Regarding his theory of development, he said that there is an absolute goal towards which all things are growing. This absolute goal is realised through the presentation of symbols, representing the various aspects of the Absolute. These symbols are called "gifts" which we shall discuss later.

Development can be produced only by the exercise or use of faculty; physical, mental or spiritual. If mind is to be developed, it should be exercised and so is with the development of the body. Effective development is possible only if the exercise arises from the thing's own activity. "Each individual must develop from within, self-active and free, in accordance with the eternal law, because full development comes only by spontaneous self-activity". Froebel advocates balanced and unified development of body, mind and soul.

2. His Concept and Aims of Education. To Froebel, education is growth from within. It is a development by which an individual realises that he is one unit of the all-encompassing unity. "It is development by which man's life broadens until it has related itself to nature; until it enters sympathetically into all activities of society, until it, participates in the achievements of the race and aspirations of humanity." Education is to unfold the child's innate powers and awaken his spiritual nature so that he may have a spiritual union with God.

Regarding the functions of education, Froebel remarks, "Education should lead and guide man to clearness, concerning himself and in himself, to peace with nature, and to unity with God. It should life him to a knowledge of himself and of mankind, to a knowledge of God and a nature and to the pure and holy life."

As regards the aims of education, Froebel wants all-round development of the individual, so that he may be able to express the spiritual, the Divine, that slumbers in him. Like Rousseau, Froebel education should lead to moral improvement, religious uplift and spiritual insight. Then the child will be able to realise that he is component of all-pervading spirit, which is Absolute Unity.

Finally, education should enable the child to enter sympathetically into all activities of society and participate freely in its achievements and aspirations.

3. Froebel's Kindergarten. Froebel, however, attached great importance to education in the child's early life. He thought that if the education of pre-school years was not properly reformed, no tangible improvement could be made in school education. This led him to establish a school for small children between the ages of three and seven. This school was named "kindergarten" or the *garden of children*. The chief characteristics of the kindergarten are:

(i) Self-Activity. Self-activity is spontaneous in which the child carries out his own impulses. Such activity directs the growth of the child along the lines of racial development. So it merges the individual spirit with the spirit of humanity. Self-activity, in fact, is self-realisation through which the child comes to know of his own nature as well as the life around him. Thus, self-activity not only fills the gap between knowledge and action but also gives joy, freedom, contentment and peace of mind. Self-activity is promoted through song, movements and construction.

(ii) Creativeness. Child is creative by nature. If he is given some material, he will at once try to create new forms and combinations with that material. "Since God created man in his own image, man should also create and bring forth like God," Froebel also believes that every man's mind, soul and hand are inseparable, although they are independent parts of him. Mind and soul express themselves through physical activity and expression. It is, therefore, that thinking must express itself in doing, otherwise education will remain unproductive.

(iii) Social Participation. Froebel believes that man is essentially a social animal by nature. It is the primary instinct of man to live in the company of other persons. So unlike Rousseau, he emphasised the social aspect of education and advocated that home, school, church, vocation and the state, should all provide opportunities to children for social participation. By participating in co-operative activities, the child not only receives physical training but also intellectual, social and moral education.

4. Methods of Teaching in the Kindergarten. Froebel's Kindergarten is a miniature state for children in which they move freely and joyfully, of course, with due consideration for each other. There are no books prescribed. The entire school programme gives training in self-expression through song, movement and construction. Out of these three, the child automatically learns the proper use of language. But these three modes of expression are not generally separated from one another, but they often go together, so that the entire process may become one organic whole. For instance, when a story is told or read, it is expressed in a song, dramatised in movements and gestures and finally illustrated by construction work from blocks, paper, clay, drawing or other material. Through such a procedure, "thoughts are stimulated, imagination vivifies, hands and eyes trained, muscles coordinated, and moral nature strengthened."

5. Teaching through Songs. In the Kindergarten, education is generally imparted through songs. It is, therefore, that songs are included in the daily school programme. All the songs, selected and included by Froebel, are about the common objects of life. They relate to nursery games and satisfy some physical, intellectual or moral needs of children. These are arranged no accordance with the development of the child. Each such song has three parts *(i)* a motto for the mother's guidance *(ii)* a verse for singing to the child and *(iii)* a picture illustrating the verse. There are in all fifty play songs of this type. Besides these play-songs, Froebel also devised such nursery rhymes, as "Jack and Jill", "Humpty Dumpty" and "Cyndrella". The main aim is to enable the child to use his senses, limbs and muscles and to make him familiar with the objects, around him.

6. Teaching through Gifts and Occupations. Gifts and occupations of Froebel are the most conspicuous contribution to the methodology of nursery education. Gifts are simple educational toys which are presented to the child in a definite order, without charging their forms. The child is given the freedom to handle them in any way, he likes.—While gifts signify the material, occupations represent activities which are suggested by that material and which can be continued with its help. Gifts are in the shape of wooden balls of different colours, wooden spheres, cubes and cylinders of different types and sizes. Additional gifts are in the form of wooden squares, triangles, tables, sticks and rings. Occupations include activities like construction with paper, clay, wood and materials.

It may, however, be noted that gifts and occupations have a definite purpose behind them. They train the senses of sight and touch. They give the idea of size, form and surface. They also develop the number sense and artistic consciousness. In this way they facilitate further instruction in Algebra, Geometry, Trigonometry and Drawing. And as Rusk says, "By his methodological arrangement of the gifts and occupations, Froebel nevertheless founded a new type of educational institution and although his system too readily lent itself to formalism by later generations of teachers who had not the spirit of the natter, it ameliorated the lot of countless children."

7. Teaching through Play. About play, Froebel remarks, "Play is the characteristic activity of childhood. It is the highest phase of child-development—of human development to this period, for it is self-active representation or the inner-representation of the inner form, inner necessity and impulse. Play is the purest, most spiritual activity of man at this stage and at the same time, typical of human life as a whole—of the inner, natural life in man and all things. It gives, therefore, joy, freedom, contentment, inner and outer rest and peace with the world. It holds the source of all that is good."

It is through play that the child discloses his real self and clearly indicates his interests. So Froebel gives a prominent place to play activities in his Kindergarten system. He has rather based the educational process in early years on play. He utilises play for cultivating in child the habits of action, feeling and thinking. Courage, instinct and motivation are also developed through play. But Froebel's play activities are all very well-directed and guided by the teacher.

9. Role of the Teacher. Teacher in the Kindergarten acts as a gardener, whose function is to see that young plants (small children) under her care, grow according to their own natural course of development. Froebel compares young growing children with plants and, therefore, he asks the teachers to let the children grow and develop in accordance with their natural endowments. He says, "The tree germ bears within itself the nature of the whole tree. So the development and formation of the whole future life of each is contained in the beginning of its existence."

So the teacher is instructed not to distort the natural endowments, powers and tendencies of children by undue and wilful interference in their activities. The teacher is simply to redirect the child's growth to natural direction when she feels that the child is going astray. According to Froebel, education is controlled development so it is the duty of the teacher to control this process.

9. Other Subjects of the Curriculum. Besides spontaneous self-activity and play activities, Froebel has also recommended manual work, nature study, natural sciences, languages, art and religious instruction. About the inclusion of manual work, Froebel says, "Scholastic education of our times leads children to indolence and laziness and a vast amount of man-power remains undeveloped and is lost. Manual work is necessary condition of the realisation of pupil's personality; through it, he comes to himself." Nature study creates a sense of wonder and admiration in the minds of children for the work of God and, therefore, he believed that it would result in religious uplift and spiritual insight. Natural sciences including Mathematics, which gives an insight into the laws that govern human life. Languages establish the inner living connection among the diversities of things. Art activities like singing, drawing, painting, clay-modelling, wood-work and leather-work provide the soul with opportunities for expression in those outward forms.

10. Discipline. Discipline, according to Froebel, is not a set of rules and regulations, imposed upon children. It is a way of living and doing which gives children a strong will. In the Kindergarten, discipline is of protective and co-operative type. Spontaneous and play activities, games and strories, art and crafts, gifts and occupations, all provide sound physical and mental training to children and teach them discipline.

11. Contribution of Froebel to Educational Theory and Practice. Froebel's Kindergarten system attracted the attention of the educational world to the proper education and training of pre-school-going-age children. Although this stage is the most important stage of child development, yet its education was so far neglected altogether. The Kindergarten system soon became very popular throughout Europe and now it has firmly established itself in the shape of reformed nursery schools throughout the civilised world. Froebel has really shown the right road to further advance. His main contribution to educational theory and practice is as follows:

(i) ***Emphasis on Nursery Education.*** As we have stated above, it was Froebel who greatly emphasised the importance of pre-school education. He often said, "All school education was yet without a proper initial foundation and until the education of the nursery was reformed, nothing solid and worthy could be attained." He was a great lover of young growing children. So he made a minute study of their nature, aptitudes, interests and endowments and then gave to the world a theory and practice of education for the pre-school period, which had very largely been neglected so far.

(ii) ***Respect for the Child's Individuality.*** All the modern educators have a great respect for the child's individuality. They consider the school as a "temple where they are to pay homage to the individuality of the child". But it was Froebel who first realised the value of "discovering and developing individuality by means of initiative, execution and co-operation in the educational process." It is in the

wake of Froebel that modern educators recognise the child's individuality and work it out by means of the child's own initiative and effort.

(iii) ***Learning through Arts and Crafts.*** Modern progressive schools fully recognise that creativeness is a great incentive to work and to learn. So the child is made to create and construct things with his own labour and effort. In Basic education also a great stress is paid on learning through arts and crafts. It was Froebel, who was an early advocate of the inclusion of manual work in the school curriculum. In "*The Education of Man*," he says, "Manual work is a necessary condition of the realisation of the child's personality. Through it he come to himself." So he included various arts and crafts like drawing, painting, wood-work, leather-work, clay-modelling, paper-cutting, card-board work and embroidery etc., in pre-school education.

(iv) ***Self-Activity in Education.*** Although the concept of education as a process of learning through self-activity is not original, yet Froebel by making spontaneous inner activity of the child as the very basis of all learning, attached a new value to the native capacities of children in scheme of studies. He said that children were not only receptive of knowledge, they were also very active in the expression. So at the pre-school stage they should be allowed to see, handle, arrange, rearrange, make and unmake things themselves.

(v) ***Sociological Aspect of Education.*** By laying stress upon activity and social participation and by transforming school into a miniature society where children develop the power of doing things in a social atmosphere, Froebel brought sociological aspect of education into limelight. It is this aspect which is greatly emphasised in modern education. Froebel wanted education to fit the individual for full life

within the group, so that he may adjust himself properly to his physical and social environment. For this purpose, he recommends that primary virtues like co-operation, sympathy, fellow-feeling and responsibility be developed in children in the school community. So Froebel is looked upon as the father of sociological trend in education.

(vi) ***Play-Way in Education.*** Modern educators stress that children should be taught through play-way. It was Froebel who based all the early education of the child on play by identifying play and work as one. This doctrine of play forms the centre of mordern education and has had the greatest influence on educational theory and practice. In modern progressive schools, the project and other new methods as well as all types of experimental and creative activities are based on play-way.

(vii) ***Inclusion of Nature Study in Curriculum.*** Froebel gave new stimulus to the aims and methods of teaching Nature Study. He regarded the study of nature as a means of realising the presence of the all-pervading Divine Spirit, in the Natural phenomena. It is, therefore, that he recommends the study of nature page to page, as a living expression of Divine life. His main aim of including this subject in the school curriculum was moral and religious uplift of the child, by coming into contact with nature.

(viii) ***Emphasis on Sense-Training.*** For sharpening the intelligence of pupils, Froebel emphasised sense-training, against merely verbal instruction. Since senses are the gateways of learning, their training must form the first step in the child's education. Froebel's gifts and occupations are especially devised for training the senses of children.

Thus, we can conclude by saying that Froebel's Kindergarten system aims at the complete development of the individual child. "It is by far the most original, attractive and philosophical form of infant development, the world has yet seen." This is the only reason why this system has now spread in all the progressive countries of the world.

Some critics of Froebel say that tiny rots of three or four years cannot understand his philosophic principle of "Organic Unity". Then symbolism involved in gifts is also too difficult to be understood by immature brains. Furthermore, there is no correlation in the subjects and activities in the Kindergarten system. Everything is taught in isolation. Another defect pointed out by them is that Froebel stresses the sociological aspect to the neglect of the child's individuality.

CONTRIBUTIONS OF MADAM MONTESSORI

Madam Maria Montessori (1870–1952) was an Italian lady-doctor, who later became a world famous educationist. She entered the field of education through her interest in mentally deficient children. She studied those children very intensively and reached the conclusion that mental deficiency was due to dullness of senses and that if their senses could be properly trained, those children could acquire some knowledge. And she actually succeeded when she tried the experiment. This lead her to employ that very method on educating normal children and she achieved far better results. Thus, her approach to education is scientific and rational as against that of Froebel's metaphysical. She is the originator of the 'Montessori Method'.

1. Concept and Aims of Education. According to Madam Montessori, "Education is the active help given to the normal expansion of the life of the child." She said that every child is different from others, physically as well as mentally. Each has peculiar powers and endowments. So the child's individuality must not be crushed or suppressed through collective teaching. Each child should be paid individual attention and allowed to progress at his own pace. Education should enable each child to adjust himself to his immediate environment. She wanted that each child should develop from within and not from without. Education should guide the process of unfolding the hidden powers of the child in a way that he becomes what he is destined to become.

2. Principle of Montessori System of Education. The important principles of the Montessori system are:

(a) ***The Principle of Individuality.*** As we have stated above, Montessori believed that each child has got his own peculiar interest, aptitude, capacities and endowments. He can, therefore, develop them in his own peculiar way and at his own rate and speed. Thus, individual differences must be recognised both physically and mentally. She says, "The child is a body which grows and a soul which develops. Such a mysterious thing should neither be marred nor stifled. Educational activities should be so planned that a child's individuality must be unfolded to the full." So she recommends observation of each child, proving him the environment, suited to his individual normal growth and thus educating him individually.

(b) ***The Principle of Sense-Training.*** Like Rousseau and Froebel, Montessori also stresses that senses play a very important part in a child's education because these are the gateways of knowledge. She believed that mental deficiency was due to the dullness of senses, and, therefore, proper training of senses was necessary for acquiring knowledge. From a study of children she realised that senses of children were particularly very active between the ages of three and seven and a such, a lot of learning could take place during this period. She, therefore, devised graded apparatus for providing sensations of weight, colours, sound, touch and temperature etc., and this enabled children to discriminate between different stimuli.

(c) ***The Principle of Self-Education.*** Montessori believed that self-education was the best method by which a child can learn in his own way and of his own speed, without any interference from outside. Knowledge gets a new meaning altogether when it is self-sought and self-caught.

She, therefore, stressed that we should never goad on the dull child and check the bright one. In case of error, she recommended the use of Didactic Apparatus, which controls every error and helps the child to correct himself automatically. This apparatus enables even dull and defective children to receive education. In fact, it is a substitute for the teacher.

(d) ***The Principle of Liberty.*** For self-education, children should have an atmosphere of freedom and liberty. This principle of liberty has come out of her concept of education as development. It means that as education is concerned with the unfolding of the child's nature, his innate faculties and latent potentialities. The child must be allowed maximum freedom to unfold himself without any check or hindrance. Thus, freedom is the most suitable medium for the development of human personality. So she says, "The school must permit the free, natural manifestation of the child if he is to be studied in a scientific manner. The method of observation is established upon one fundamental basis—the liberty of the pupils in their own spontaneous manifestations which necessitates independence of action on the part of the child.

3. Practical Working of Montessori Method. Froebel called his school "Kindergarten" or "The Children's Garden". Montessori called it "the Children's House". It is the place where children are taught in homely atmosphere, which is very congenial to the development of pupils individuality.

"The children house" is a many-roomed school with a nicely laid-out garden. It has separate rooms for study, lunch, manual work, games, amusement and rest etc. All these rooms are properly equipped and furnished. These are looked after by the children themselves, who not only clean and dust them but also lay the tables and set the chairs. The Montessori school has no fixed time-table because class is only a unit of organisation and not a unit of teaching.

There are no punishments and rewards. The child's sense of achievement is the only rewards and self-development is the greatest pleasure. Each child is free to choose his own activities, interest and inclinations.

For children below the age of six, three types of exercises are given in a Montessori School:

(a) ***Exercise for Practical Life.*** In Children's House, pupils are given exercises for practical life. They are taught how to wash their hands and clothes, how to sweep the rooms, dust the furniture, set the tables, clean their nails, brush their teeth, polish their shoes and comb their hair. Exercises are also given to train children in movements, necessary for dressing and under sing themselves. It is, in fact, a training in liberty, for freedom. According to Montessori, it does not consist in having others at one's command to perform the ordinary services, but in being able to do these oneself and in being independent of others.

Montessori has also devised certain formal gymnastic exercises, which develop coordinated movements in the child. For these exercises she has also devised special apparatus. Muscular education and training is given through walking, holding objects and hand-work, Rhythmic exercises are also provided. These exercises not only make children healthy but also give them training for practical life.

(b) ***Exercises for Sense-Training.*** Montessori attached more importance to sensory training than learning, thinking or reasoning. She, therefore, devised apparatus for providing exercises in sense-training. The Didactic Apparatus sharpens the pupils' senses and accelerates learning. The varied material includes blocks, cylinders, paper, cabinets; coins, tables, pencils and wools of different colours, boxes, balls, cubes, rods, and water of different temperatures.

This material is meant to give perception of size, form, weight, touch, hearing and colour etc. The sense of touch is developed by presenting water at different temperatures to the child. Sand-papers of graded roughness are also used for this purpose. Perception of size is developed through handling a series of wooden cylinders of varying heights and diameters. Series of blocks and rods of graded diameters are also used for this purpose. Sense of hearing is developed through boxes, containing pebbles and other sound-producing material. Sense of weight is cultivated through blocks and tables of wood of varying weights. Colour sense is trained through samples of wood of different colours, arranged and graded according to the depth of colour, as we have already stated under the 'Principle of Self-education'.

(c) ***Didactic Exercises for Teaching 3R's.*** After sensory training, children are taught reading, writing and arithmetic. In her system writing starts before reading. For this purpose, she depends upon the psychological principle of "Transfer of Training". In her own words, "Preparatory movements could be converted and reduced to a mechanism by means of repeated exercises, not in the work itself, but in that which prepares for it."

(i) Teaching of Writing. The procedure of teaching consists these steps:

(a) ***Recognition of the forms of Letters.*** For this purpose, letters of the alphabet are cut in sand-paper and pasted on cardboard. The children are asked to pass their finger over these letters. In this way they gradually learn to manipulate a pencil. The same exercise is then practises with closed eyes.

(b) ***Learning of Phonetic Sounds.*** While the pupils are tracing out letters, the teacher tells them their sounds, which they are asked to reproduce. This prepares them for reading.

(c) ***Control of Pen.*** Then the pupils are asked to place the metal frame on a piece of paper and draw a line round it with a coloured chalk. The same thing is repeated by placing the metal inset. In their way, two figures are produced on the paper. The intervening figure is then filled up with another piece of chalk. While making upward and downward strokes, the pupils are not allowed to move their pencils or pieces of chalk, outside the outline. Thus they learn the necessary control of pen.

(ii) Teaching of Reading. About reading, Montessori says, "Reading is the interpretation of an idea from the written signs and not merely breaking at print. Until the child receives a transmissions and of ideas from the written word, he does not read." Her material for reading consists of slips of paper or cards, on which words and phrases are written in bold scripts. The child is given a card, containing the name of a familiar object. He tries to utter the sounds and then repeat them faster and faster. When the child is able to pronounce the word correctly, he is asked to place the card under the object, whose name is written on it. Similarly sentences, describing actions or expressing commands are written on paper or card-board. The child selects a card, reads it mentally and does the action contained in it.

(iii) Teaching of Arithmetic. After sufficient writing and reading, Montessori wished that children should be introduced to the four fundamental rules of arithmetic. But there is no originality in the methods of teaching arithmetic as advocated by her. It is the same old procedure of teaching by means of coloured beads, numerical rods, wooden spindles, sand-paper numbers, simple boxes, printed shells and such other attractive material as could be made available. Thus addition, substraction, multiplication and division were taught. The device, generally used, was the 'Long Stair'. Consisting of a set of ten rods, varying in length, from one to ten decimetres. Each rod was divided into a number of parts, painted red and blue respectively.

4. Place of the Teacher. Montessori recommends "consciously controlled and systematically directed" education for young children.

This control and direction is to be provided by the teacher, who should be an expert guide and excellent organiser. The teacher in Montessori system is called a "directress", who should be well-versed in child psychology. Montessori says, "The broader the teacher's scientific culture and practice in experimental psychology, the sooner will come for her the marvel of unfolding life and her interest in it. The teacher must allow full freedom to the child and not to interfere with his activity. She is simply to observe and intervene only when absolutely necessary. She is to act as a stage director in this self-educative process. Virtues and not words are the main qualifications of the teacher. She should be partly a scientist, partly a doctor completely religious."

5. Montessori's Contribution. Dr. Maria Montessori's work has considerably influenced modern educational theory and practice, especially in case of children at nursery school stage. Her gospel of love, respect and sympathy for the child has been accepted all over the world. Her system of child education has become so popular that the word "Montessori" became synonymous with "child". All values her system have been absorbed and put into practice by the modern nursery school. Her main contribution is as follows:

(a) Scientific Concept of Education. Dr. Montessori started life as a doctor and, as such formulated her method of teaching young children in the light of her experience and experiment.

She gave us observation, experimentation and other scientific methods in education. She never insisted on material and method as the last words in the field of child education. She rather gave a scientific approach to education by breaking away from old traditions.

(b) Psychological Approach to Education. Like Froebel, she has also given emphasis on sense training, which is based on psychological principles. By introducing exercises for practical life, she has enabled children to meet everyday situations themselves. She has advocated auto-education in an atmosphere of freedom and in the spirit of play. She has also emphasised child's development from within through his own efforts. All these principles have made *learning* more important than *teaching*, which is universally accepted today.

(c) ***Emphasis on Individual Teaching.*** As against collective and class reading, Montessory stresses individual treatment of each child. Because of individual differences in physical and mental make-up, each pupil should be observed, studied and handed in a different manner. Thus, like the modern educators, she made child as the "unit of teaching" in place of class.

(d) ***Love and Respect for Small Children.*** Montessori often said that child-education was the most important problem of humanity. It is, therefore, that it should receive the best attention of the Government and the public. In her own words, "The child's soul which is pure and very sensitive, requires our most delicate care". For her "child was God, her school was the temple and deity of the temple was the essence of childhood." The profound love for children, that she had compelled her to travel from one corner of the world to another to start institutions for them, based on her system. She also stayed in India from 1939 to 1951 and conducted a number of training courses for teachers in her system of child education.

(e) ***Learning through Exercises.*** The most conspicuous contribution of Montessori is the Didactic Apparatus, which she devised for imparting sense training, muscular co-ordination and instruction in 3 R's. It was really a new experiment to teach writing before reading, but the experiment was successful in actual practice.

6. Limitations of her Method. In spite of such a unique contribution to the field of child education, the Montessori Method also suffers from certain limitations. Firstly, she has neglected play activities of children, which are most valuable in a child's education. Secondly she gives too much stress on Didactic Apparatus. In fact, her entire method rests upon this apparatus. Exercises with this apparatus, as recommended by Montessori, are so limited that a child cannot express himself fully. Thirdly, she has neglected social factor in the education of children. She looks only to individual development. This is the reason that in Montessori method there is a little of music songs, dramas, dances and group activities, which are all so essential for social training. Lastly, her method is very costly. Teachers of the concept of Montessori are not available to majority of our schools, especially in villages. So this method is not suited to Indian conditions.

6. Special Role of the Teacher. In her system of education there are no teachers because they do not teach. They are simply directors because they direct and guide the movements of children. They only provide the proper environment and material at the right moment and then observe auto-development of children. Thus, in Montessori system, the child is more active than the teacher. He learns by participating fully in the reading-learning processes. Thus, the teacher has to play a different role altogether. "Instead of facility of speech, she has to acquire the power of silence, instead of teaching, she has to observe, and instead of the proud dignity of one who claims to be infallible, she assumes the venture of humanity."

Montessori *Versus* Froebel. Both Montessori and Froebel have oganised schemes of educating pre-school age children. Both of them consider education as the process of unfolding. Both lay stress on self-expression and self-activity in an atmosphere of freedom. Both advocate play-way methods of imparting education. Both respect the child's individuality and have profound love for the child. Both are in favour of sense-training for sharpening the intellect of children. Both recommend self-education on the part of the child, with his own efforts, while teacher should be in the background, to play the part of an observer and a guide. Both are idealist thinkers. To Montessori, child was God, while Froebel wished education to lead and guide a man to unity with God.

However, there are also certain points of difference between these two educators. While Froebel's theory is based on metaphysical, assumptions, Montessori's method has a scientific background, and, therefore, her approach is based on practical considerations. Secondly in the kindergarten, the children are taught in groups while in the Montessori, individual work and individualism is emphasised. Thirdly, kindergarten, social training is one of the basic principles. It is imparted through movement, plays, action songs, group activities and cooperative occupations. Fourthly, Froebel advocates a good use of stories, fairy-tales, fables, songs, dramas and poetry for stimulating the imagination of pupils. Montessori neglects altogether the training of imagination in her system. Fifthly, in Montessori system, writing, reading and arithmetic are provided, while there is nothing, of the sort in kindergarten. Sixthly, in Montessori, sense training is provided through Didactic Apparatus while in kindergarten, it is given through gifts. Seventhly, while in Montessori, daily life activities are given prominence, in kindergarten, manual activities like clay-modelling gardening, wood work, paper-cutting, etc. emphasised, Eighthly, teacher in a kindergarten school is like a gardener, looking after tender plants. She is to guide children's activities and may interfere when they go a stray. In a Montessori school, the teacher is simply to observe children, handling didactic apparatus. Lastly, kindergarten system can be introduced in any infant school without much difficulty as gifts can be got prepared locally according to needs. It can therefore be medium of mass education. On the other hand, the Montessori Method cannot be applied in that Didactic Apparatus. Moreover, teachers with knowledge of experimental psychology and laboratory procedure are not available.

❐

5

Education in Indian Constitution

Values are derived from the Constitution, culture and religion of a nation and country. Indian values are determined by the Indian constitution, Indian culture and Indian religion.

What is a Constitution? A Constitution is a fundamental legal document according to which the government of a country functions. It is the basic law which defines and delimits the main organs of government and their jurisdiction as well as the basic rights of the citizens. A Constitution, thus, is superior to all other laws of the country and no law can be enacted which is not in conformity with the Constitution.

A government looks after law and order in a society. It does so by making laws and maintaining order. But a government cannot make laws and administer a country according to its own whims and forces. Every government has to function in conformity with basic law of the land. The Constitution contains those laws which act as the source according to which the rules and regulations of governing a country are framed.

A democratic government is one in which the citizens participate in the functioning of the government, directly or indirectly. It is a government in which the government's powers are limited and clearly spelt out. Conversely, it is also a government under which citizen's rights are also given clearly. Now, how are these limits placed on the activity of the Government? This is done by what is called a Constitution.

A Constitution is considered the source of powers and authority of government. It lays down precisely what the powers of a particular government agency are, what this it can, or cannot do. The idea is to minimise confusion and conflict of operation between the various organs of the government. A Constitution is concerned with two aspects—the relation between different organs of government; and between the government and the citizens. More than anything else a Constitution is an instrument of controlling the abuse of power by the government. That is why the Constitution is a very important document.

INDIAN CONSTITUTION

Preamble. "We, the people of India, having solemnly resolved to constitute India into a Sovereign Socialist Secular Democratic Republic and to secure to all its citizens: Justice, Social, Economic and Political; Liberty of thought, expression, belief, faith and worship; Equality of status and of opportunity; and to promote among them all Fraternity assuring the dignity of the individual and unity and integrity of the Nation; in our Constituent Assembly this twenty-sixth day of November, 1949, do hereby adopt, enact and give to ourselves this Constitution".

The Preamble sets out what the objectives of Indian government the kind of value system the Constitution wishes to set up in India. It declares India a sovereign state. Sovereignty means absolute independence, a government which is not controlled by any other power. When India was under British rule, it could not be called a sovereign country. Besides, the Constitution provides for democratic society in India. Here every citizen enjoys equal political rights. The country is governed by the elected representatives of the people. There is no state religion of India. The state does not favour people of any particular religion. The citizens are free to follow and practise the religion of their own choice. The Constitution also declares socialism to be one of the objectives. The ideal of equality remains incomplete if it is restricted only to the political sphere. It must extend to social and economic life too. The Preamble declares India to be a Republic. It means that the head of the state is not a monarch, but a president indirectly elected by the people.

Secular Government. The government under the Indian Constitution has to be secular. This means that the government must not formulate policies which discriminate between various religious communities which live in India.

Universal Adult Franchise. Indian Constitution establishes a system of universal adult franchise. Under this system, every Indian citizen above the age of 18 years has the right to vote and participate in choosing the government.

Building a Just Society. Indian Constitution has one part dealing with the fundamental rights and fundamental duties of the citizens. Another part contains provisions which are called directive principles of the state policy. These are instructions which the Constitution gives to the States (the government at both the central and the state level) for achieving a just society in India. Indian Constitution, also, has several provisions which seek to protect the interets of those people who have been traditionally poor and socially deprived, the Scheduled Castes and Scheduled Tribes and Other Backward Classes of Citizen (OBCs).

Emergency Provisions. Finally, Indian Constitution also foresaw that there could be situations of danger when government could not be run as in ordinary times. To cope with these difficult times, it lays down some emergency provisions. In case of national emergency fundamental right can be restricted.

Fundamental Rights. The Indian Constitution mentions some of the most important rights of the citizens. These are called fundamental rights. These rights, are fundamental in two different ways. First, the Constitution gives us these rights. and guarantees them because it believes that the rights are necessary if citizens are to act properly and live democratically. Secondly, effective procedures for the enforcement of these Fundamental Rights have been guaranteed in the Constitution itself. A citizen has the right to go to the court of law if he/she is denied these rights. The Constitution is their guarantee.

This Constitution guarantees to six fundamental rights. Apart from these rights, the Constitution also mentions some 'Directive Principles of State Policy', and a list of fundamental duties of Indian citizens.

To understand the fundamental rights it is necessary to know about the directive principles and the fundamental duties.

Indian Constitution guarantees to Indian citizens six fundamental rights. These are:

(i) Right to equality;

(ii) Right to freedom;

(iii) Right against exploitation;

(iv) Right to freedom of religion;

(v) Cultural and educational rights; and

(vi) Right to Constitutional remedies.

Directive Principles of State Policy

The name Directive Principles of State Policy, shows that these are actually directions given by the Constitution of the state to adopt policies, which would help to establish a just society in India. The aim of these instructions is to create proper economic and social conditions in which citizens of India can lead a good life. The idea of democracy need not be only a political idea. It can also be extended to the social and economic life of the people. Some of the principles are in the form of social and economic rights, for example, the right to work, the right to free and compulsory education of children up to the age of 14, right to equal wages for equal work; or the right to an adequate livelihood. These rights are not fully enjoyed by all Indian citizens today. The government has to try to provide conditions under which these can become legal rights of citizens. Unlike fundamental rights the rights mentioned in this part are not justiciable. The Constitution, however, tells the state, *i.e.*, whoever runs the government that it must not forget these long-term aims, and it should try to achieve them in reality. If the government makes a law to enforce any of these principles it cannot be questioned in a court of law on the grounds that it violates any of the guaranteed fundamental rights. Indian Constitution mentions that the state should strive to give the right of work, right to education, right to assistance from the government in case a citizen is unemployed, sick, retired, or disabled. It should try to give free legal aid to poor people; so that poor people, who suffer greater injustices in society, can also go to courts and defend their rights.

All the Directive Principles, however, are not concerning social and political rights. Some of them are instructions to government in other matters. For instance, the Constitution says that state should try to prevent concentration of wealth, it should ensure that workers in factories can have a share in decision-making. It instructs the state to promote and look after the interests of scheduled castes and tribes. The state is asked to promote cottage industries. It is instructed to protect forests, the wild life of the country and ancient monuments.

Fundamental Rights and Directive Principles

Fundamental Rights are justiciable. They can be enforced by courts. The government cannot take away these rights. But the provisions of Directive Principles are not ineffaceable by courts of law. If a citizen is out of work, he cannot get a writ from the courts of law. If a citizen is out of work, he cannot get a writ from the courts directing the state to give him work. But if he is jailed by the police without reason, he can go to the courts. And the courts will direct the government to free him. The government must obey courts' order.

Fundamental Duties

Fundamental Duties have been incorporated by the forty-second Amendment of the Constitution, with the purpose of making citizens patriotic, help them to follow a code of conduct that would strengthen the nation, protect its sovereignty and integrity of India.

(i) to defend the country and render national service when required,

(ii) to promote the common brotherhood of all people in India and renounce any practice derogatory to the dignity of women,

(iii) to value and preserve the rich heritage of the nation's composite character,

(iv) to protect and improve natural environment and have compassion for living creatures,

(v) to develop scientific temper, humanism and spirit of inquiry,

(vi) to safeguard public property and abjure voilence, and

(vii) to strive for excellence in all spheres of individual and collective activity.

DEMOCRATIC EDUCATION

The Education Commission (1964-66), said that the development of values such as a scientific temper of mind, tolerance, respect for the culture of other national groups, etc., will enable us to adopt democracy, not only as a form of government, but also as a way of life. This clearly shows that in a democratic country like India the first and the foremost goal of education should be development of democratic values. Indian democracy is made by the people who profess different religions, speak different languages, belong to different races, castes, classes and communities. keeping in mind these and several other characteristics of Indian democracy following should be the most appropriate goals of education:

1. Development of Democratic Values in the People. These values apart from those given above include a spirit of large-hearted tolerance, of mutual give and take, of the appreciation of the ways in which people differ from one another. No education is worthwhile if an educated man does not translate these values in his behaviour and no democracy in that case can survive for long. Hence, education has to make deliberate and planned effort on development of these values in the people.

2. National Integration. It means harmonising religions, language, caste, class and community differences as they exist in India causing social tensions. It is essential that the people of India in spite of these differences live peacefully and cooperatively and utilise their varied talents for the enrichment of the national life as a whole. Education through various programmes and tailored curricula should make efforts to develop in the people such attitudes and values. It is difficult but possible. These changes include realising the importance of knowledge and education, learning various social skills, developing scientific attitude, computer literacy considering science and technology important, and so on. The Commission (1964) said that, "The most important tool in the process of modernisation is education based on science and technology." But, the Commission, further said "Modernisation, if it is to a living force must derive its strength from the strength to spirit."

The Secondary Education Commission (1952-53), has formulated three social or national aims of education. These are:

1. Development of democratic citizenship.
2. Improvement of vocational efficiency.
3. Development of leadership which means training pupils for discharging their duties efficiently.

Ishwar Bhai Patel Committee (1977), also reiterated the importance of development of citizenship as a social or national goal of education.

The Adiseshiah Committee Report (1978) formulated the following goals to be achieved through education:

1. Removal of unemployment.
2. Removal of destitution, *i.e.*, poverty.

3. Rural Development.

4. Adult literacy.

All these foregoing aims are social or national objectives to be achieved through education. They are the tasks completion of which is imperative for strengthening the society. These aims have been discussed here with special reference to India. Hence, they may be considered national goals of education or educational aims of national development.

Our schools should develop a strong tradition of striving to generate a sense of national unity and national consciousness, in the pupils. This can be achieved as suggested by the National Commission on Education (1964-66), by *(i)* making pupils understand and revaluate our cultural heritage and *(ii)* by the creation of a strong driving faith in the future towards which we aspire. The first may be promoted by well-organised teaching of the language and literature, philosophy, religion and history of India as well as by introducing the students to Indian architecture, sculpture, painting, music, dance and drama. Faith in future would involve an attempt to bring home to the students the principles of the Constitution, the great human values contained in preamble of the Constitution.

3. Development of Physical Resources through the modernisation of agriculture and rapid industrialisation should also be an important aim of education in a democracy like India. To achieve this purpose education should be linked with productivity, science should be made a basic component of education, work-experience should be considered important, vocational education should be expanded, scientific and technical education should be improved.

4. Development of Human Resources should be considered still more crucial an aim of education in Indian democracy. This aim implies changes in the knowledge, skills, interests, and values of the people as a whole. In a democracy the individual is an end in himself and the primary purpose of education should be to provide him with the widest opportunity to develop his potentialities to the full, through social reorganisation and emphasis on social perspectives. Cultivation of essential values in the people, development of dedicated and competent leadership and educated electorate are essential for strengthening democracy. Education, therefore, must develop such human resources needed for the defence of Indian democracy.

5. Development of Social, Moral and Spiritual Values. In a democratic country like India it is inevitable to inculcate social, moral and spiritual values in the people. Knowledge in the absence of essential values may be dangerous. The success of democracy, its strength and stability are contingent upon people's developed sense of social reponsibility and a keener appreciation of moral and spiritual values. Hence, education must make efforts on developing these values in the people. Prime Minister Nehru in his Azad Memorial Lectures (ICCR, 1962) said "Material riches without toleration and compassion and wisdom may well turn to dust and ashes."

EDUCATION FOR DEMOCRACY IN INDIA

Democracy in India. India is not merely a modern democratic state but a country which is traditionally inclined towards democracy. A democratic Constitution was adpoted after independence. In 1938, Jawaharlal Nehru had said, "The Indian Constitution seeks to establish a popular government in the country on the basis of democratic principles outlined earlier. For this every citizen must participate in the administration, through his right to vote and to be elected. Every individual is guaranteed and given equal status and opportunity, because no one is discriminated against on the basis of religion, race, caste, community, sex, or on any other grounds. The government is responsible to the people and its elected representatives."

Provisions in Indian Constitution. In order to achieve this objective of democracy, education is as necessary in India as anywhere else, a truth which the Indian people have been quick to realise. In the words of **F.W. Themes,** "Education is no exotic in India. There has been no country where the love of learning had so early an origin or has exercised so lasting and powerful an influence. From the simple poet of the Vedic age to the Bengali philosopher of the present day there has been an uninterrupted succession of teachers and scholars." Not only did the Indian Constitution accept the ideals of democracy, it considered education the prime responsibility of the state. In Article 45 of the Constitution it has been stated that every state must arrange for the provision of free and compulsory education to all children upto the age of 14, within ten years of the date of inception of the Constitution. After the achievement of independence, a new phase began in the history of education. Articles 29 and 30 of the Constitution give fundamental rights to every individual in connection with education and cultural development. According to article 20, every Indian national living in any part of India will have the right to maintain his own specific language, script and his culture. No person can be refused right of admission to any educational institution, established by the state, by reason of religion, race, caste, language or any other similar consideration. According to article 30, every minority community will have the right to establish and maintain educational institutions of its own choice, irrespective of whether the minority is a linguistic or religious one. The state will also not refuse aid to any such institution created by a religious or linguistic minority. Articles 45 and 46 determine the policy for education as part and parcel of the directive principles. According to article 45, the state will make every effort to provide free and compulsory education, within ten years, to every child below the age of 14. According to article 46, the stage will pay special attention to the educational and economic interests of all backward classes, especially the scheduled castes and scheduled tribes. It also entrusts the state with the duty of protecting such tribes from social injustice and exploitation of every kind. The Indian Constitution laid the foundation for a federal government in which the functions of the state government have some duties with respect to education. It has been realised that there must be coordination between the central and state authority on education for a balanced development of the country. The modern Indian state is a welfare state whose objective is the complete development of its people. This welfare can be achieved only through education. Little surprise therefore if all the leaders of the nation stress the importance of education as a first step to improving the future of the nation.

Views of Secondary Education Commission

The democratic ideals which the existing educational policy is trying to achieve have been outlined most precisely in the Secondary Education Commission's explanation of the objectives of education:

1. *Development of Democratic Citizenship.* The success of democracy depends largely upon the people's awareness of their rights and duties and the extent to which people fulfil their responsibilities. Education aims at developing this ability in the people, because education teaches the man to think and distinguish between right and wrong. He can understand social, economic and political issues, and reflect on the possibility of solving such problems. He can decide upon the political party or the leadership which should be entrusted with the task of forming a government and undertaking administration. He does this after thinking on the problems facing the country and considering the ability of each group or leader to face such problems. He can express his ideas and suggestion through lectures, essays, articles, etc. He can organise new movements or constitute various kinds of committees to solve the problems facing the country. It is the duty of the state to insist upon a syllabus which can be expected to generate such democratic awareness among the children being educated.

2. *Training in Skilful Living.* Democracy can be said to have succeeded only if it translate the democratic ideals to its society. And, for this, socialisation of the individual through education is essential. It is desirable to develop such social qualities as collective feeling, cooperation, discipline, tolerance, sympathy, brotherhood, etc., in the individual. Education must also aim to create faith in social justice and the willingness to rebel against injustice. Education helps people in adjusting to each other, and the educated individual is generally tolerant and liberal. Although he may differ from other prople in their opinions, he has the ability to adjust to such people because he can understand their attitudes. Hence, education is the only means of removing the obstacles in the path of democracy and also of achieving some adjustment between people who differ from each other in respect of language, race, caste, religion, sex, etc.

3. ***Development Vocational Skill.*** The Secondary Education Commission has pointed out that another aim of education is to develop some vocational skill in the educand. No nation can progress in the absence of economic progress. The first duty of the state is to provide a system and means of education which imparts some vocational and professional skills to the educands so that they can earn their livelihood at the same time as they contribute to the nation's economic growth. The country urgently needs skilled craftsmen, engineers, doctors, teachers and administrators. For this, specialised colleges are required. Every child should be given the right to choose a profession of his own liking, and he should be given the opportunity to acquire the highest training and education in this profession.

4. ***Development of Personality.*** The success of a democratic society also depends upon whether mature men and women form the majority or minority in its population. Democracy can succeed only if most of its members have developed mature personalities, because a mature person has gone through physical, mental, social, ethical and spiritual development. Hence, education should aim at the development of all aspects of the educands' personality through various kinds of training. Keeping this in view, most schools and colleges now provide many kinds of extra curricular training, which supplements all that is taught as part of curriculum.

5. ***Developing Leadership.*** The success of a democracy depends upon the capabilities of the leadership. The democratic government is a decentralised government, and for that reason it requires skilled leadership at many different levels of administration. The democratic government is run by the elected representatives of the people, who should be possessed of special qualities. Expert leadership is required for development and progress in every sphere—political, social, economic, artistic, scientific and cultural. Education should aim at evolving such leadership, because without doing this education cannot make any real contribution to democracy, for then it is leaving unfulfilled one of its important responsibilities. The element of leadership can be encouraged through many kinds of curricular and extra curricular activities in schools and colleges.

Apart from these objectives of education laid down specifically by the Secondary Education Commission, it is desirable to reflect upon some other objectives, which have significance in view of the fact that India is a democracy. In fact, the aims of education vary a little bit with the level of education—the primary, secondary and university education—a fact which has been recognised by the different education commissions established from time to time. The aim of education, at the primary level, is to develop the child's mind by presenting the fundamental elements in the various areas of knowledge, and also to give him an opportunity to develop all his abilities—physical, mental, moral, motor, creative imagination, etc. At this stage attention should be paid to physical development no less than mental development, but attention must also be paid to the burden such an education places on the child. The education imparted should not become a burden.

At the secondary level, attention should be focused on discovering the interests and abilities of every adolescent, and then developing such abilities. Education should be concerned not merely with the general welfare of society but also with the self-realisation and personal development of each individual.

Recommendations of Indian Universities Commission. The Indian Universities Commission has laid down the following objectives of university education in the country:

1. Providing leadership in politics, administration, professions, industry and commerce;
2. Training intellectual leaders of culture and creating inventors;
3. Causing spiritual development in the educand;
4. Protecting the culture and civilisation of the country and instilling the youth with the ideals of this culture; and
5. Discovering the inherent qualities of individuals and developing them through training.

IMPACT OF DEMOCRACY ON EDUCATION

It is only in recent times that democratic principles and values have entered the field of education. The credit of this revolutionary change goes to the American educationist Johy Dewey. He emphasised that in a democratic society, educational planning should be done in such a way that each individual member is made capable to shoulder social responsibilities efficiently and discharge them effectively and profitably. According to him, education should inculcate in the individuals the sense to welcome needful changes in the social structure and reoriented one's behaviour smoothly to the ever changing social milieu. The impact of this philosophy has brought about revolutionary changes in the thinking about educational planning and schemes of public education have begun to emphasise the provisions of the education of the masses so that general people become conscious about their rights and duties, about their individual and social responsibilities and about their national and international obligation. As the democratic rule is by the people for the people, they should be made to understand their obligations and to discharge their duties intelligently. Hence, in all democratically ruled countries, more and more emphasis is being laid upon free, compulsory and universal education.

The impact of democratic tendency on education is evident on the working of the following elements:

1. Provision of Equal Oportunities and Recognition of Individual Differences. In a democratic set up, each child is a sacred and valuable entity of society. As such, equal opportunities are made available to one and all for their fullest development. In this connection the principle of individual differences is given proper recognition and therefore each child receive proper support according to his interests, aptitudes and capacities to develop his individuality to the fullest extent.

2. Universal and Compulsory Education. In democracy, the reigns of government remain in the hands of the people. Hence, common people must be so educated that they develop themselves as responsible and dynamic citizens conscious of their rights and duties, fully conversant with their national and international obligations, well aware with the government procedures anti-administration processes.

3. Provision of Adult Education. Under the influence of democratic tendency, in different countries, emphasis is being laid upon adult education, women education and education of the mentally retorted and physically handicapped. Schemes are under operation in our country also for the effective education of the adults who constitute a bulk of our entire population. Night-schools, short-term courses, one day schools and the schemes are being launched to solve this stupendous problem.

4. Free Education. The principle of universal and compulsory education involves free education to all irrespective of their social or monetary status. Hence, education is now regarded as the birth right of each child irrespective of colour, caste, creed and sex. In almost all democratic countries, education has been made free up to a certain standard. In addition, education of the physically and mentally handicapped is also receiving proper and increasingly effective attention.

5. Methods of Teaching. Under the impact of democratic tendency, method of teaching are undergoing revolutionary changes. Old, traditional and mass education methods are being gradually replaced by individual attention methods. Nothing is now enforce or thrust in by force. Self-learning devices are encouraged and such methods are promoted which motivate children to pay attention and learn by their own efforts. Such wholesome and welcome environment is created wherein children search for truth, gain knowledge by their own efforts and learn by their own experience.

6. Child Centred Education. Democratic way of thinking emphasises the importance of each child as sacred individuality. Hence, educational schemes and plans are so structured that each child receives full attention and full facilities to develop his individuality to the fullest extent.

7. Social Activities. Bookish and academic activities are not over-emphasised in schools now-a-days. Proper attention is paid to social, cultural and co-curricular activities, so that children develop in a wholesome way and gain more and more social experience.

8. Importance of Individual Attention. As discussed above, each child receives individual attention. His family background, his own interests, likes and dislikes, his needs and capacities are fully taken care off in all plans of educational development, the purpose being to achieve the maximum development of personality.

9. School Administration. To inculcate in children the sense of self-discipline and self-administration, their association with school administration is being welcomed. Such schemes are being formulated in various institutions where student participation in actual educational and school administration is a fact.

10. Student Unions. Student unions and student welfare associations are formed in institutions to promote student welfare in all spheres with the aim of achieving balanced, dynamic, efficient and socially motivated personalities.

11. Respect of Teacher's Personality. Democratic philosophy respects teacher as a very dynamic and effective agency of social change for social progress. Thus, teachers are now made to participate more and more in curriculum construction and educational planning. Side by side, they are allowed to experiment freely in respect to methods, techniques and devices of teaching as well as materials which aid teaching procedures and processes. Not only this, more and more plans are being laid and worked out for increasing the professional competency of teachers.

12. Physical Health of Children. To promote physical well-being of children, facilities for games and sports, gymnazia, medical tests and medical help are being provided freely and on an increasing scale. Medical check up, advice and medicines are now provided to the needy.

13. Intelligence Tests. Schemes of intelligence tests are under operation in various institutions all over the world to evaluate the mental capacity, growth and achievement of children. Diagnostic tests are proving very useful for this purpose.

14. Co-operation between all Agencies of Education. In a democratic set up, all the agencies of education co-operate actively for the development of children. Hence, under the influence of democratic tendency, schemes are being formulated now-a-days to establish co-operation between all the agencies of education namely—family, school, community, and state.

15. School. School is now regarded as a centre of promoting national consciousness and international understanding. Education for dynamic citizenship is associated with education for national and international understanding, amity and fellow-feeling. Thus, school is now regarded as a miniature of society.

SOCIOLOGY OF EDUCATION

Dualism has always been a popular view with the philosophers. It is quite natural also, for we always live in two worlds, namely, the world of things and the world of our own inner experience. Some philosophers have considered the inner world and the individual more important, while a few others have stressed the world outside the individual, *i.e.*, the environment or the society. Rousseau, for example, focussed on the individual while Dewey emphasised the social setting in which the individual has to live. Rousseau was the forerunner of psychological tendencies in education. Dewey may be considered a pioneer to shift the emphasis to sociological tendency in education. He maintained that philosophy must be described in terms of the problems with which it deals and which originate in the conflicts and difficulties of social life. He defined the problem of education as "...the harmonising of individual traits with social ends and values." He considered education a difficult process because effective coordination of psychological make-up of the individual with the demands of the social environment was, to him, extremely difficult. He lamented that such a coordination in the schools of his time was ignored. It was held by him that the process of mental development is essentially a social process. He said that "man is a social being who attains mind and self only when nourished in social experience." By "social" he meant individual's social adjustment to the group or to contemporary social realities. The business of education, as emphasised by Dewey, was "habituation of an individual to social control, subordination of natural powers to social rules." Thus, social efficiency aim of education was emphasised which appealed to many people of his times as it was more in line with democratic thinking of nineteenth century. The great social change emerging from the nineteenth century industrial revolution in Europe may also be considered responsible for the origin and development of sociological tendency in education. The pragmatic philosophy of education also emphasised the social aspect of education for it believed that socially oriented minds alone could forge a better state of society, one in which human wants are fully satisfied.

Thus, the sociological tendency has its origin in the philosophy of Dewey, the pragmatists and the nineteenth century social change resulting from the industrial revolution and acceptance of democracy as a form of government and a way of life. The tendency emphasised the social aim of education. Its watch words are "education for social service" which means that education should be directed in a broader more elastic way to the good of the community. It emphasises that the individual must be trained to be unselfish, to put the needs and desires of others before his own. Prof. Bagley in America said that, "Social efficiency is the norm against which educational practice must be judged." He, further, emphasised that social efficiency aim of education ought to have the position of primacy in a rational theory of education. The activities of the individual should be valued with reference to his social obligations.

The sociological tendency in education focussed on the interaction between the individual and the social milieu in which he lives. Education, according to this tendency, was defined as reorganisation and reconstruction of this interaction so that the child learns what is socially desirable. Dewey said that education should develop individual's ability to "share in the experiences of others and thus, widen the individual consciousness to that of the race." Emergence of a new branch of knowledge known as sociology in the first half of the nineteenth century contributed significantly to this aspect of the sociological tendency in education. Study of human relations in the schools was emphasised. Scientific study of the process of interaction of persons was considered important. Study of education in relation to social needs and social change was emphasised. Several new trends emerged in the field of education as a result of sociological tendency in education. The relationship between the school and the society, relationship between the school climate and education of the pupils, education as an instrument of social change, influence of various social groups on education, education as related to social mobility of the people in the society, etc., many issues figured for discussion and for being resolved. The aims, content, method and other aspects of education were also affected by this tendency.

The Relationship between Education and Society. Sociological tendency in education made several thinkers in the field of education to discuss and classify the relationships between education and society. Education was considered as a sub-system of the larger society. The character of society and social changes taking place must influence the system of education also. It was emphasised that these social changes and emerging social needs must be rejected in the theory and practice of education also. This point was very mush emphasised by Dewey in his book, *"The School and Society"* wherein he said that while proposing to bring about a change in education the social point of new should always be kept in mind, otherwise it will be considered merely an arbitrary fad. "Education for the society" emerged as the focus of educational thought.

Education and Politics. The relationship between education and politics also was emphasised as an aspect of sociological tendency in education. Education for democracy was, particular emphasised. Democratic aims of education, democratic methods of teaching-learning, democratic organisation: of the classroom and the school, democratic discipline, etc., were several new concepts which were extensively discussed.

Education and Economic Factors. Sociological tendency in education forced the educational thinkers to analyse and see how economic factors affect education. It was realised that economic factors are important constraints of educational activities. How they affect education and how education affects the economy of the society were some of the themes which emerged for discussion. A new kind of thinking began in the field of education.

Cultural Aim of Education. The sociological tendency in education resulted into a greater stress on cultural aim of education. It was emphasised that education help in the transmission of cultural heritage.

The Curriculum. Sociological tendency in education resulted into a ranged approach to curriculum construction. These views took the form of sociological principles of curriculum construction. It was emphasised that the curriculum should conform to the conditions, problems and needs of the society. A functional curriculum which could serve the needs of the society was said to be the need of the hour, curriculum for international understanding, curriculum for citizenship, curriculum for vocation, etc., were the ideas about curriculum which gained popularity as a result of sociological tendency in education.

The Method of Teaching. In the context of method of teaching, the sociological tendency resulted into considering the classroom and the school as the society-in-miniature. Hence, it was emphasised that teaching should take help of the principles of group dynamics. Group methods of teaching, group discussions, social interactions, group planning, group activities, project method, etc., were considered important.

Thus, sociological tendency in education tried to approach education, its purposes, methods, content and other aspects from the point of view of the society and sociological forces working within it.

IMPACT OF DEMOCRACY ON VARIOUS ASPECTS OF EDUCATION

In the following lines we are throwing light on the various aspects of education in a democratic set up:

Democracy and Aims of Education. In a democracy, the aims of education are as under:

1. *Development of Democratic Values.* The success of democracy does not depend upon Legislative buildings and massive structures of Parliament houses, but it rests upon the quality of the citizens devoted to democratic values. As such, the prime aim of democratic education is to promote in children a sense of devotion to democratic values. No book teaching can achieve this aim unless children are provided with opportunities to practise democratic norms and standards of behaviour. In fact, a child learns to live democratically by living democratically.

2. *Development of Vocational Efficiency.* For the success of a democratic set-up, economic contentment of citizens is a must. An indigent and poor person can be a victim of all kinds of allurements, inducements and exploitation by the resourceful and the powerful. Hence, the third aim of democratic education is to develop vocational efficiency in children, so that they are able to become self-reliant and serve the nation as much as possible.

3. *Development of Thinking Power.* The fourth aim of democratic education is to develop thinking power of children. In fact, children of today are citizens of tomorrow when they will be confronted with all kinds of problems in political, social and economic fields. Education should develop in children the capacity to think clearly and take decisions confidently.

4. *Development of Interests in Children.* The third aim of democratic education is to develop useful and worthy interests in children. Interests form character and enrich a child's life. Hence, the famous educationist, Herbart has insisted upon the fullest development of diverse interests. To achieve this aim, children should be provided with various and varied opportunities to participate in diverse activities and programmes in all fields of human life. If a large number of worthy interests are developed in children, they will be happy, well-balanced and efficient as citizens.

5. *Development of Social Outlook.* Development of social outlook is the sixth important aim of democratic education. This aim emphasises upon the fact that children should be imbued with the sense that they are the integral parts of society, the welfare of which should be their ideal. Not only this, they should learn to live and die for the nation. Education should develop this sense of service and sacrifice making them learn the sacredness of obligations and duties for the welfare of the nation to which they belong.

6. *Development of Leadership.* The seventh aim of democratic education is to develop leadership qualities in children. For this, education should instil in children the leadership qualities from the very beginning. They are the future citizens who will have to shoulder the multifarious duties and reponsibilities of their nation in all areas. Their character, strength of will, insight, courage of convictions, clarity of thinking and decision-making will be the foundations on which the national edifice will go up and up.

7. *Development of Sound Habits.* The fifth aim of democratic education is to develop sound habits in children. Habits are the sources of good or bad conduct. Hence, education should develop good habits in children from the very beginning to make democracy a successful venture.

8. *Development of Harmonious Personality.* The eighth aim of democratic education is to develop the individuality of a child into balanced and harmonious personality. In the modern world of strife, stress and strain a balance and harmonious personality can only seek and find adjustment with the surroundings. Hence, education should develop character, dynamism and social outlook for this purpose.

9. *Development of National and International Feelings.* For the success of democracy, the ninth aim of democratic education is to develop in children the sense of ardent nationalism and devotion to international brotherhood. It may be noted that the two are not contradictory. On the other hand, they are mutually complementary and supplementary. In fact a nation cannot exist in isolation. All the nations of the world are mutually inter-dependent. Hence, education should foster the sense of inter-dependence, international good-will and fellow-feeling.

10. *Training for Citizenship.* Democratic education should impart of children training in dynamic and healthy citizenship. For this, education should instil in children—(1) Capacity to understand and solve the diverse problems of the country, (2) Capacity to distinguish between propaganda and reality, (3) Capacity to think and decide about issues, (4) Economic efficiency, (5) Consciousness of one's rights and duties, (6) Capacity to shoulder responsibility, (7) Development of diverse interests, (8) Sense of service and sacrifice, (9) Good use of leisure hour, (10) Development of human qualities as love, sympathy, fellow feeling, co-operation, sense of nationalism and internationalism, (11) Healthy and dynamic outlook about problems, good behaviour and respect for moral values.

Curriculum. In a democratic country curriculum construction is done with the purpose of realising democratic values. Hence, those subjects, activities and programmes are included in the curriculum which instil and promote healthy attitudes, dynamic habits, insight and understanding so that children are able to lead successful lives as happy citizens. The bases of such a curriculum are as under:

1. *Diversified.* Democratic curriculum is divisively to suit the needs of all children with basic differences of interests and aptitudes. Classroom activities, games, sports and other co-curricular activities bear an imprint of variety to suit various needs of children.

2. *Emphasis on Local Needs.* Democratic curriculum is constructed on the basis of local needs and available resources. It may be changed according to the needs of time, place and local requirements.

3. *Achievement of Social Aims.* While constructing a democratic curriculum emphasis is laid upon social aims and values. In other words, development of social sense in children is kept in view. As such, student activities, associations, corporate programmes and fellowship programmes are liberally provided.

4. ***Flexibility.*** Democratic curriculum is flexible to accommodate various needs and requirements which are in a state of constant change. A portion of it is made compulsory in the form of co-curriculum and diversified subjects are made optional for children to choose according to their interests and aptitudes.

5. ***Emphasis of Activity.*** Democratic curriculum is laid on the foundation of an important principle known as learning by doing. It is through practical work and activities that development of mind and intelligence is fostered. Instead of enforcing and compelling cut and dried ready-made concepts into the minds of children, they are allowed to search for truth through their own experiments and experiences. This is real learning. It develops confidence, foresight and far-sight, the three important ingredients of wisdom.

6. ***Place for Leisure Hour Activities.*** Democratic curriculum also contains such relevant and useful activities in which an individual can profitable indulge leisure time. Thus, it ensures the total development of personality.

7. ***Provision of Vocational Needs.*** Democratic curriculum very well meets the needs of vocations, professions and economic requirements of a region or the whole country. This explains the country to develop economically.

Discipline. Discipline is the corner-stone of democracy. But democratic discipline does not believe in respiration or compulsion. It advocates self-discipline. In schools where democratic set up is in vogue, the following ideas are emphasised for fostering and developing self-discipline:

1. In democratic schools the headmasters, the teachers and the administrators are not despots or police officers. Instead, they are friends, philosophers and guides. Through their friendly and affectionate behaviour, they mould the behaviour of children and

thus promote self-discipline by creating a congenial and cordial atmosphere.

2. In democratic schools, such activities and programmes are structured which cater to the interests and needs of children. This develops self-discipline among children.

3. In the administration of a democratic school, children participate actively, discuss problems and decide them freely. They, thus, feel their integral and intimate relationship with the school and feel internal kinship with its progress and development.

4. In democratic schools, students unions, students parliaments and all kinds of student organisations are encouraged for the benefit and development of children. They learn self-government, co-operation, fellow-feeling and other human qualities together with qualities of self-discipline and leadership.

5. In democratic schools full freedom is given and opportunities provided for each child to develop his individuality to the fullest extent. Hence, no problem of indiscipline arises at any time.

6. In democratic schools, the sense of rights and duties is instilled in children. They, thus learn self-control through social service and social consciousness. Nothing is imposed on them from above. They discuss, decide and carry out the decision with perfect co-operation and cordiality.

Teacher. In a democratic set up a teacher is a friend, philosopher and guide. He often works as a social reformer. Such teachers process the following qualities:

1. The teacher is devoted whole hearted to the ideals and values of democracy. Hence, he tries to impart the same faith to children through gently persuasion and affectionate rapport.

2. The teacher regards every child as a sacred legacy to society. Hence, believing in the principle of individual differences he allows every child to develop his individuality to the fullest extent according to his interests, aptitudes and capacities.

3. The teacher tries to solicit maximum co-operation from the guardians, parents and other social agencies for the greatest possible development of children as dynamic and socially oriented citizens of the future.

4. In a democratic set up, each teacher is fully conscious of his rights and duties towards society. Hence, he tries to instil the same sense of responsibility in children and also to make them capable and intelligent citizens of tomorrow.

5. In a democratic set up, a teacher lays greater stress upon environment rather than on heredity. Hence, he tries to structure such a wholesome environment for the child that fullest development is naturally achieved.

6. Each teacher is well-versed in knowledge of his subject and has full academic competency to make children develop physically, mentally, morally and spiritually so that they are able to shoulder national and even international responsibilities in times to come.

❐

6

National Integration and Socialisation

If we wish to retain our hard won freedom, national integration has to be our natural tune. In this integration lies our strength, dignity and hope for future progress. The basis of National Integration is emotional integration. It is through training of mind and heart, that a sense of oneness among the people of the country can be inspired. By emotional integration we mean a feeling of national pride and faith in the nation's greatness. When the emotions are conditioned by the idea of national loyalty and are directed towards national welfare, the result is national integration. It is a feeling among people to share certain common objectives, ideas and giving them high share over smaller. It is feeling of oneness which transcends all groups of cultural differences and connects the different religions, castes and linguist communities into a compact whole.

According to **Pandit Jawaharlal Nehru,** "By emotional integration I mean the integration of our minds and hearts, the suppression of feelings of separatism."

Emotional integration brings about an emotional synthesis of diverse elements. With the development of this national consciousness, all individuals forget about their selfish interests, personal or group motives, pursue national ideals, contribute to national aspirations and solve all the national problems with all sincerity and devotion. India is also a nation and we all people, belonging to diverse religions, castes and groups, are its inhabitants. Thus it is a joint responsibility of us all to defend the freedom of our nation.

Nationalism. An individual is an integral part of his nation. An individual is for the nation, the nation is not for the individual. Isolated from his nation, the individual loses his identity, his existence even. Hence every individual is duty bound to uphold the integrity and strength of his nation and offer his best co-operation in its advancement.

Nationalism is that feeling which inspires all big or small units of a society to raise above the narrow self-centred activities and work in unity and co-operation for national development. It is an aggressive, dynamic-social organisation interlinked with threads of unity and propagates the ideology and policies of national government. Nationalism is not mere love of one's place of birth. It includes the essential constituents namely love and regard for the history, culture, religion, language and traditions of the nation. In short, nationalism means whole-hearted devotion to nation, sense of duty together with obligation and unquestioning faith in its glorious future based on its present well-being and prosperity.

According to **Humayun Kabir,** "Nationalism is that which depends upon our feelings towards the nation."

There are two concepts of nationalism—Narrow and Broad. When a country is interested only in its narrow limited interests, it is known as narrow nationalism. My country right or wrong is the spirit behind narrow nationalism. This concept is full of dangers and shortcomings. Broader concept of nationalism is related with emotional integration. The whole world is now so intimately inter-connected that no national can dare live alone and the development of a sense of world citizenship has become just as important as that of national citizenship. In its broader sense, it means bringing about economic, social and cultural differences within tolerable range.

Meaning of National Integration. National integration is unity in diversity. It means a feeling of oneness. It implies social, political, economic, linguistic and cultural unity. It is the development of a mental climate that would help react in terms of oneness, irrespective of the region, language or religion of the people concerned. It means a heaven of freedom where the world has not been divided into fragments by narrow domestic wells. It is based on feeling of oneness, common ideals of life and a common code of behaviour. It implies confidence in nation's future, deep sense of values and obligatioin of citizenship, mutual understanding and respect for the culture of different sections of the nation.

Need for National Integration. National integration is the feeling that binds the citizens of a country. Its aim is to put individual's best efforts for the optimum growth, prosperity and welfare of the country as a whole. It does away with inter-state, inter-linguistic, inter-religious and inter-cultural differences. It promotes a spirit of tolerance and respect for the view-point of other cultural groups. To **Kanungo**, "Every country at every time needs national integration but India needs it the most."

India's passing through a critical period these days. The integrity of India is in danger. Therefore Indians will have to act carefully. In India national integration is needed due to following reasons:

Threat of Foreign Aggression. National integration is vital for India's survival especially at a time when the country is under the threat of foreign aggression and internally the people are divided on the basis of castes, religions, regions, communities, languages and races.

For the Development of National Character. National integration is an essential element for the development of national character. These days there is lack of national character. Corruption is increasing day-by-day. We are sacrificing national interests for the sake of money. National character can be formed only when we have the feeling of national integration.

For Success of Democracy. India is a democratic country. National integration is an essential pre-requisite for the success of our democracy. It is a basic need for the success of democracy, otherwise, the fissiparous tendencies in the country may lead to serious consequences.

For Peace. National integration is essential for keeping peace at national and international level. Modern age is the age of science. It has changed the whole world in a family. Every nation is dependent on one another. Therefore, scientific achievement should be used for constructive work in order to provide peace to humanity. This feeling can develop only when we have the thought of national integration.

For Diversity. National unity is essential for any country at any time. There is unity in diversity in India but now unity is in danger. Therefore, national unity is essential in order to maintain the eternal value of unity in diversity.

Obstacles to National Integration. Following are the obstacles in the achievement of National integration:

Casteism. The germ of casteism is cutting the roots of the Hindu society gradually. It has so compartmentalised this society into Brahmans, Kshatriyas, Vaishyas and Shudras that the people of one caste don't mix up freely with the people of the other castes. Casteism is fully exploited during elections. Such a situation creates bitterness and tension.

Communalism. Communalism divides the people having different religions. In India, people belong to different religions like Hinduism, Islam, Christianity, Sikhs etc. It were these forces which led to the partition of our country in 1947. Even in free India, these fanatics spread the rumours of mal-treatment to the minority groups which results in ill feeling and creates tension. Communal riots are taking place in the country. It has become a serious threat to national unity.

Linguism. Language is the connecting link for the people. It is an important means of national unity. India is a country of many languages. This has led to much dissension and destruction. Separate provinces were demanded on the basis of languages and were formed too.

Provincialism. It is a very big obstacle in the way of our national progress and national integration. Every person loves his/her province but he/she should not forget that nation is greater than the province. The inhabitants of one province should not look upon those of another province with hatred and feeling of inferiority.

Economic Disparities. The growing gulf between the haves and the have-nots is also responsible for bringing about fissiparous tendencies in our Indian society. The ways of life and the standards of living of the lower and upper classes are so different that there can be no meeting point between the two.

Frustration in Youth. The young generation of today is getting frustrated because it sees no future for it. The ghost of unemployment haunts their youth all the time. This results in agitations, strikes, raising of slogans, destruction of public and private property, looting, arsoning and other such anti-national activities. There is scant respect for teachers, leaders and law. There is unrest, indiscipline and lack of values in the students of today.

Political Disparities. Unfortunately in India, the political disparities are increasing day-by-day. Political parties are organised in the name of community, language and province etc. which is a serious threat to national integration. Changing of parties time and again, making politics an arena of "Aya Rams'' and 'Gaya Rams', creates political instability in the states. In some states the political changes are so rapid that the administration comes to a virtual standstill. This creates frustration in the people.

These are some of the factors which put hurdles on the way to national integration. The history of India shows that India has always existed as one nation despite all these diversities. In fact, the Indians believe in unity in diversity and they have shown themselves as a nation during the three aggressions on them after the attainment of independence.

Education for National Integration. Education is a powerful means of bringing about national integration. In the words of

Dr. Radha Krishnan "National integration cannot be built by brick and mortar or with chisel and hammer. It has to grow silently in the minds and hearts of people and the process by which it could be achieved was by education."

Education alone can develop the feeling of nationalism in the masses and it has to accomplish this task compulsorily. Without the active co-operation of education we shall not be able to defend the structure of the nation..

Objectives of Education for National Integration. The objectives of education for national integration can enumerated as below:

- To train the emotions for developing an emotionally integrated personality.
- To develop attitudes, dispositions, values and tolerance.
- To equip students with an intimate knowledge of the different aspects of the country, including the events which led to freedom.
- To encourage all studies and activities which lead to greater understanding between communities and states.
- To create a feeling that the country and its resources belong to the citizens who thereby acquire certain rights and privileges alongwith corresponding duties and responsibilities.

RELIGION IN EDUCATION

In the beginning, the idea of Religion might have been a divine inspiration, the basis of which might have been logic personal belief. Now the modern advanced religious belief developed in men in a subject for research. Today one may wonder how the modern religious concepts come to imagination? In the beginning the nature of religion has quite liberal, but today it has become narrow; Superstitions have crept into it. Some people hold different views regarding the same religion. Science has hoped in removing many superstitions, fears; doubts and orthodox views from religion.

Today if *Dharma* (religion) is taken in a wider perspective, man can create conditions of peace, hope, love, sympathy and contentment by bringing an end to frustration, mental-tensions, quarrels, unjealousy, discontentment and discomfort. Faith in religion can lead the world to brotherhood and peace. Religion establishes human values, cultural traditions; ideals and moral understanding in human society. Religion in India pervades throughout the whole life of an individual. Here we have many religions.

Relation of Religion to Human Life. The most developed period from the view point of religion has been the Vedic period when religion was considered as a basis for human life and source of inspiration for virtuous conduct. Since then religion has been inspiring people to follow the right path, improve their conduct and imbibe human virtues. It is possible that certain superstitions, conservation, frustrations, fears and doubts might have crept into religion due to some ignorance. Self-confidence has always been with man in the form of religion. Religion by adding to the human qualities, has made man capable of self-confidence, self-reform, self-realisation, self-discipline, self-reliance and self-development.

True Meaning of Religion. Vedas are the oldest books. Vedas are the repository of all knowledge. Here in religion has been described in its wider perspective. According to the Vedas, the efforts, which inspire man for various conduct and develop human qualities, fall in the category of religion. Hence, than in characteristic of religion is inspiration for virtuous conduct. The modern word 'Religion' can not be a synonym for 'Dharma', bacause 'Dharma' has been considered as all-pervading in Indian scriptures. All activities from rising in the morning to sleeping a night and death and actions after death are all included in 'Dharma'. In fact, whatever qualities a person acquires are his Dharma. Here qualities mean human qualities which are universal.

In Islam '*mazhab*' is a way of imparting education for virtuous conduct. According to the philosophy of this religion, '*namaz*',

'*Roja*' and '*Haj*' are considered, a method for creating universal love and feeling of neighbourhood. To give some benefit to the society or social service are considered as a part of this religion.

Religion and Sects (Belief). Some narrow minded people evince unnecessary opposition by equalling religion with sects. We should clearly understand the meaning of religion and sects. Religion is taken in the wider sense which means spiritual development of human society through the welfare of mankind. In other words; religion means human religion which every society is prepared to accept. A sect (belief) is a specific religious view point of a group of persons. That is the individual belief of the persons of that group, based on the wider values of religion. It is not necessary for other sects to accept that belief. Hindu religion accepts the opinion of Vedas, Islam that of the Quran and Christians of Bible. Hindu Dharma has been divided into Buddha sect, Jains, Sikh, Vedic (Sanatan and Arya Samaj) according to the different methods to philosophers and thinkers of these sects, although all these sects are parts of Hindu Dharma. Some agitators and diplomats propagated it as different religions in order to create faction in Hindu Dharma. The idea behind this propaganda was to cut of the organisation and unity of Hindu Dharma. It is amazing that some Hindus also accepted the sects as different religions.

Islam Dharma has its original from the word 'Salm'. 'Salm' means peace which has been interpreted as knowing God peacefully and surrendering the self before Him. This is the true nature of Islam. Whenever some one seeks the shelter of God, forgetting his vanity and pride, he attain all-round development and divinity is radiated from his personality. In Christian religion, christianity was formed from the word 'christos' which means 'bathed in Divine wisdom'. Thus Christian religion extends that divine wisdom which creates brotherhood, love, sympathy and tolerance in the human society.

Vedic religion, is based on Vedas, 'Ved' means knowledge. Hence Vedic Dharma means that scientific knowledge which by recognising the existence of 'Inner self' and 'Supreme self' *i.e.*

'Antaratma' and 'Parmatma', develops human qualities like, non-violence, truth, humanism, love and compassion, etc.

Thus religion is a source of morality. Science can be of great help in this direction, but science devoid of religion is meaningless. Religion is all-pervading and Universal. So it should be included in education.

Mis-use of Religion and Violence. Due to ignorance and superstitions some universe followers of religions have strangulated humanity and have committed great atrocities. The reason for such violent attitude is misinterpretation of religion. These religions hypocrises of violent nature committed so many atrocities on humanity that man began to hate religion. These committing oppressions in the name of religion were non-vedic (unwise) and selfish. Religious reformers born from time to time led the people to the right path and presented the true nature of religion. Buddha, Mahavir, Shankaracharya, Dayanand, etc., were such great personalities. In the Western countries Rousseau and Locke suggested to save education from wrongly interpreted religion. Corrupt practice, in various religious bodies in the name of religion created hatred for religion.

Relation between Religion and Education. Religion and Education are closely associated with each other both are of spiritual tendencies. Spiritual, material or physical urge are dealt with by religion as well as by the education. "Both seek to emancipate man, not from contract with his environment, but from slavery to it." As has already been discussed, *education creates certain values of life and help in the modification of behaviour*. It gives certain mouldings to the life, while religion beautifies the life by cultivation of truthful heart with the moral and spiritual values.

In this way religion and education have different ways but the same aim of achieving God through cultivating three absolutes truth, and goodness.

Religion must be given a suitable places in the curriculum because it is the core of our culture and 'heritage'. Gentle given a fine statement in regard to the place of religion in the curriculum.

He writes. "National cultures have never been more conscious than now of the higher needs of the mind, needs that are not only aesthetic and abstractly intellectual but also ethical and religious. For a school without an ethical and religious constant is an absurdity." Thus, religion should find a suitable and proper place in the sphere of education. Education, according to Pestalozzi, is aimed at "natural harmonious and progressive development of man's innate powers." Wider education mean an education which broadens the outlook, awakens the inner powers and teaches us to respect all the religions. In this manner, a teacher should enable the pupils to cultivate religious attitude and mentality through education. Religion, in this sense does not mean merely a bundle of rites and of dogmas followed by symbols and emotions but it is applied to all that what noble. Religion and education with this collective and mutual efforts lead a person towards self-realisation and self-understanding. Rousseau and Wordsworth believed in nature and education on the lane; of nature. The essence of their philosophy was to worship nature in practical way. In other words, we should obey natural laws and must follow the path traced by her.

Truly speaking, religious education does not mean something separable but pure, honest and beneficial. Education is nothing but religion, because both the religion and the education aim at harmonising the person to the ultimate truth. Religion is the pure form of education.

Education has been defined as "a process of development in which consists the passage of human being from infancy, to Maturity, the process by which he adopts himself gradually in various ways to his physical and spiritual environment." In this definition the ability of social adaptation means the development of the social qualities like cooperation, coordination among social groups and communities. This ability of the adaptation is religious, because religion in a wider sense says clearly that all are one. We are brothers and sisters borne of the same father. The same ideology of cooperation is found in this interpretation alike education. Therefore, curriculum construction should be based on the principle that education and religion are not the separate entities but they are one in nature and consequence.

What is man and what is God? These are the main problems dealt with by religion. These are the truth of a vital significance and are at the basis "of the whole structure of knowledge whether of fact or value, and deprived of them education as well as life is radically defective, without centre, balance or proper subordination of part to part."

The aim of education is all-round development of man. The same is the aim of religion. So because use of this common aim the correlation of education and religion quite natural. Now to include the various forms of religion in education, is a great problem. Some people due to their ignorance of the true nature of religion, do not and to give any place to religion in education, whereas some people want to give it an important place. Since earliest times in India, education and religion have been related to each other. With the break of this relation, indiscipline, violence and immorality have increased. According to **Dr. Sarvapalli Radhakrishnan** the reason for all vices and troubles pervading the world is want of morality which has been created due to education being not corelated to religion. Here in India there were those centres of education in which people from all parts of the world came to receive education. In Western countries also Movements were started for, educational organisation by correlating religion and education. Sunday School Movement, Religious Education Movement were some such movements in which the demand for integration of education and religion was asserted. The world has witnessed the evil effects of materalism. Hence it has rightly realised that humanity cannot be saved without relating education to religion. Now, the need for education integrated with religion is being felt throughout the world. Some politicians and economic groups do not think it proper to give a place to religion in education. In fact, if religion is treated as 'human religion' a revolution can be brought out in the improvement of education. Peace can be established in the world through a religion integrated education based on thinking of universal peace, universal-brotherhood and universal-good.

On the basis of the view point expressed above, it seems useful to impart religious education by integrating education and religion. But it is necessary to consider points both in its favour and against.

ARGUMENTS IN FAVOUR AND AGANIST RELIGIOUS EDUCATION

Those who want to separate religion and education, argue in the following way:

1. To give place to religion in education is not practicable, because children of all religions come to receive education in schools. In such a situation which religion is to be taught in a school? If one particular religion is taught in the school, the followers of other religions will not accept this position. It will lead to mutual ill-will quarrel and disturbance.

2. Religion education is generally based on preaching. So long as desired changes are not brought about in the environment and ideal examples are not presented till then good conduct cannot be spread through religious education. Hence mere teaching of religious doctrines in schools will not achieve the goal of education.

3. Doubts and mental conflicts are created in children as they cannot understand the abstract processes of sin virtue, reward and punishment as explained in religious educational schools.

4. Religious education emphasises, religious sermons and religious knowledge. But life is not conducted according to these sermons. Man cannot become virtuous simply by getting knowledge of religion. He become virtuous only when he puts the same into practice. This is not done in schools.

5. It is not possible for the modern teacher to analyse religious knowledge dispassionately because he may be faithful only to one particular religion. Consequently, the students will be incapable of understanding the true and obscure meaning of religion. It willl be better to analyse religion with the help of science but the teachers will not accept it because science may injure the personal beliefs. In fact, it will be difficult to get able and suitable teachers for religious education. It is a difficult task to correlate education and true human religion. Every teacher may not be capable of this.

6. We have already observed that religion means human religion through which human qualities should be developed. But history bears testimony to the fact that humanity has been oppressed in the name of religion and in place of love, compassion, sympathy and cooperation, the feelings of enmity, hatred, jealously and opposition have grown. Such examples in the history of religion may create irreligious feelings in children.

7. Man imbibes 'religion' through self-realisation. Self-realisation is individualistic. Hence inclusion of personal elements in religious conduct is natural. In the school environment, collective and social tendencies are found. So personal view point of religion cannot be given importance. This view point may be suitable to those children who agree with that line of thinking but not to others who follow other view point.

There may be some strength in thc above arguments. But this strength will be there only to the extent to which education is imparted on the basis one particular religions without understanding the true meaning of religion. Religion is universal, omnipresent and eternal. It is necessary to present its universal form. The following arguments may be presented in favour of religious education:

1. "All-round development of man is not possible only through physical, mental and intellectual development, as this requires, spiritual development also. Physical comforts alone do not provide real pleasure and peace. The more a man is absorbed in wordly pleasures, the more he is attached towards them. He tries to get the physical comforts of this material world through all possible means (even though in human action). He becomes prepared to commit atrocities and cruel actions. This disturbs world peace. Various subjects such as geography, science etc., lead to physical, mental and intellectual development, but they do not develop him spiritually. For spiritual development religion oriented education is needed. Only then the goal of an all-round development of the individual may be achieved.

2. Lack of religious faith in man is the cause of his troubles. All the vices of the world are due to irreligiousness and materialistic

tendencies. Selfishness is the outcome of materialism which creates vices like enmity, jealousy and intolerance. Hence, religious education is necessary in order to get rid of inhuman tendencies.

3. We have said earlier that religious education becomes defective only when religion is teated in its narrow form. Religion is not be identified with any sect or opinion. The essence of all sects, is the true religion. This religion alone can be named as human religion. If it is taught through education, the follower of any religion will not be ignored. It will be worthwhile to provide education in high human ideals which are adored by people of every religion instead of giving place to the rituals of different sects.

4. In such countries which are mainly religious, the religious education will be useful from educational point of view. Education based on religion will be easily understandable and interesting in such countries. India is one such country. But religion should not be taken into its narrow form. By adopting essence of all the sects, religious education should be given in its wider perspective.

5. The aim of education is all-round development of the individual in which development of character is the main aim. Religious education is the best source for character development. Today education being devoid of religion, the character of many of our youths is not what it should be. Evidently, religion is to be given due place in education for the sake of character development.

6. In the modern world scientific experimentalism, scientific invention, scientific thinking, intellectual and materialistic development have been continuously going on. Consequently, the progressive countries have achieved material affluence. But have these countries become happy and peaceful inspite their affluence? The two World Wars are the consequences of the materialistic selfishness. Humanity had to suffer due to the menace of these wars. Some people tried to bring peace in the world and efforts are still continuing. But world peace has not been achieved so far. The sole reason for it is the neglect spiritualism. The truth is that materialism and spiritualism should be integrated through religious education. That a hungry

nation can survive with spiritualism alone, is not true. Along with physical hunger of soul should also be satisfied. Religious education alone can satisfy the hunger of soul. So it will be necessary to impart universal religious education in schools. One or two persons alone have not stressed the need of religious education. In India, Shri Syed Ahmed Khan, Radhakrishnan, Madan Mohan Malviya, Mahatma Gandhi, Dayanand, Rabindranath Tagore and Arvind and such other great men have advocated religious education. Smt. Annie Besant and Mira Behn, Mataji considered it necessary to integrate education with religious education. While integrating education and religious education we shall have to keep it in mind that the religion to be integrated should be human-religion. Religious education should not be based on the belief of one particular sect.

CAUTIONS IN THE TEACHING OF RELIGION

An evaluation of advantages and limitations of religious education leads us to be conclusion that religion should be given a place in education. But religion should be included in such a way that the above mentioned defects religious education may be avoided. One of the objectives of religious education is self-realisation and to inspite virtuous conduct. It is necessary to make efforts in this direction. Self-realisation and virtuous conduct are inner-impulses. They can not be imposed on anyone. Sermons and instructions alone will not achieve religious aims. Moral development and virtuous conduct through religion is possible only when opportunities are provided for such behaviour. A religious atmosphere in schools can make it possible. The incidents are greatly influenced by the ideal behaviour of teachers. So the teachers themselves should present examples of ideal behaviour by leading a religious, moral and virtuous life. The teacher religion alone cannot create a religious atmosphere in schools. All teachers should cooperate in this process.

Religious education should be kept away from narrow mindedness. It will be better to give religious education based on logic, analysis and criticism, otherwise it may lead to superstitions fanatics, jealousy and narrow-mentality.

In schools, religion should not be taken as an end in itself. It is simply a means for all-round development of the individual. The schools are not to be made temples, mosques, or churches by titling religious education to a particular sect. Schools are not to fulfil the functions of religious institutions other the religious institutions should work as schools. If religious institutions make an attempt for the all-round development of children through spiritual development, they will certainly lessen the burden of schools. It is, therefore, necessary for the religious bodies to take the form of educational obligations to the extent possible.

Educational Functions of Religion. A man is attracted towards religion only when he is mentally, healthy and a sound mind are sides in a sound body. So it is the function of religion to co-operate in the physical development of children. In vedic religions behaviour the ideal of celibacy is for the sake of physical development. The child who observes restraint up to maturity and takes physical exercises for the development of body makes himself sturdy. This restorative power prepares him for household life and his regulated behaviour keeps him healthy till death. Some religious people think that good physical health creates a liking or worldly pleasures and happiness. So a person desirous of religious knowledge should not pay any attention to physical development. This is their fanaticise. Religion should first of all educate the individual for his physical and mental development. Body, mind and senses are means of inhibiting religion.

Religion should always mean performing of duties. To think only of the next world (Parlok) through religious knowledge and to forget this world (Ih-lok) is not fair. The first field of performing duties is this world Karma-Kshetra (the field of action) is another name for Dhama-Kshetra (fields of religious). The man who succeeds in the Karma-Kshetra of this world is entitled to reach the other world (Parlok). Therefore, religion should prepare man for the Karma-Kshetra (field of action). The field of action of the individual is determined on the basis of his aptitudes. So religion should inculcate in the child the ability to choose his field of action according to his interest and aptitude and to get success engaging himself in it.

The basis of religion is knowledge. An ignorant person cannot be religious. A person may be familiar with religion and religious behaviour after he has attained knowledge. The basis of religion are logic, analysis, observation, contemplation and freedom of thought. So the child should be provided opportunities for independent thinking, logic, meditation, analysis and observation with an open mind. The doubt of some persons that the child does not believe in religious facts on the basis of arguments, analysis, observation etc. is baseless. The permanent religious feeling is always based on perception. To have faith in religion without independent thinking, logic and analysis will be blind-faith and fanaticism.

Some people consider aesthetic sense and artistic sense as hindrance to religion. But this is not true. Satyam, Shivam, Sundaram (Truth, Bliss and Beautiful) and the bases for artistic and aesthetic senses. Satyam and Shivam are the bases of religion. A thing which is not true or for happiness cannot be beautiful. The carving of Jain idols in Ellora caves and Jataka stories connected with the life of Lord Buddha and their carving in Ajanta, the poetry of Sur, Tulsi and Mira and all considered unique for propagation of religious feelings. So religion should diffuse an aesthetic sense also.

Although it is true function of schools to develop the moral and character of the child, but religious institutions can bring about better moral and character development, if they pay attention in this direction. The very meaning of religion is to inspire virtuous conduct and virtuous conduct develops moral and ethical qualities. Today the country needs able and noble citizens. The religious institutions can fulfil their national duties by giving education virtuous conduct.

Thus, after studying the merits and demerits and functions of religious education we come to the conclusion that religion should be included in schools as a means of all-round development of children. Religious institutions can perform at least those educational functions which are difficult to be achieved in schools. Thus, it is necessary for schools and religious institutions to shoulder the responsibility of developing noble citizens.

SOCIALISATION

Socialisation is a social process, and it has been variously defined. Some of these definitions are the following:

V.V. Akolkar. "The process of adoption by the individual of the conventional patterns of behaviour is described as his socialisation, because it occurs on account of his integration with others and his expression of the culture which operates through them."

E.A. Ross. "The development of we feeling in association and the growth in their capacity and will to act together."

E.S. Bogardus. Socialisation is, "The process whereby persons learn to behave dependably together on behalf of human welfare and in so doing experience social self-control, social responsibility and balanced personality.

Socialisation then, is process by means of which the individual learns to behave according to the social traditions and conventions. The human child has a remarkable capacity to imitate others, and hence he develops according to the environment into which he is born. Man, being a social animal, tries to win the appreciation of the group in which he lives and hence he naturally tries to imitate the culture of that group. It is through socialisation that he is transformed from the animal into the human, and it is socialisation which gives— him a balanced personality. The social aspects of the personality is no less inportant than the individual aspect. Socialisation teaches him to retain control over himself in the interest of others. It evolves a we feeling or community feeling in him and there by invests him with a sense of responsibility.

The Process of Socialisation

Individuals influence each other by imitation, suggestion and sympathy, besides which the process of socialisation is furthered by many social institutions. Man is the product of many social processes such as praise and blame, cooperation and conflict, submission and ascendancy, and these forces create the individual's personality.

Education is the most potent agency of socialisation available to society.

Factors of Socialisation

1. ***Socialisation in the Family.*** The family plays a very significant part in the individual's socialisation because the child spends his early formative years in the home. He learns much by observing the people around him, by imitating them, by indulging in activities which win their approval and avoiding those which bring their disapproval and immediate punishment. It is the family environment which can create good habits in him, because the child's moral code is conditioned by the system of reward and punishment which prevails in the family. And, it is also in the family that criminal tendencies are first generated. In the book *New Light on Delinquency and its Treatment*, Healey and Bronner have pointed out that juvenile delinquents are frequently found in those families in which the fulfilment of social relationships has been hindered at one time or the other. Freud and other psychoanalysts have demonstrated that the child remains throughout life whatever he is made out to be in the family. In his *"Psychological Factors in Marital Happiness"*, Termann has theorised that only those individuals can enjoy marital bliss whose own parents had been happy and contended. In the preface to *'Women of the Street'*, a depth study of the prostitutes of London, it has been commented that the problem of prostitution is, in reality, a problem of the relationship between the children and parents.

The family plays a very significant, perhaps the most significant role in the individual's development. Freud and other psychoanalysts believe that the impressions made upon the child's mind at home determine the child's personality as an adult, for in childhood, the child's mind is very flexible and susceptible to any influence. The parents' love for the child makes a deep impression on him. And, although it is true that exclusive love and affection have detrimental effects, the complete absence of affection creates complexes in the child's mind, which later disbalance his personality. His personality is also influenced greatly by the behaviour of his brothers and sisters towards him. Adler, the famous psychologist, has stressed the fact that the order of the birth of children in the family distinctly and separately influences the personality of each child. The eldest child's mental make up differs from that of the last. Besides, all great thinkers and philosophers have admitted the importance of their mother's love as far as their personality development is concerned. In India, people often gauge the personality of a young marriageable girl by observing her mother. And, as far as marriages are concerned, more attention is paid to the prospective bridegroom's parentage than to his own personality, for the family makes a lot of difference.

The family's influence does not end with the individual's entrance into adolescence, for even then the influence continues. Complete absence of control often results in moral degeneration among the young people, while excessive control manifests itself in repressed personalities and narrow minds. Only reasonable restraint and freedom can help the individual to develop a balanced personality. After marriage, the individual's personality is also exposed to the influence of his partner's personality, his or her health, mental attitudes, family background, physical beauty, attainments, etc. The ability to beget children or not is another factor which plays a significant role in the individual's personality development. In fact, considerable literature has been devoted to the subject of family's influence upon the personality by sociologists, psychologists and anthropologists.

2. ***Socialisation in the School.*** After the home, the child is exposed to the school which also influences him, for the school is nothing less than a miniature society to him. It socialises him, gives him an opportunity to manifest his qualities, instincts, drives and motives, and helps to develop his personality. For the child, the educator's personality and character provide a model which he strives to copy, thereby consciously or unconsciously moulding his personality. This is ture only of those teachers who succeed in arousing in the child's mind an attachment and love for themselves. Every little action, every movement, speech, etc. impresses itself on

the child's mind. On the other hand, he is often repelled by some teachers, and he wants to contradict them through every act. This repulsion may be conscious or unconscious, but it drives the child away from such a teacher. The child is attracted by the other teacher who wins his sympathy, and it is from this teacher that the child wants to win praise and appreciation. He fears the frown of his teacher, he imitates him persistently. Apart from the teacher the child is also influenced by his colleagues, and his status and role in his school groups plays a large part in determining the status and role he is to occupy in society in later life. During the process of education, the child's personality develops under the impact of the other personalities with whom he comes into contact. In the school the child is disciplined. He is aware that disobedience brings immediate punishment, but too strict a system of discipline restricts the child's mental growth and may even drive him to criminal activity. On the other hand, complete absence of control may either make him liberal, free and independent or impulsive and impish.

In this manner, the human personality is profoundly influenced both by the home and the school, of the two, family influence lasts for a longer time and is more comprehensive.

INDIVIDUAL AND SOCIAL AIMS OF EDUCATION

Apparently it seems that individual and social aims of education are two rival camps, two rival claims of the individual and of the society. All educational aims tend to lay stress on either the one or the other. But the difference is merely one of emphasis and a synthesis of the two is possible if the extreme view of these is avoided.

The extreme view of social aims of education originates in the totalitarian philosophy of the state which says that the state is an entity over and above the individual citizen, superior to him in every way and transcending all his desires and aspirations. Hence, it follows, the aim of education should be the GOOD OF THE STATE. In the interest of the good of the state, it is argued that the state has a right to determine and dictate what shall be taught and how it will be taught. Similarly, who will be taught what is determined by the consideration that how best he will serve the state. From the primary stage to the University the children should be taught that the state or the society is absolute.

The extreme view of individual aims emerges from the philosophy of individualism which emphasises the individual rather than the society. Expressed in **T. Percy Nunn's** words it says that "nothing good enters into the human world except in and through the free activities of individual men and women, and that educational practice must be shaped to accord with that truth." This is an attempt on asserting the importance of the individual and safeguarding his indefeasible rights. Hence, it stresses that the aim of education should be to secure for everyone the conditions under which individuality is most completely developed. Except this ideal of developed personality, according to this extreme view, there is no other aim of education. Nunn claimed that laws of nature would support this aim. In a slightly different way it means "self-realisation". Thus development of "individuality" and the "Self" is the only aim of education according to the extreme view of individual aims of education.

These two extreme views as such have no possibility of any compromise or synthesis. But, in their moderate form a synthesis is possible. If both these aims are interpreted and understood slightly in different ways, they may appear to be the one and the same thing. And this way of understanding them alone is more, positive and realistic more so in a democratic country like India.

Synthesis. If instead of "education for the state" we say, "education for social service" or "education for citizenship" emphasising the good of the community only on the one hand and "spiritual individuality" instead of only "individuality" or "self emphasising the importance of the development of the responsible man" the compromise between the two becomes possible. If we believe that the greatness of a society or the state is an outcome of its democratic institutions and responsible citizen the two aims appear just one as one cannot take rise without the other. It is the virtues of the individuals that make a society or the state great and glorious. The interests of the state are enhanced by the development of virtue and wisdom in the individual and individuals find their best chance of self-development in the service of the state or the society. It is a fact that only in a social medium man's individuality can be fostered and personality exalted. The individuality of a person or his so called personality can be expressed and understood only in social terms. The very concept of individuality will be meaningless without a reference to what he is expected to be in relation to his society. A charming personality, for example, means what the society means by being charming how the society defines and describes it. As **Nunn puts** it "man's nature is social as truly as it is self-regarding". Thus as **Ross** has expressed it "the individuality is of no value and personality is a meaningless term apart from the social environment in which they are developed and made manifest." Self-realisation can be achieved only through social service and social ideals. At the same time social ideals of real value can come into being only through free individuals who have developed valuable individuality.

Professor **Bagley** of America tried to synthesise these two aims into one by saying that education should aim at developing "social efficiency" in the pupils. It was defined by him as consisting of three components: *(i)* economic efficiency, *(ii)* negative morality and *(iii)* positive morality. This point of view stresses that all the activities of the individual are to be valued with reference to his social obligations. On the other hand social institutions exist only to make the individual life better, fuller, richer, happier, more secure and more fruitful.

Thus, there should not be any conflict between the social and individual aims of education. They are the two sides of the same coin, self-realisation and social service are complimentary to each other. They can not be separated and pulled apart. If one single heading, theme or title has to be found for both of them, it may be "Welfare Aim of Education", meaning, thereby, seeking welfare of the individual as well as of the society, the state through education.

SOCIAL CHANGE

Social means concerning society and change means deviation from existing pattern. In this sense, social change means change in the structure and functions of human society. In fact human life is not static. It is under a constant change in the ideas, attitudes and values of an individual. This changing process brings changes in the social structure and in other social attributes also. In fact, styles of living are changing so fast today that it is difficult to keep pace with the changing ideas, beliefs, life-styles and material pursuits for more and more human welfare. This change in social structure is known as social change.

To understand the meaning of social change, it is essential to know the meaning of 'change' and 'society'. 'Change' means alteration of an item under consideration either in part or whole. It is a variation from previous state or difference through time. Therefore going by these two definitions we can say that social change is the change in social relations.

According to **Jenson,** "Social change may be defined as modification in the ways of doing and thinking of people."

According to **Davis,** "By social change is meant only such alterations as occur in social organisaton *i.e.*, in the structure and functions of a society."

According to **Ginsberg,** "By social change I understand a change in social structure, *e.g.*, size of a society, the composition or balance of its parts or the type of its organisation."

According to **MacIver and Page,** "Social change is the change in society. Society is a network of social relationship. Social relationships include social processes, social patterns and social interactions. Social change can be defined as change in social relations itself."

According to **Dawson and Gettys,** "Cultural change is social change, since all culture is social in its origin, meaning and usage."

Some scholars depict the process of social change in the following manner:

Change in the experience of individuals

↓

Change in the attitude of individuals

↓

Change in the social interactions

↓

Change in social relations

↓

Change in social structure

Social change

On the basis of above definitions, we can say that any change in the social structure or its functions is a social change.

Social change is accepted as such only when the majority of individuals in a society accept it in their life, behaviours and beliefs.

In short, social change means replacing the old with the new in the society. It can be a modification of the old also if not total replacement. It can be a new mode of thought, a new attitude towards work, worship and wealth, a new behaviour pattern and so on. It can take various forms.

Different Aspects of Social Change. Social change is related with all types of changes related to society. It includes all aspects of society.

Economic Aspect. Change relating to industry, business, agriculture, productive process etc. comes in this aspect.

Political Aspect. It is related with change in administration and political power.

Moral Aspect. It is related with change in values and thoughts.

Scientific and Technological Aspect. It is related with change due to scientific and technological development.

Religious Aspect. It is related with change in religion and religious institutions as—Church, Temple and Gurudwara.

Factors Affecting Social Change. Social change is the product of the interaction of many factors which are as follows:

Geographical Factors. Change in the Geographical environment has great effect on human society. Climate is the only reason of rise and downfall of civilisations and cultures.

Geographical factors comprise all the inorganic (Non-living) phenomena which exert an influence on human life. Theoretically, such a definition would include even the physical state of other planets in our solar system. Practically, however, the geographic factors may be limited to the climate and its influences including temperature, sunshine, rainfall, relative humidity, prevailing winds and other climatic possibilities. Every man lives in particular geographical conditions which do affect the social life, *e.g.* social life of people living in plains is different from those living in hilly areas.

The inhabitants of West Bengal and other regions near sea depend more on fish for their food as fish are available in these areas in large number and at ease.

When natural calamities such as flood, drought, famine etc. uproot innumerable families, the individuals involved from new social relations which as a result bring about social change. Natural catastrophe encourages geographical mobility and people moving to a different place and culture adapt themselves to it.

Biological Factors. The important biological factors affecting social changes are: The plants and animals in the area and the human beings themselves. Man uses the available plants and animals according to his culture and traditions. He destroys the enemies like insects, poisonous plants, bacteria and dangerous animals with the best available means. The biological environment is dynamic and we find change in the climate, change in soil composition, drying up of lakes or streams etc. which spell the doom of some organisms and encourage new opportunity for others.

Psychological Factors. The psychology of human being may itself become the cause for social change. Man by nature loves change, desires to invent new things in every sphere and is always anxious for novel experiences.

As a conequence of this, attitude changes and rituals, customs, traditions etc. also go on changing in the society in a continuous manner. This does not imply that whatever is new is considered superior to the old. On one side man wants to preserve the good elements of what is old and simultaneously attends to what is new. In this process of interaction between the two tendencies change in social relationships takes place which leads to social change.

Technological Factors. Social change is brought about mainly due to the following technological factors:

(1) Development of new methods and processes of agriculture.

(2) Development of means of transport.

(3) Development of means of communication.

(4) Use of machines in industries.

Technology is nothing but applied science, which helps in bringing social change with the changing needs of the society. The development of technology has led to the establishment of factories, urbanisation and industrialisation. Therefore, new classes emerged. People of different regions started migrating to industrial areas for want of work and stayed there which led to the mixing of different cultures. The increase in the number of educational institutions, facilities of bank, opening of new business centres and expansion of trade and commerce are also its products. As a result of industrialisation joint family system has broken and is fast being replaced by single family system.

Technological development has resulted into many material and non-material changes in our society such as:

— Abolition of untouchability and weakening of caste relationships.

— The manner of preparing our food, standard of living, decrease in the death rate, development of scientific attitude and emergence of new values such as equality, liberty, justice, secularism, brotherhood, co-operation and fellow feelings etc.

Cultural Factors. Culture encompasses values, styles, ideals, beliefs, traditions, emotional attachment etc. These affect the society to a great extent.

Main Factors in Bringing Social Change in India

The main factors of social change in India are as follows:

Science and Technology. Scientific and technological discoveries and inventions have caused several far-reaching social changes in the lives of people in developing as well as developed countries. Television, Films, Video, and other scientific inventions have completely changed our mode and style of living, modes of thinking and consequently social relations.

Sanskritisation. It is the process by which a low Hindu caste, or tribe or other group changes its customs, rituals, ideology, and way of life in the direction of high caste. Generally such changes are followed by a claim to a higher position in the caste hierarchy than that traditionally conceded to the claimant caste by the local community.

Social Mobility. Social mobility means position in social sphere. This mobility occurs in 'vertical' or 'horizontal' directions. It can be 'individual' or 'group mobility'.

Vertical mobility implies movements up the social or occupational ladder, accompanied by rise in status, position, income and economic condition etc.

Horizontal mobility means change in place without accompanying rise in social or economic status.

Indianisation. A glimpse of Indianisation is noticed in dress, meditation, religious songs, prayers, celebration of Indian festivals and customs. Integration with Indian culture and civilisation is known as Indianisation.

Modernisation. Modernisation means the change in the values, attitudes, relationships, associations, social institutions etc. on the pattern of the so called modern culture of U.K., U.S.A., Japan, France etc. A country can evolve its own model of modernity as well by developing its own ideas on style of living and technology.

Westernisation. This is the process of social change in India by which the culture, traditions style of living and values are changing as the western culture considerably affected the Indian culture and society. Under the British rule the Indians have not only adopted the western technology and educational system but also they have accepted the western manners and habits in the matter of food, dress, social relations, mode of living, recreation and system of marriage etc.

Secularisation. Secularisation implies rationality, differentiation, religious toleration, naturality, broad outlook and unorthodoxy. It implies that various issues in personal and social life are evaluated not from religious point of view but from utilitarian point of view.

Urbanisation. A significant feature of this change is the continuous migration from rural areas to the urban areas. This social change leads to the same problems as that of industrialisation. Urbanisation leads to growth of towns, cities and urban centres, industrial towns, business projects, educational, commercial and trade centres and religious cities etc.

Hinduisation. The tendency and efforts of several tribal communities in India to enter the broadfold of the Hindu social structure are implied by this process. For example a section of the

Bhil tribals has now become Bhil caste in Hindu social structure. By doing so they think that they have gained social status.

Politicisation. There was politicisation due to leaders' political outlook, manifestos of political parties and awareness about the rights and duties of citizens, regional, national and international relations. The advancement of democracy, the spread of education and the mass media greatly promoted politicisation throughout the country resulting in vast social changes.

Industrialisation. The spread of industrialisation gives rise to crimes, strikes, prostitution, drinking, trade unionism and agitations. Other changes which take place due to industrialisation are: growth of educational institutions, banks and business centres, extension of roads and other civic amenities.

Planning and Law. Law also helps in bringing social change in the society. People have the tendency to oppose new changes in the society but they are forced to accept these changes if enacted as law. And then these changes become the part of their life, for example Zamindari system, privy purse, slavery, exploitation and untouchability etc. have been abolished by law.

Role/Importance/Functions of Education in Social Changes

Education is an important instrument to bring social revolution. Among all the instruments education is considered as the most powerful. Education for all, at all levels, and at all ages of children is the only remedy to bring about the desired social change in Indian society.

The relationship between education and social change takes a dual form—education as an instrument and education as a product. This implies that education as an instrument is used as a means for bringing about desired changes in the society and in the later case changes in the educational structure follows as a consequence of changes which have already taken place in the society.

There are three types of relationship between education and social change which are as follows:

1. *Education as a Necessary Condition of Social Change.* Historical experience of advanced countries has shown that for any social revolution education is the pre-condition. Illiterates remain satisfied with their existing conditions and feel that they are destined to be what they are. They never bother to exert to bring change in their present social and economic conditions. They are guided by orthodoxy, traditions and fate rather than by rationality in their actions. Education helps people to make them rational in their thinking and approach.

2. *Education as an Instrument of Social Change.* Education as an instrument of social change means how education helps people to bring social change. Education changes the outlook and the tradition approach towards social and economic problems. It sharpens the skills and knowledge of the children. Technical education helps in the process of industrialisation which results in vast changes in society. Education not only preserves the cultural traditions *i.e.*, customs, traditions and values etc. of the society but also transmits them to the next generation. It also motivates the children to adopt new pattern in order to remain dynamic and forward looking. Education fulfils the needs of the society and propagates such ideas which promote social changes in all fields of life.

3. *Education as an Outcome of Social Change.* There is interdependent relationship between education and social change. On the one hand it brings change in social conditions. On the other hand it is influenced by social change, which means social change helps spreading education. Education follows social change. It has its place before and after social change. First come social changes and then teaching process is changed according to those social changes. Education system changes according to the needs of society.

Functions of Education as an Instrument of Social Change

Education fulfils the needs of society and propagates such ideas which promote social change in all fields of life. In this way, education becomes a social process by means of which society moulds children according to its needs and approved patterns of behaviour. Functions of education as an instrument of social change are as follows:

(1) ***Stabilizing Eternal Values.*** Education protects eternal values, saves them from pernicious effects of social changes and promotes their knowledge and acceptance in such a manner that inspite of social changes, people in general keep faith in these values. In our society such eternal values are of moral and spiritual nature. Education should protect, preserve and promote these values.

(2) ***Increasing the Areas of Knowledge.*** Education promotes in the individuals the capacity to increase the scope of knowledge more and more for their benefit. It opens new areas for investigations and researches, which bring about desirable changes in material as well as non-material aspects of culture. Thus education prepares ground for the advent of social change.

(3) ***Evaluation of Social Change.*** Education lays down the required standards and criteria of values with reference to which this process of evaluation takes place effectively, and only after that, desirable social changes are propagated wheres the undesirable ones discarded.

(4) ***Leadership Role in Social Change.*** Education provides leadership in social change. Education makes people capable to initiate and guide for needed social changes by fighting succesfully against social evils, customs and blind traditions. Thus people become capable for realising their own true personality to the full and promote social welfare to greater and greater extent.

(5) ***Education Accelerates Social Change.*** Education tries to banish social evils, blind customs and traditions through various social reformation projects, political movements, social service schemes and also tries to bring in 'needed social changes and reforms'. For example, in India public movements and agitations against child marriage, forced widowhood, untouchability and social injustice resulted in desirable social changes.

(6) *Education Prepares People Mentally for Social Change.* It prepares the mentality of people to welcome and adopt desirable social changes easily. It may be noted that people will welcome and adopt any technique or pattern only when they become convinced of its utility and desirability. Education, thus structures a wholesome and conducive environment for these social changes to become acceptable to all.

It tries to remove the mental reservations and complexes in the minds of people which obstruct the progress of change.

Education provides necessary training in skills and occupations and thus produces the needed competent personnel for manning the different specialised jobs in modern industry, business, educational and research establishments and other secondary associations.

Education is expected to change the values and attitudes of thc people and to create in them the urge of the necessary motivation to achieve social class ascendency, social mobility and/or their sanskritisation.

Modern education can mould people into enlightened, emphatic, risk-taking, thick-skinned, industrious and mobile personalities.

Education can be of immense help in bringing about democratisation, secularism, national integration as well as economic prosperity and proper political socialisation.

Education can cut down the thick roots of traditions, superstitions, ignorance and backwardness etc.

Education prepares the society for the initial cultural stock inherent in determined plans of modernisation. Elvin Toffer's thrilling book '*Future Shock*' tells us about it.

Education can prepare the society for the cultural imbalances that inevitably characterise the social transitional situation, and should endeavour to prevent, as far as possible, shocking conditions, and, during the long transitional phase, it can discipline the people to withhold immediate gratification in the interest of future inputs for the furtherance of the long-range plans of modernisation.

INDIAN SCHOOLS OF PHILOSOPHY

The Indian schools of philosophy are:

1. Vedas (Vedanta).
2. The Gita.
3. Jainism.
4. Buddhism.

The Vedanta Philosophy

In the beginning, we had Vedas. The word "Veda" means knowledge. The Vedas are four—Rig, Yajur, Sam and Atharva. They contain hymns or Mantras.

These 'Mantras' stand explained in Upanishads. These Upanishads are known also as 'Vedanta' as it comes at the end of Vedas.

The Upanishads have two terms for ultimate realiy—The Brahman and the Atman. The "Brahman" is the ultimate source of the outer world and the 'Atman' the innerself of man. Both are complimentary. The subjective side is 'Atman' and the objective side is "Brahman".

The "Brahman" is the supreme reality.

The 'Brahman' is the Absolute. It is called Sanchi-Ananda—pure existence, pure knowledge and pure bliss—all rolled into one. It is also Truth, Beauty and Goodness. These are the three values which Indians cherish the most and beauty being the highest value.

The Implications in Education

1. *Perfect the Individual.* It is said that the spiritual personality of the individual is the central core of the Vedanta philosophy. We must thus repeat the individual personality.

2. *Teacher-Taught Relations.* These relations are bound to be excellent if a student is to learn anything from a teacher.

3. The knowledge is to be acquired through detachment. The methods are Hearing, Reflection and Meditation.

4. The four ideals of life or the core of our culture are 'Artha', 'Kama', 'Dharma' and 'Moksha'. These are stressed by Vedantas.

THE GITA

Holy Gita is also called the 'Gospel of Humanity'. It is also called the Song Celestial. Its teachings are well known. Duty. Do your Duty. Do not expect any fruit. Duty itself is a reward in itself. It is Action which is important and only action will take you to salvation. And Fight the evil. 'Karma' is supreme.

Implications in Education

1. Act. Act now. Act boldly: Do not be despondent. Education should teach us to be manly.
2. Be of service to others.
3. Do your duty fearlessly and with devotion.
4. Renounce. Your only need should be 'Being needless'. No greed. But at the same time renunciation should not be of extreme type. And do not be over attached to the world.

"The Gita's message is for all men and women living in world doing all kinds of work. It shows a way of life by which people shouldering responsibilities can achieve all round success and happiness. The ideal of Gita is not only to produce great seers and sages but to produce also great warriors, statesmen, industrialists, artists and scientists. Anybody in any station-in-life can lift himself through his own self-effort."

JAINISM

Founder is Bhagwan Mahavir. Jainism is from "Jiva" which means to conquer.

It refuses to believe in God. It encourages a pessimistic outlook on life.

Main Points

1. Two aspects. There are two aspects of universe—Jiva and Ajiva—The conscious and the unconscious spirit. Jiva is expansion and contraction. It is life. Ajiva is divided into Kala, Akasha, Dharma, Adhara and Pudgala (motto).

2. Ignorance means slavery. Right knowledge is the act of liberation. Right faith, Right knowledge and Right conduct are the three pillars of Jainism.

3. Jainism believes in strict discipline. There are five vows—the last two are not for laymen; Ahimsa, Astega, Non-stealing, Celibacy and Renunciation.

4. Jainism is a religion of self-help. Jainism denies God. But every liberated soul is God.

5. Development of personality—individual and social are its aims.

The implications in education are:

1. One of the aims of education is obviously development of personality. The many sides of personality should be taken care of.

2. Right conduct should be always stressed.

3. Curriculum was based on three Ratnas—right faith, right knowledge and right conduct.

4. Memory is stressed.

BUDDHISM

Lord Buddha and his teachings are well known. We sum these up.

Three Fold Teachings of Buddha are:—1. The Four Noble Truths—There is suffering; There is a cause of suffering; There is a cessation of suffering; There is a way leading to the cessation of suffering.

2. The Eight-fold path to Nirvana are:

— Right Faith,

— Right Resolve,

— Right Speech,

— Right Action,

— Right Living,

— Right Effort,

— Right Thought,

— Right Concentration.

3. Dependent Organisation. All things hang between reality and nothingness. Each object of reality is relative. Everything is conditional, dependent. Everything is merely a link in its chain.

Implications in Education

1. You can achieve peace here and now. Teachers need not despair.
2. Buddhistic philosophy is pragamtic. Everything is in a state of flux. Nothing is permanent. Change is the rule of universe.
3. It is democratic. It encourages enquiry.
4. It believes in the teaching and learning of manual skills.
5. It is ethical. Our education should be ethic based.

ENVIRONMENTAL EDUCATION

Environment is a word which describes all the external factors, influences and conditions which affect the life, nature, behaviour, growth and development and maturation of living organisms. Environment stands for all those circumstances which assert their influence on the human beings since birth to death. Whatever is present around us, above the land, on the surface of the earth and under the earth is environment. It covers the whole natural surrounding that is spread over around us. It includes vegetation, like trees, plants, animals, birds, forests, rivers, mountains, lakes and tanks etc. The environment has been playing an important role since times immemorial. Environment is of two types—Natural environment and social environment.

1. Natural Environment. Natural environment is related with nature which includes air, water, forests, land, minerals, animals, birds, etc. or organic and inorganic substances. All the components of the environment keep themselves in balance but man has polluted the environment by his ignorance and carelesseness.

2. Social Environment. The social environment is expressed in the action and reaction of social relationships. All the aspects of man's life are included in the scope of social environment *e.g.*, political, economic, religious, spiritual, physical and intellectual etc.

Importance of Environment

Modern age is the age of science. We have conquered nature. Attention was paid to available and new resources because of explosion of population and explosion of knowledge. The explosion of population has a direct effect on our ways of living. India is a vast country having a population of about 100 crores.

In India explosion of population has given birth to various problems pertaining to environment. Our population depends upon the natural resources to meet their basic needs, particularly of fuel, fodder and housing material. It has led to deterioration in the quality of life. Man has cut off forests to satisfy his endless hunger and adopted artificial means of irrigation. The fertility of soil is decreasing day-by-day. As a result of increasing pressure of pupulation land is becoming limited. Cultivable land is decreasing due to increasing population, industrialisation and urbanisation. Increase in population leads to pollution of air and water and spread germs of many diseases. Apart from this, industrialisation has given birth to noise and smoke. It increases slum dwellings. It compels a large number of people to live in dirty surroundings having dirty lanes permeating bad smell. The smoke emmitted by cars, motors and scooters pollutes the atmosphere.

Increase in pollution has given birth to several diseases such as tuberculosis, deafness, heart attack and high blood pressure etc. The carbide gas factory at Bhopal made thousands of people blind. Pollution also creates mental diseases.

The tendency of urbanisation also contributes to this problem at a rapid rate. The rural population started moving towards the cities and the cities went on expanding. Due to the housing problem the life of metro cities became more complex.

According to the Report given by United Nations, 22350 lakh acres of land has become sterile because of soil erosion and saltishness. 2/3 jungles of the world have been cut down. 200 kinds of animals and birds have become extinct because of human carelessness. This tendency continues in all areas. If attention is not paid to this side the future of man will become dark.

These days man is moving towards the planet whereas humanity is moving towards the jungle. Insecurity, restlessenss and disorder prevail in the society because human beings have been intellectually polluted. If environmental education is given.to future citizens in the present day schools by formal and informal methods, humanity can get rid of this danger. We find around us air pollution, water pollution, noise pollution, nuclear pollution, ecological imbalance and increase in heat and radiation. Today's environment is not pure and natural due to these pollutions.

— For checking pollution, more and more parks should be created in order to make the environment healthy and clean.

— Factories should find place at long distance from the dwellings.

— Rivers are to be protected from dirty water and filth.

— Vehicles are to be checked from emmiting smoke.

— They should be fitted with silencers to reduce noise.

— Drinking water should be drawn from greater depth and put in clean and well covered pots.

— Vanmahotsav programme should be a continuous process.

— Ways and means are to be adopted to check soil erosion.

— Special cleanliness drives should be undertaken at regular intervals in the cities.

— Milk dairies are to be established at the outskirt of the city.

— No factory should be allowed to work in and around the localities.

— There is need to take steps to prevent the spread of various diseases. In this, family planning should form an integral part of the whole scheme.

Methods of Providing Environment Education

There is dire need to educate people about environment balance. Earlier we did not bother about our environment and took it for granted. We are now worried when we see that ecological and environmental (Air, Water and Noise) imbalances have started to occur in our life and have started to take their toll.

It is imperative that we carefully manage our renewable resources of soil, water, plant and animal life to sustain our economic development. Over exploitation of these is reflected in soil erosion, siltation, floods, rapid destruction of our forests, floral and wild life resources. It is only towards the end of nineteen seventies that Ecology has caught the imagination of people—of planners and educationists alike. It is the time to wake up or face tragedy or catastrophe of unimaginable dimensions. We shall fall victims to chronic and fatal diseases.

Some suggestions to educate people in this direction are as follows:

1. ***Environment Education in Curriculum.*** Environment education should be included in the curriculum. At the primary stage environment studies should be correlated with the nature-study, social studies and health education. Form class 8th onwards, environment studies should be made a compulsory subject.

2. ***Arrangement of Extention Lectures.*** Lectures on environment education should be arranged in schools and colleges. Today's children are the citizens of tomorrow. It is they who have to face the ecological imbalance. They must be warned of and educated about impending disaster of ecological imbalance. For this, experienced persons working in the field of environment education can be invited for delivering lectures on different aspects of environment education.

3. ***Environment Education Corners.*** In the primary schools environment education corners should be set up. The pupils should be encouraged to carry out projects like cleaning up the environment, cleaning up vacant spaces, parks, school compound, lawns and other physically polluted areas of one's surroundings.

4. ***By Arranging Discussions and Seminars.*** Students can be made aware about the ill effects of different types of pollutions through discussions and seminars which can be arranged in schools and colleges.

5. ***By Organising Co-curricular Activities.*** Co-curricular activities can be more helpful and useful in this field. Education for healthy environment can be given effectively with the help of various co-curricular activities being organised in the school. Co-curricular activities like organisation of exhibitions, seminars, workshops, excursions, declamation contest, organisation of clubs etc. can help a great deal in this respect.

6. ***Publicity.*** Our general public and policy makers should be effectively exposed to environmental issues. We must broadcast talks over Radio, T.V. on these issues. Films can also be shown to make people aware of the need to maintain ecological balance. Posters can also be displayed. Hoardings at crossings can make people conscious of their duty in this regard.

7. ***School Magazine.*** Teacher can invite the students to write articles on pollution and its ill effects on the humanity. They can take part in essay competitions. The teacher can guide the pupils regarding the literature available in this field. He can arrange poster competitions, declamation contests, dramatisations etc.

8. ***Legislation.*** In view of disastrous effects of different types of pollutions, there is urgent need to adopt suitable measures to prevent air and noise pollution, over exploitation of fisheries, control of impact of mining on environment. A provision for taking over the treatment of industrial effluents by the Government and preservation of landscapes is also of special significance. Old legislations should be suitably amended and strictly enforced. In 1974, Government passed a law for the prevention and control of water pollution and set up a Cental Water Pollution Board.

9. ***By Encouraging Research in the Field of Environmental Education.*** To control the problem of environmental imbalance, the need to encourage research today is stronger than ever before. Latest technology should be utilised in industries.

10. ***By Involving Students.*** Schools should take up cleaning campaigns, campaign against social evils like drug addiction, cleanliness of the surroundings, etc. The teacher should involve students in solving local environmental problems. The teacher should make the students familiar with their close relationship to the environment surrounding them and tell about its contribution for them.

11. ***By Celebrating Environment Day.*** To make students aware about environmenal problems and their ill effects, there is urgent need to celebrate environment day in schools every year. On

this day students should be made to understand the use of protecting the environment. Tree plantation programme can be organised and cleanliness drives can be taken up.

12. *By Encouraging People Initiative.* In order to create awareness about environmental problems and their bad effects people should be encouraged to take part in "chipko" like movements. Such movements can be launched from time to time in different parts of the country against indiscriminate felling of trees. These movements can draw the attention of the government as well as general public. We should give whole hearted support to such movements.

Teacher is an important means of process of education. Therefore when education plays important role in the formation of healthy environment, teacher can make as much important contribution. He is the architect of the future whom the children copy.

The responsibility of guiding the society lies on the teacher. He is the agent of social change and modernisation. He can impart current information to the new generation and develop outlook towards new values. He can prepare the students mentally for the healthy environment. Its effect is not only there on the student community but he can expand his area.

❑

7

New Educational Policy

The need for National Education Policy was felt after 1947. Kothari Commission had recommended for National Education Policy in 1966 and for the first time Policy for Education was declared in 1968. Due to political instability during 1971-79, Congress has to leave power and the then Government also declared its own National Policy on Education. Again, Congress came into power and deceased Prime Minister Shri Rajeev Gandhi took interest in Education and declared his National Education Policy in 1986 and proposed an action plan.

This document was published in 1986. Honourable Governor of Gujarat, Mr. R.K. Trivedi expressed his views on this policy—"Considering the all-round development of the country, the structure of Education Policy was erected. Education is not considered within four walls of the schools. Teaching is not limited to the curriculum but it is a source of developing national unity, cultural preservation and indication of moral, social and ethical values.

Education Policy provides a sound basis to National Progress. Every ruler in India gave preference to Education according to its need. Present Government declared its National Policy on Education. Following are the main features of National Policy on Education 1986:

1. Role of Education. Education is responsible for the all-round development of the individuals. It is also responsible for cultural assimilation and provide strength to democracy, secularism. Education constructs the nation at every level, creates self-sufficiency and search new areas of development.

2. National System of Education. Though Education is a state subject, this policy provides a National System of Education, *i.e.*, 10 + 2 + 3 system.

3. Equality. This policy provides equal opportunities to all for education. Navodaya schools have been opened for socially and economically deprived but to talented children. Regional imbalances are also being removed.

4. Women Education. New Education Policy gave special emphasis to Women Education. This statement owes that women are the keys to nation's progress. Education of illiteracy vocational curriculum, nutrition and child care courses, home management, etc., are given priority.

5. Education of Scheduled Castes. Socially and economically deprived scheduled castes are the backbone of our society. They need proper development and place in the society. Scholarships, hostel facilities, adult education programmes are being introduced.

6. Adult Education. Education Policy gave a programme for adult education to remove the illiteracy from the masses. For this, adult schools, libraries, distance education, T.V. programmes are being introduced.

7. Education for Tribes. This policy gave main emphasis to the education of tribes. Residential Ashram Schools have been opened for them, scholarships for higher education are given.

8. Education for other Backward Classes. A large number of backward classes, minority classes have not been given any opportunity for education. These classes have a very crucial situation. They are socially and economically deprived due to their profession, but they usually linked themselves with higher varnas. Thus upper castes do not give them social sanction. Education is the only way to give them chance to co-operation with the society.

As far as the secondary education is concerned, vocationalisation of it is introduced. At Higher education stage, autonomy will be given to good colleges.

Though, New Policy gave a new direction in the field of education in the light of national unity and development this is the preparation to welcome the 21st century. Life deal, family structure, social organisation, national consciousness are influenced by the scientific and technological advancement. Moral, social, ethical and human values need development. This is a felt need of our new policy. Common man is on the cross roads. He does not find his way to destiny. Growing population, expansion of social distances and economic disparities put some questions before the new policy. Those questions are as under:

1. Whether new policy will create class difference?
2. Is this policy competent to shape the socialistic society?
3. Will it be possible to make free and compulsory education to all the children upto the age of 14.
4. Reservation policy will not give the passage to new policy.
5. What will be the shape of future? This indication is not given by the policy.
6. How will this be helpful to reconstruct the nation?
7. Will social justice be possible through it?
8. Language problem is a very big problem before new policy?
9. No equality is possible through it.

Though these questions are before our policy makers, even then they are much hopeful to build new India. In the word of our deceased Prime Minister Rajeev Gandhi—"We will have to build our society, such a society where education must be honoured. Education does not end after learning school or college. It is a life long process. We cannot progress until our education be honoured and we could not face the challenges in future to save our country."

In the end past is gold, present is full of dust and future is indefinite. New Education Policy is the determination of youth. This will create a faith for future, develop our determination, thus distance will be dispersed.

INTEGRATED EDUCATION FOR DISABLED CHILDREN

It has been established scientifically that disabled children with mild handicaps make better progress academically and psychologically if they study with the normal children. To integrate these children with others in common schools, a revised scheme of Integrated Education for Disabled Children was started during 1987-88. Under it, cent per cent financial assistance is given to State Governments/UT administrations/voluntary organisations for creating necessary facilities in schools. Admissible items of expenditure are books and stationery allowance, transport allowance, uniform allowance, readers allowance (for blind children), escort allowance (for orthopaedically handicapped with lower extremity disabilities), equipment allowance and wherever necessary hostel charges. Besides, the scheme also provides, among other things, to meet cost of salary and incentives for teachers, setting up of resource rooms, carrying out assessment of disabled children, training of teachers, removal of architectural barriers in schools, development and production of special instructional material for them. Assistance is also given through the University Grants Commission to the selected universities/institutions to run training courses in special education for teachers of handicapped children. Training facilities are also provided by NCERT and four regional colleges of education. The scheme is at present in operation in Andhra Pradesh, Bihar, Goa, Gujarat, Haryana, Jammu and Kashmir, Himachal Pradesh, Karnataka, Kerala, Madhya Pradesh, Maharashtra, Manipur, Mizoram, Nagaland, Orissa, Punjab, Rajasthan, Tamil Nadu, Uttar Pradesh, Delhi, Andaman and Nicobar Islands and Daman and Diu. By the end of 1993-94 about 40,000 disable children in over 9,000 schools were covered under the scheme.

Educational Concessions to Children

The Centre and most of the State Governments and Union Territories offer educational concessions to children of the defence personnel and paramilitary forces killed or permanently disabled during Indo-China hostilities in 1962 and Indo-Pakistan operations in 1965 and 1971.

During 1988, these concessions were extended to children of IPKF/CRPF personnel who were killed/disabled during action in Sri Lanka and children of the armed forces personnel killed/disabled in action in 'Operation Meghdoot' in Siachen area.

Education of SC/ST/OBC

Pursuant to the National Policy on Education, the following special provisions for SCs and STs have been incorporated in the existing schemes of the Departments of Elementary Education & Literacy and Secondary & Higher Education:

(a) Relaxed norms for opening of primary schools;

(b) A primary school within one km walking distance from habitations of 200 population instead of habitations of 300 population;

(c) Abolition of tuition fee in all states in government schools at least up to primary level. Most of the states have abolished tuition fee for SC/ST students up to senior secondary level;

(d) Providing incentives like free text-books, uniforms, stationery, school bags, etc., to these students;

(e) The major programmes of the Department of Education, *viz.*, District Primary Education Programme (DPEP), Lok Jumbish, Shiksha Karmi, Non-Formal Education (NFE) and National Programme for Nutritional Support to Primary Education accord priority to areas of concentration of SCs and STs;

(f) Reservation of seats for SCs and STs in Central Government institutions of higher education including IITs, IIMs, Regional Engineering College, Central Universities, Kendriya

Vidyalayas and Navodaya Vidyalayas, etc. Apart from reservation, there is also relaxation in the minimum qualifying cut off stages for admission in universities, colleges and technical institutions. The UGC has established SC/ST cells in 104 universities including Central universities to ensure proper implementation of the reservation policy;

(g) To improve academic skills and linguistic proficiency of students in various subjects and raising their level of comprehension, remedial and special coaching is provided for SC/ST students. IITs have a scheme under which SC/ST students who marginally fail in the entrance examination are provided one year preparatory course and those who qualify are then admitted to the First Year of the B. Tech. Course;

(h) Out of 43,000 scholarships at the secondary stage for talented children from rural areas 13,000 scholarships are exclusively reserved for SC/ST students, seventy scholarships are exclusively reserved for SC/ST students under the National Talent Search Scheme;

(i) SC/ST candidates are provided relaxation upto 10 per cent cut off marks for the Junior Resaerch Fellowship (JRF) test and all the SC and ST candidates qualifying for the JRF are awarded Fellowship;

(j) 50 Junior Fellowships are awarded every year in science and humanities including social sciences to SC/ST candidates who appear in National Eligibility Test (NET) and qualify the eligibility test for lecturership;

(k) UGC provides relaxation of 5 per cent from 55 per cent to 50 per cent at the Master's level for appointment as lecturer for SC/ST candidates. The Commission has also reduced minimum percentage of marks required for appearing in the NET examination to 50 per cent at Master's level for SCs/STs;

(l) The Central Institute of Indian Languages, Mysore has a scheme of development of Indian Languages through research, developing manpower, production of materials in modern Indian Languages including tribal languages. The Institute has worked in more than 75 tribal languages; and

(m) 146 districts have been identified as low female literacy districts to be given focussed attention by the Centre as well as States/UTs for implementation of programmes/schemes.

The allocation of Rs. 889.98 crore and Rs. 436.54 crore have been made under the Special Component Plan and Tribal Sub-Plan (TSP) for SCs and STs respectively. This accounts for 16.33 per cent and 8.01 per cent of the total outlay.

Minorities Education

In pursuance of the revised Programme of Action (POA) 1992, two new Centrally-sponsored schemes, *i.e.*, *(i)* Scheme of Area Intensive Programme for Educationally Backward Minorities and *(ii)* Scheme of Financial Assistance for Modernisation of Madarsa Education were launched during 1993-94.

The objective of scheme of Area Intensive Programme for Educationally Backward Minorities is to provide basic educational infrastructure and facilities in areas of concentration of educationally backward minorities which do not have adequate provision for elementary and secondary schools. Under the scheme cent per cent assistance is given for:

(i) establishment of new primary and upper primary schools, non-formal education centres, wherever necessary;

(ii) strengthening of educational infrastructure and physical facilities in the primary and upper primary schools; and

(iii) opening of multi-stream residential higher secondary schools for girls belonging to the educationally backward minorities.

GROWTH OF DISTANCE EDUCATION IN INDIA

Peter Says. 'Distance education is a method of indirect instruction, implying geographical and emotional separation of teacher and taught whereas, in main stream education, the relationship between a teacher and student in classroom is based upon social norms, in distance education, it is based upon technological rules.' **Jack Foks** stated the Distance education—'Distance education is a mode of learning with certain characteristics which distinguish it from the campus based mode of learning.'

About 40 years ago, correspondence education in India was started as a pilot project in the University of Delhi. The success of this experiment encouraged other universities to take up instructions through the distance education. By 1985, 31 universities adopted this scheme. About 40000 students at various levels were enrolled by the universities under this scheme. Though the universities are providing education through this media, but there was a great demand for an open university. As a result in 1985, the Govt. of India decided to set up Indira Gandhi National Open University. The focal points of this university are as under:

(i) to promote open university and distance education system.

(ii) to determine the standards of teaching evaluation and research in such system.

(iii) to allocate and disburse grants to colleges, whether admitted to its privileges or not, or to any other university or institution of higher learning as may be specified by the statutes.

Indira Gandhi National Open University is providing Degrees in B.A., B.Sc. and B.Com., Diploma Course in Distance education, Creative writing, Nutrition, Management, Local Self-Government, Library Science, Banking, etc.

Separate Radio and T.V. channels have been started to broadcast and telecast the educational programmes.

As a measure for implementation, the programme of Action has also favoured and recommended Open Universities System to provide higher education through non-formal channel. The main suggestions and recommendations of this Action Programme are given as under:

(i) Action Programme suggested the Open University System. This should be cost-effective, flexible and innovative.

(ii) Indira Gandhi National Open University has been established and is running effectively.

(iii) Non-formal education system should be structured on modular pattern.

(iv) Network of course be framed.

(v) Quality of programmes be ensured.

(vi) Minimum level of learning should be objectively assessed.

(vii) Separate Radio and Television channels be used for the use of distance education.

(viii) Financial Assistance will be ensured very carefully.

Advantages of Distance Education

National Education Policy, 1986 has rightly stressed that distance education will provide many opportunities for education and will lessen the burden of formal education. The advantages of Distance Education are as under:

1. *Reliable.* Distance education is reliable. It has the cost-effective alternative and new means of communication.

2. *Education at Learners' Door.* Distance education is the only way which provide the education to the learner at his door. It provides equal educational opportunities even to those who used to live in remote areas.

3. *Variety of Programme.* Distance education provides variety programmes according to the needs of the learners.

4. ***Beneficial to Adults.*** Distance education provides many benefits to adults. They may up-to-date themselves for the development of skills and knowledge.

5. ***Co-ordination.*** Distance education is the co-ordination of various educational factors, *i.e.*, general, basic, professsional, technical, life-long, inservice and expansion.

6. ***Learner Centred.*** Distance education is learner-centred, therefore, there is no doubt in its success.

7. ***Minimizing Pressures.*** Distance education minimises the educational pressures caused by the explosion of population.

8. ***Freedom.*** This system provides freedom to learner. A learner, learns according to his needs, conditions and facility.

9. ***Educational Needs.*** Distance education fulfils the need of society through variety of educational programmes.

Distance education is still in experimental stage. Even then nobody will disagree that this system will be helpful to solve our educational problems and minimise the pressure of population over the traditional system of education.

ROLE OF EDUCATION

Before we discuss the role of education in the eradication of pollution let us keep in mind a few things like its impact on health, the radio-active waves, rise in respiratory and eye diseases, the growth in diseases caused by virus, the gastroenteritis diseases, various diseases relating to noise resulting in deafness, and other diseases of lungs and heart. The growing adverse effect on all types of vegetation cannot be ignored.

Now it shall be worthwhi e to discuss the role of education in the eradication of pollution. Following are the measures if adopted in letter and spirit in the right earnest, may bear fruitful results:

1. New ways of looking at the environment so that its value can be reflected in the national accounts, better planning and legislation, more careful and wider use of existing and new environmental

technologies, including the all-important environmental impact assessment—a way of appraising the effect of any proposed project on the environment before it is launched.

2. The new Environment (Protection) Act, 1986, is far better in approach than the earlier laws. The Water (Prevention and Control of Pollution) Act, 1974, and the Air (Prevention and Control of Pollution) Act, 1981, were weak and merely regulatory in character.

3. There is a section on hazardous industries and environmental disasters. Thus, hazardous industrial pollution is also covered. A hazardous substance is defined as "any substance or preparation which, by reason of its chemical or physio-chemical properties or handling, is liable to cause harm to human beings, other living creatures, plants, micro-organisms, property or the environment."

4. There are stringent measures to check hazardous pollution. Section 8 of the Act states clearly: 'No person shall handle or cause to be handled any hazardous substance except in accordance with such procedure and after complying with such safeguards as may be prescribed.' Section 6(f) empowers the Central Government to make rules for 'the procedures and safeguards for the prevention of accidents which may cause environmental pollution and for providing remedial measures for such accidents.' Morevoer, it is now mandatory for a person responsible for the discharge of any hazardous substance in excess of the prescribed norms to immediately inform the concerned authorities and to render all possible assistance. Earlier there was no such responsibility.

5. Vigilant citizens can initiate proceedings against an establishment that is polluting the water supply or otherwise ruining the environment. The penalties for defaulters have been made more stringent. The Water Act provided for a maximum imprisonment of six years and/or a fine upto a total of Rs. 5000; in the Air Act the limits were a maximum imprisonment upto three months and/or fine upto a total of Rs. 5000. The new Act provides for imprisonment of defaulters for upto a total of seven years and/or a fine which may extend upto Rs. 1 lakh.

6. However, there are some flaws even in the new Act. One, all power and authority is vested in the hands of the Central Government.

7. **Stress on Ecological Balance.** Addressing the first meeting of the National Land Use and Wastelands Development Council on February 6, 1986, Prime Minister Rajiv Gandhi called for a nation-wide "people movement" to protect the country's ecological balance. He suggested a time-bound land reclamation and afforestation programme. The approach to this problem could not be departmentalised or compartmentalised but had to "respond to the differing needs of every section."

8. **Strategy Needed.** Having experienced the ill effects of industrial development, it is high time a long-term strategy for environmental protection is evolved. In this respect, the Parthasarathy Commission has strongly pleaded for a Regional Development Strategy and a National Urban Development Policy with a view to contain metropolitan choas, for developing secondary cities and to ensure development of existing small and medium towns as well as establishing new ones, as part of a regional strategy generating employment and promoting decentralised urbanisation. In addition, a clear industrial location policy will ensure setting up of specific large industries at specific locations with a predetermined time-frame. It will ensure not only systematic industrial growth but also facilitate in taking measures for environmental protection economically and in a coherent manner.

9. Apart from increasing the forest wealth, the programme generates additional earnings to the Panchayats, more employment to labour, and it provides cheap fuel to the village poor. In Dhanoli, a village in Valsad district of Gujarat, social forestry has achieved remarkable progress. By adopting the scheme of raising village forests in only four hectares of land a net income of over Rs. 43,000 was generated.

10. All state governments, semi-government bodies and municipalities as well as social organisations have been propagating "grow more trees" campaign. To boost the idea of growing more and

more trees, the government has taken up the project of "social forestry" on a large scale. The project aims at planting trees singly or in groups wherever they can be grown.

11. Social forestry not only prevents felling of trees but also tries to distribute the produce of the project directly to the people of the area. The scheme also aims at growing more trees and forests on unused land and promotes research in the science of trees and their varieties.

12. Community lands in villages are wasted and used only for grazing village cattle. This unproductive use of land yields the village panchayats hardly Rs. 4,000 to Rs. 5,000. But the same land, if utilised for a cluster of trees for which the Government provides free seedlings, can fetch a much higther income to the panchayats. The Gujarat Government has decided to give 50 per cent of the net profit realised from the sale of village wood-lot to the Panchayat. Crores of trees are required to strengthen and support agricultural and animal husbandry, to combat pollution and to attract adequate rains and also to stop erosion of fertile soil.

13. **The Ganga Plan.** The Government of India has launched a Rs. 292-crore project to clean up the mighty Ganga, which has been greatly polluted as a result of the inflow of effluents and dirt from various sources. There are about 100 cities situated along the banks of the river, in the States of U.P., Bihar and Bengal. Nearly 4200 small and medium units are responsible for polluting the holy river. The Ganga Project is the largest and most ambitious of all the environment protection plans launched in the country.

14. The cleaning up work began at Rishikesh and Hardwar in September, 1985. Cleaning the Ganga is also in progress at Varanasi waterfront, which is heavily polluted. A Central Ganga Authority had been constituted under the chairmanship of the Prime Minister himself.

15. The wanton destruction of natural wealth, including forests, and the indiscriminate setting up of chemical industries endangers the

lives of both human beings and animals. The greed for personal gain, the general decline in values, the knowledge that one can flout the laws with a vengeance and get away with it, or at worst to pay a small fine, have cumulatively rendered ineffective the agencies enstrusted with the duty of protecting the environment. There are poachers galore, but it is only rare that legal action is taken against such offenders.

16. In February, 1986 the Supreme Court directed the Union Government to examine the possibility of setting up environment courts. The court judgement in the Shriram Foods and Fertiliser Industries case may well provide a basis for action by the Government to safeguard the environment in areas where potentially hazardous industies are located. The court has in fact set out a framework for appropriate governmental action. It has also set up a monitoring committee to ensure that the expert bodies recommendations are implemented. Even more significant is the suggestion that measures should be taken to educate the workers and provide early warning systems for the public.

While the increasing awareness and rethinking about the importance of preserving all aspects of the environment, including forests, clean air, and wild life is welcome, there is an urgent need for earnest implementation of declared policies. So far, the implementation has been poor and, consequently the environment has been deteriorating; forests, in particular, are disappearing at a disconcerting pace. It is time to recall the farsighted Chanakya's observation in the 4th century B.C. that "the stability of an empire depends on the stability of its environment." Strong and committed machinery is needed and it must have sufficient resources.

Ecology also has some effect on poverty. Undeniably, an ecologically and scientifically sound afforestation programme can provide a solution to the problem of India's poverty, if it is not based on the profit motive alone. More research is undoubtedly needed to evaluate the costs of monoculture based social forestry. Unless afforestation programmes are linked with the basic needs of the rural poor, they will prove economically counter-productive and ecologically disastrous.

Obviously, the plunder of what Nature has built over billions of years has to be stopped. We need a new life-style with environmental ethics as an integral part of it, not only for this generation but also for the future generations to live and enjoy the freedom of this planet and beyond. It is important in this regard to reduce the rate of population growth to one per cent from the present 2.2 per cent, as China has done. Industries generating high pollution should be moved out of the perimeters of cities. Environmental education should be made compulsory at every level of learning.

❑

8

Learning Psychology

Learning pervades our life from cradle to grave. It is the phenomenon with which we come across in almost every walk of our life. It occupies an important place in the field of education. All educational processes appearing in formal, non formal and informal contexts aim at development of learning. Learning influences our life at every turn, as parents in family, as the teacher in a school, as a friend in society, as a boss in an office, as a leader in a group.

Learning is not a thing that exists somewhere outside the individual. It is a process or product which results into some potential behaviours and capabilities or an activity which causes some change in the behaviour of an individual.

Learning means the modification of behaviour of an individual. It is said to be equivalent to change, modification, development, improvement and adjustment. It is not confined to school learning, reading, writing, typing, cycling, cooking but it is a comprehensive term which leaves permanent effect on the individual. While approaching a burning match stick the child gets burnt and he withdraws. By this incident he learns to avoid not only the burning matchstick but also all burning things. Learning has been defined in many ways as follows:

According to **Walker,** "Learning is a relatively permanent change in performance that occurs as a result of experience."

According to **Jones and Simpson,** "Any change of behaviour which is result of experience and which causes people to face later situations differently may be called learning."

Garden Murphy, "The term learning covers every modification in behaviour to meet environmental requirements".

Woodworth, "Any activity can be called learning so far as it develops the individual (in any respect, good or bad, and makes his behaviour and experiences different from what that would otherwise have been."

Henry P. Smith. "Learning is the acquisition of new behaviour or the strengthening or weakening of old behaviour as the result of experience."

Kingsely and Garry. "Learning is the process by which behaviour (in the broader sense) is originated or changes through practice or training."

Pressey, Robinson and Horrocks. "Learning is an episode in which a motivated individual attempts to adapt his behaviour so as to succeed in a situation which he perceives as requiring action to attain a goal."

Crow and Crow. "Learning is the acquisition of habits, knowledge and attitudes. It involves new ways of doing things, and it operates in an individual's attempts to overcome obstacles or to adjust to new situations. It represents progressive change in behaviour.... It enables him to satisfy interests to attain goals."

Nature of Learning

1. Learning is the acquisition of new behaviour.
2. Learning is the process by which an activity originates.
3. Learning is the perceptual reorganisation of the situation.
4. Learning is the total reaction of total situation.
5. Learning is goal-directed activity.

6. Learning is universal in nature. Man is rational and he learns the most.

7. Learning is the change in behaviour as a result of experience.

All Animals Learn

1. Learning is motivated by adjustment.

2. Learning is a never ending growth. We always aspire to learn more and more.

3. Learning is acquisition, retention and modification of experience.

4. Learning is process and product.

5. Learning is a life long process. It starts with birth and comes to an end when the individual dies.

Main Characteristics of Learning

Yoakman and **Simpson** have enumerated nine general characteristics of learning which we discuss below:

1. *Learning is Growth.* The word growth is generally associated with the body which is growing, but through the mental growth of the learner. Although it is latent yet we can perceive its growth. Through his daily activities the child grows both mentally and physically. Therefore, we say that learning is growth through experience.

2. *Learning is Adjustment.* Learning helps the individual to adjust himself adequately to the new situations. Children meet with new situations which demand solution. Repeated efforts are required to react to them effectively. Life is full of experiences, and each experience leaves behind some effects in the mental structure. These effects modify his behaviour.

3. *Learning is Organising Experience.* Learning is not mere addition of knowledge. It is not mere acquisition of facts and skills through drill and repetition. It is the reorganisation of experience.

4. *Learning is Intelligent.* Meaningless efforts do not produce permanent result. Any work done mechanically is without any soul. When a child learns something unintelligently, he is likely to forget it very soon. He does not assimilate but simply commits to memory. Only efforts made intelligently have lasting effects.

5. *Learning is Purposeful.* All true learning is based on purpose. Purpose plays a big part in learning. According to **Ryburn**, "This purpose is always connected with the use of some instinctive power, with the use of the energy with which we are endowed with birth." We do not learn anything and everything that comes in our way, in a haphazard manner. All schools activities should be purposeful so that the child should feel real urge for learning.

6. *Learning is Active.* Learning does not take place without a purpose and self-activity. In the teaching-learning process, the activity of the learner counts more than the activity of the teacher. The principle of learning by doing is the sole principle and has been recommended by all modern educationists. It is the basis of all progressive methods of education such as the Dalton, the Project, the Montessory and the Basic.

7. *True Learning Affects the Conduct of the Learner.* There is a change in the mental structure of the learner after every experience. By **Colvin** learning has been described as the "modification of the reactions of an organism through experience."

8. *Learning is both Individual and Social.* Learning is more than an individual activity. It is a social activity also. Individual mind is affected by the group mind consciously as well as unconsciously as individual is influenced by his friends, relatives, classmates, parents etc., and learns their ideas, feelings and actions. Social agencies like the family, church, film and gangs of playmates have a tremendous influence on the child and are always moulding and remoulding him.

9. *Learning is a Product of the Environment.* Environment plays an important part in the growth and development of the individual. Environment should be healthy and rich in educative possibilities.

Factors Affecting Learning

Learning is influenced by various conditions of life and school. Our attempts should be to create such conditions as are conductive to effective learning and which help students to make the most satisfactory adjustment to life. The following factors influence learning:

1. ***Hereditary Factors.*** Neither we can change nor increase hereditary endowment. Of course, we can use it and develop it. This differs in different individuals. Some are very rich in the matters of hereditary endowments while others are very poor. The native intelligence is different in individuals. Children vary also in particular abilities. The intelligent children can establish and see relationship very easily and more quickly. Our ability to learn and the rate of learning are conditioned by our heredity. Maximum use should be made of the hereditary endowment.

Attempts should be made to see to it that children get opportunities to use and develop their hereditary endowment.

2. ***Physical Conditions of Children.*** The physical conditions of children also affect learning. Bodily weakness, chronic illness, malnutrition, fatigue and bad health are a great hindrance in learning. The home conditions—bad ventilation, unhygienic living, bad light, overcrowding etc., affect the rate of learning and the general response of the child. Sometimes children have to walk long distances to and from the school and this also influences learning.

Physical conditions of the classroom are the other determining factors.

It may also be remembered that learning is affected by the physical teachers—their health, voice and speech.

3. ***Goals Set before the Pupils.*** A definite goal should be set before each child according to the standard expected of him. Immediate goals should be set before small children and distant goals for older ones. It must be remembered that the goals should be very clear and the children must understand these goals.

4. *Stimulation.* Best learning takes place when the teacher is successful in arousing the interest of the students. "The guidance of the teacher is mainly a matter of giving the right kind of stimulus to help him to learn the right things in the right way", write Ryburn.

5. *Association of Things.* Thorndike points out that things which we want to go together should be put together as a part of one process. Then it becomes easier to make the students understand their connection.

6. *Guidance and Instruction.* Suitable guidance should be given to the students in selecting the best response to their environment. Demonstration is very helpful to teach various skills.

7. *Emotional Conditions.* Children should be praised when they show good results. This gives them encouragement to show all the more better results and they develop confidence, hope, self-reliance and self-respect. Sympathetic attitude on the part of the teachers gives stimulus and a sense of security to the students. We should discard our habit of fault-finding. This develops fear and feelings of insecurity and of inferiority.

8. *Result of a Total Situation.* Learning is affected by the whole situation. It is not always possible to estimate the result of one individual factor. Learning is fruitful and permanent if the total situation is related to life.

THEORIES OF LEARNING

Psychologists differ at the nature of learning process. Accordingly they have propounded different theories.

Some of the important theories of learning are as follows:

1. Learning by trial and error.

2. Learning by insight.

3. Learning by imitation and observation.

4. Learning by conditioning.

1. Learning by trial and error

The chief exponent of this theory was Thorndike. He make many experiments on rats and cats. He concluded that an individual makes many random efforts to reach a goal. Most of his efforts go useless in his aim. By further trial and error he goes on eliminating useless movements and synthesising useful ones. At last he reaches the aim. In further trials he need not repeat the useless movements. He will perform the activity quite easily in further attempt as he learnt to perform the real needed movements after eliminating the useful ones. His typical experience in his connection is given below:

The Cat Experiment. He shut-up hungry cat in a big cage. An attractive piece of food was placed outside the cage. The cat looked at the piece and tried to get at it. It extended its paws through the bars of the cage but the piece was far away. It tried every part of the cage but all its efforts failed. It thrust its nose through the bars but all in vain. There was a latch inside the cage. While it was making random movements its paw struck against the latch. The door of the cage opened. Next week the experiment was repeated. The cat made some random movements again but was successful in opening the door sooner than before. In the third or fourth trial there was no random movement. The cat pushed against the latch and went ouside. It learnt the method of opening the door by trial and error.

The experiment sums up the following stages in the process of learning:

(1) *Drive.* In the present experiment it was hunger and was intensified with the sight of the food.

(2) *Goal.* To get the food by getting out the box.

(3) *Block.* The cat was confined in the box with a closed door.

(4) *Random Movements.* The cat, persistently, tried to get out of the box.

(5) *Chance Success.* As a result of this striving and random movement the cat, by chance, succeeded in opening the door.

(6) *Selection (of proper movement).* Gradually, the cat recognised the correct manipulation of latch. It selected the proper way of manipulating the latch out of its random movements.

(7) *Fixation.* At last, the cat learned the proper way of opening the door by eliminating all the incorrect responses and fixing the only right responses.

Educational Utility. In solving problems of mathematics in the school and those of life in the world we do follow this method in many cases. There is a tendency in animal as well as in men to find out the solutions of difficult problems by trial and error method but the whole behaviour of man is not based on this sort of learning. Skills like walking, talking, running, swimming, cycling, reading and writing can be well explained by this theory. Pupils should remember the motto of 'practice makes a man perfect,' 'work hard' 'try, try again'.

2. Learning By Insight

Kohler and **Koffka**, were the chief exponents of this theory. They stressed on the totality of the process of learning. They took the process of learning as a synthetic activity which brings forth complete solutions of problems. They referred to the sudden appearance of solutions in many cases. Insight means penetration into the nature of things to find out the solution of a problem without necessary trial and error.

Experiment 1

In one of his experiments **Kohler** shut up his chimpanzee, Sultan by name, in a big cage. Out placed a banana at a considerable distance of the cage. Close the cage there were put two sticks—one of them a long one and the other a bit shorter. The shorter stick could be screwed into the long one. The long stick could not reach the banana but if the other one was screwed into it, the banana could be touched. Sultan tried to get at the banana. He tried the longer stick but it did not reach the fruit. The other was still smaller. He sat down and began to play with the sticks. But he was still brooding over the matter. Suddenly an idea flashed to him. He thrust the smaller sticks into the hole of the longer one and thus managed to get at the banana with the help of the combined sticks.

Experiment 2

In another experiment the chimpanzee was shut up in a room with unscalable walls. A banana was hanging with the ceiling. The animal was hungry. He jumped at the fruit but it was too high. He left the efforts and sat down. There was a box lying in the corner of the room. The animal began to play with the box. He then suddenly got up and pushed the box to the centre of the room below the banana, jumped from it and got the fruit.

Kohler says that learning is a question of perception and not mere motion-activity or mere trial and error. He insists that this sort of learning is very useful in difficult and complicated institutions.

In fact, man does not always learn through trial and error. He often learns through insight. Anyhow learning by insight is much superior to learning by trial and error and we should encourage the children in this process.

Educational Implications

(a) Learning by insight leads to transfer of training.

(b) It saves time and energy because it is quick, efficient and permanent.

(c) It can be used while teaching lessons because the teacher can proceed from whole to part.

(d) The teacher can arouse the motivation of pupils psychologically in the classroom.

3. Learning by limitation and observation

We find that children learn much by mere imitation. They observe doing various things. They then try to intimate the same activities and learn many things in this way. Even in school the children learn reading and writing and many other processes by imitation, and most of our behaviour is imitated.

Thorndike put some cats in a cage and studied their behaviour as regards the process of imitation. He came to the conclusion that cats do no imitate. Therefore, he does not give value to this theory. But the apes of Kohler imitated. In fact animals differ in this tendency. There is no doubt in it that man learns a lot by initation.

4. learning by conditioning

By conditioning we modify the behaviour of an individual in such a way that the response originally connected with a particular stimulus comes to be aroused by a different stimulus. The classical experiment of Pavlov will make the process of conditioning clear.

Pavlov was Russian psychologist. In one of his experiments he fitted a tube in the lower jaw of a dog. The dog was kept hungry and was offered food at a fixed time. Simultaneously with this act of offering the food to him, a bell was rung. It was natural that the dog secreted saliva when he saw the food. The saliva went into the tube and it was measured. The experiment went on for some days. After that the bell was rung one day but no food accompanied it. The dog secreted the saliva even then. It was observed that the saliva went on coming in the same quantity with the ringing of the bell for some days. The actual stimulus to bring forth the response, *i.e.*, the secretion of saliva, was the sight of the food but it was conditioned in such a way that another stimulus which ordinarily had nothing to do with secretion of saliva began to stimulate it.

Educational Implications. Most of the habits are conditioned reflexes only. Similarly, some sentiments are also conditioned reflexes. The school can exploit this mechanism to a great extent. The children learn to speak with the help of this process. Direct method of learning, the use of audio-visual aids, associating various subjects with incentives are based on this theory. It may be helpful in formulating principles regarding rewards and punishments. It is also useful in the learning of languages.

All the theories explained above help in the process of learning but man does not learn through any one of the theories exclusively. The child does learn through trial and error as the cats of Thorndike did but he does not stop there. Often he benefits from the power of insight but he does not stop there too. He observes and imitates others also—insects, animals, men and inanimate physical forces. Many times different stimuli combine to develop conditioned reflexes in him. He synthesises all those modes of learning and goes on developing.

LEARNING

I.P. Pavlov (1849-1936), an eminent Russian physiologist and a noble prize winner for his work on physiology of digestion, while experimenting on the gastric secretion in dogs observed that any stimulus frequently associated with the presentation of food aroused salivation. This observation led to the famous conditioned response theory of learning. He noticed that an incidental stimulus was sufficient to bring salivation. Then his attention was diverted to the possibility of producing saliva to an unnatural stimulus.

Likes trial and error, conditioning deals with certain basic principles of learning process. It holds that the formation of SR connection, its strengthening or weakening depends upon association between two things.

Presentation of a stimulus arouses a response in every normal organism. When you see a friend you welcome him, when you see a snake you run away from it. Sight of food arouses salivation. Here friends, snake and food are natural or unconditioned stimuli and responses like welcome, running away and saliva are natural or unconditioned responses.

However, when an unnatural or conditioned stimulus is frequently associated with a natural or unconditioned stimulus, the 'O' starts showing his conditioned response to the stimulus. The conditioned response here is equal to the unconditioned responses, *i.e.*, saliva. In other words, saliva is the natural response to food. If food is associated with bell for several trials, bell alone brings out saliva. In short, due the association between the unconditioned (Food) and conditioned stimulus (Bell) the 'O' responds to the conditioned stimulus (Bells) in the same way (Saliva) as he responds to the unconditioned stimulus. This is called conditioned response learning. In case of Pavlov's dog, bell is the conditioned stimulus (CS) and Saliva is the conditioned response (CR).

Conditioning is supposed to be a process by which a response (Saliva) is attached to a stimulus (bell) different from the one which originally elicits that response. In simple words, a response is said to be conditioned when some stimulus other than the already effective one comes to arouse of modify it for the establishment of a definite stimulus response connection. A non-effective stimulus, therefore, brings an effective response due to conditioning. This pattern of behaviour is observed when learning by conditioning is complete.

The nipple in the mouth of an infant in an unconditioned stimulus and sucking is an unconditioned reflex. But when the sight of the bottle produces sucking response in the baby, it is called conditioned response. Similarly, happiness at the sight of a friend's letter, fear for the doctor, crying at the sight of water, are certain examples of conditioned responses. When an injection needle pricks the muscle of the baby he cries out of pain. Next time when only he sees the needle or the doctor, he cries with the anticipation that the needle would now prick him again. Here the pricking of the needle is the U.S. crying is the U.R., sight of the needle is the C.S. and crying is C.R. Strengthening of the SR connection therefore depends upon the association between two stimuli.

CLASSICAL CONDITIONING

The conditioning technique developed by Pavlov is famous as the classical conditioning technique. The following experiment conducted by Pavlov on a dog is known as classical conditioning experiment. Pavlov made a minor surgical operation in the cheek of the dog to measure the rate of salivation. The animal was kept in a sound-proof room. During the experiment a servant was feeding the dog. Pavlov to his great surprise noticed that one day, only the sound of the footsteps of the servant made the dog to salivate. The very incident created such an interest in Pavlov that he devoted most of his time to study the phenomenon of conditioning.

To start with the experiment, when food was placed in the mouth of the dog, it brought saliva. On other occasions, only a bell was rung, but it did not bring any salivary response from the dog.

Then Pavlov rang the bell first and after an interval of 5 seconds placed the food in the mouth of the dog. In this first trial bell alone did not bring saliva until food was not placed in its mouth. Only after the repetition of bell-food sequence for several days, when the dog could connect the bell with the food and anticipated food at the sound of bell, did it salivate to the bell only, even before seeing the food. Pavlov noticed that the dog salivated to the presentation of bell only after several trials when learning by conditioning was firmly established. From this Pavlov inferred that stimulus response connection has been established. The dog has finally learnt to respond to the C.S. This technique of establishing a response to a conditioned or artificial stimulus is called classical conditioning process. Pavlov, in course of his many experiments, demonstrated that the dog can be made to salivate to any stimulus, however, unnatural and irrelevant it may be. This discovery of Pavlov made a significant contribution to the learning theory.

Pavlov's classical conditioning can be explained by the following pattern, which Pavlov used in his experiment on dog :

1. Natural or unconditioned stimulus (U.C.S.) food.	Natural or unconditioned response (U.C.R.) Salivation
2. Conditioned stimulus (C.S.)	—No salivation
3. C.S. (Bell) 5 seconds interval U.C.S. (food)	—Unconditioned response U.C.R. (Saliva)

Condition 3 is repeated for several trials until an association is established between bell and food (C.S. and C.R.)

4. C.S. (Bell)	—C.R. (Saliva)

In any classical conditioning experiment in the C.S., U.C.S. pattern, the C.S. should always precede the U.C.S. and the time between the two must be constant and very close in all trials. If the time gap is too large! Conditioning may not be established because lack of close temporal pairing of the C.S. and U.C.S. will not be able to establish the association between C.S. and U.C.S. While establishing the salivary response to a tone in one experiement the following observations were recorded:

No. of presentations of sound and feeding	*No. of drops of saliva in 30 seconds*
1	0
9	18
15	30
31	65
41	64
51	69

[From Munn, O.N.L. (1954) Psychology page 118, Time sequence in conditioning.]

In this experiment after 9 presentation of the C.S. and U.S. in close proximity, conditioning was established. It is also noticed from this table that the number of drops of saliva increased with number of repetitions of the conditioning process.

The strength of conditioning can be found out in terms of saliva and in terms of latency (the time elapsing between the bell and the saliva).

Time Sequence in Conditioning

Usually is conditioning technique the C.S. precedes the U.S. by a fraction of second. Sometimes it is almost simultaneous. As a matter of fact, about 3 seconds give the best result as studies show.

It is also found that if we measure the effectiveness of conditioning, the strongest conditioning occurs with shorter latency period, *i.e.*, near about 3 seconds.

The most vital point in Pavlov's classical conditioning technique is that food always follows bell irrespective of the salivation of the dog. Whether the dog salivates or not, does not matter. Food is always presented after bell with the lapse of a very short time interval.

Besides Pavlov, Bechterev, Watson and many more psychologists have conducted experiments on conditioning. Wever made respiratory conditioning to belt. Pavlov and his associates have observed certain important phenomena in conditioning which are discussed below.

Stimulus Generalisation

It is a tendency for the CR to be aroused by a similar stimulus other than the stimulus aroused in training. Generalisation in conditioning occurs to a certain class of stimuli rather than to a specific stimulus. Pavlov noticed that when a C.S.C.R. bond has been established by conditioning, a stimulus which is similar to the C.S., can produce the same response and he called this stimulus generalisation. The more similar the new stimulus, the greater is the probability for generalisation and *vice-versa*. If the dog is conditioned to salivate to tone, it will salivate to any type of tone like electric bell, worship bell, college bell, buzzer, ding dong bell and other sounds.

Watson in an experiment on the development of fear in children has demonstrated stimulus generalisation. Albert, a small child, used to play with a rabbit without showing any fear. Watson produce a loud sound whenever the child started playing with the rabbit. After a number of trials, the child started showing fear towards the rabbit, associating rabbit with the occurrence of loud sound. Then the child showed fear in gerenal towards while furcoat, bunch of cotton and to all other stimuli having similarity with white rabbit. Stimulus generalization in conditioning happens usually more in childhood particularly when the child has not developed the capacity of differentiate between two stimuli. This is why, during infancy the baby considers every women to be his mother. This tendency of generalization Pavlov attributed to a spread of effects from the region stimulated to other parts of the organism.

Stimulus Differentiation

Differentiation develops out of generalisation. Though in the beginning mostly generalisation in conditioning is found, the organism can be conditioned to make a response only to a specific stimulus by appropriated conditioning procedures.

Suppose you want to positively condition a dog to a tone of 400 cycles and negatively condition to 800 or 1200 cycles. You present the reinforcement only after 400 cycles tone and do not present reinforcement when the other tones are presented. If this is done for several trials the dog will learn to discriminate between these tones eventually. In this case the animal is positively conditioned to 400 cycles and negatively conditioned to 800 and 1200 cycles. Since it is not given any reinforcement at 800 or 1200 tones, these are not reinforced.

Children gradually learn to differentiate one stimulus for another in their own environment. In the early period they consider any woman as their mother. But gradually, as they grow up, they differentiate their mother from other woman. The woman who fondles, nurses, feeds and takes every care of the child and sleeps with him is considered as his mother.

Discrimination in conditioning has certain utilities in learning. Though usually stimulus generalization facilitates learning making, it is easy and quick, sometimes it also inhibits learning, creates confusions misunderstanding and many emotional problems. Like Albert, if one is afraid of any stimulus which has some similarity with white rabbit, he will have many adjustment problems. Differentiation at this point can prove useful. It can overcome the interfering and inhibitory effect of stimulus generalization. At the same time, if the differentiation is pushed too far, it leads to experimental neuroses. Munn, therefore, remarks "Sometimes as the difference is reinforced and unreinforced, stimulation becomes too small for the animal to discriminate, a nervous breakdown occurs."

Experimental Extinction

Once a C.R. is set-up, if one goes on repeating it without giving reinforcement, it tends to be extinguished. Sometimes people ask, how can one eliminate a conditioned response once it is established? The answer to this is experimental extinction. The process by which a C.R. can be weakened and finally eliminated is called the process of experimental extinction. It is a process by which a well established C.R. is eradicated by repeating the C.S. without the application of reinforcement. Take the case of Pavlov's dog. After the dog has learnt to salivate to the sound of the bell, it will continue to salivate to the bell for a certain period, although food is not given after bell. However, after some such trials when the dog will see that no food is coming after bell, the connection between bell and food will grow weaker, the flow of saliva will decrease. At last, the dog will not salivate to the bell at all. The salivation will practically be zero which will indicate the operation of the phenomenon of experimental extinction.

Similarly, in a study of "The Eradication of a tactile conditioned reflex of man the shoulder region of the subject was conditioned so that is elicited a galvanic skin reflex. Vibration of this region was then repeated without presentation of shock. There was a gradual weakening of response and finally complete elimination".

Internal Inhibition

After the establishment of a C.R. if the reinforcement is not provided check to salivate becomes stronger and stronger. So much so that it becomes inter-natural in nature.

Internal inhibition is a kind of negative learning not to salivate and can be applied to Ebbinghaus's curve of forgetting. But when the inhibition becomes weaker it leads to spontaneous recovery like reminiscence in forgetting. The idea of Ebbinghaus's curve of forgetting was applied to the concept of internal inhibition. It was said that this check or block was something which is acquired, *i.e.*, learning not to salivate. The negative learning not to forget is also forgotton to the same extent. However, this extinction is only a temporary suspension of response because of an internal set.

Spontaneous Recovery

Pavlov was of opinion that complete or permanent extinction of a C.R. is not possible. When the experimentally extinguished response reappears again after a period, it is called spontaneous recovery. This concept can be compared with reminiscence in forgetting. In this process even without the presentation of food, bell produces a few drops of saliva. Pavlov noticed that once the flow of saliva was completely extinguished, after about 30 minutes of rest interval the dog again salivated to the C.S. without U.S. But if again no reinforcement is provided after the C.S., spontaneous recovery will grow weaker and weaker and would at last fail to reappear.

Higher Order Conditioning

In course of his experiments on dog, Pavlov found that once conditioning was firmly established, for further conditioning, he could use the conditioned stimulus as unconditioned stimulus. When the dog is conditioned to salivate to Bell, Pavlov used this Bell (instead of food) as a U.S. for establishing further conditioning. Pavlov was of opinion that a conditioned stimulus can be used in much the same way as an unconditioned stimulus. He stated that more elaborate forms of behaviour can be developed by the process of chain of conditioned response.

First order or original conditioning

Food	—	Salivation
Bell	—	?
Bell	—	Salivation

Second order conditioning

Bell	—	Salivation
Light	—	?
Light	—	Salivation

Third order conditioning

Light	—	Salivation
Colour	—	?
Colour	—	Salivation

The arousal of the same response, *i.e.*, saliva to light by frequently associating it with bell but without presenting the food is called second order conditioning, as it could conditions a second neutral stimulus.

Though Pavlov claimed that a third order conditioning can be possible in the same way he could not proceed after the second order in case animals. However, with human beings, all sorts of complex learning can be possible by the process of higher order conditioning, he asserted.

Negative Conditioning/Unconditioning

Otherwise known as backward conditioning or negative adaptation it is learning not to make a response. The 'O' by the technique of backward conditioning can be made not to show a response to a neutral stimulus. Thus, instead of U.S. (Food) following the C.S. (Bell), C.S. will follow the U.S., *i.e.*, reverse to the pattern of classical conditioning technique, food (U.S.) will be given first and Bell (C.S.) will be presented next with an interval of 5 to 6 seconds between each presentation. As the 'O' will get the reward first it will not have any motivation or need to make a response (to salivate). So the C.R. would not be strengthened. If at all there will be any salivation, it will be marginal.

Many of our bad habits like nail biting, bed wetting, moving the leg all the while, various ticks and mannerisms, thumb sucking, smoking, alcoholism, breast feeding in case of older children, irrelevant fears can be removed, withdrawn by negative conditioning. Various habit patterns can be broken by this procedure. Thus, negative conditioning has valuable implications in practical life.

Whenever the rat proceeds for food, if it get electric shock, it will avoid food. A child who is punished while entering into a river will avoid the river in future. Mann reports that is sexually mature male rat is given electric shock everytime is approaches a female rat, it soon avoids female rats. When cockroaches are given electric shock for running into the dark, they learn to go to the lighted place instead of approaching for darkness. Tigers of Sunderban (West Bengal) over the last decade have killed at least 650 persons officially and the unofficial record is about 1000. The forest department worried over the increase in human deaths introduced something which was new in India, the use of electrified dummies. These dummies which look extremely life-like have been placed at a few corners of the sanctuary. Officials explain that when the tiger attacks the dummies, it gets electric shock and this persuades it from further attacks on humans. The projects officials claim atleast an 80% reduction in the death rate due to this method of withdrawal conditioning.

When alcoholics are given to take alcohol containing a drug which produces violent vomiting, they develop aversion for alcohol. Similarly, for babies who do not give up breast feeding, quinine is smeared on the nipples and then only they develop aversion for breast feeding. Negative conditioning is, therefore, known as aversive conditioning.

Withdrawal Conditioning

Becheterev, another Russian physiologist and a follower of Pavlov, taking animal and human subjects, found that when the 'O' gets a painful stimulation in a part of his body, it withdraws from it. Withdrawal may take place from electric shock, beating or any painful stimulation. Bell or light is presented before shock. After some trials by seeing the light or hearing the sound of the bell the 'O' withdraws that specific part of the body where shock is anticipated.

Experimental Neuroses

In recent times, the phenomena of neuroses has been studied by the process of generalisation and differentiation. If differentiation is pushed too far the 'O' fails to discriminate between two stimuli, becomes completely non-adoptive and is unable to salivate to any stimulus due to conflict. Consequently, nervous break down occurs. The animal suddenly becomes wild. It resents the situation.

An experiment on circle and ellipse can be referred to demonstrate experimental neuroses. When the circle and ellipse became very much similar, the animal unable to discriminate became wild. Physiological changes in respiration, heart beat, blood circulation etc., took place. It showed abnormal symptoms and behaviour disorders.

In experimental neuroses there is a clash between positive and negative forces to or not to salivate. Anxiety neuroses is produced experimentally by this method.

The concept of experimental neuroses which threw light on various abnormal behaviours opened new avenues for research. Nessermen, Meyer and Sears have made such experiments on experimental neuroses.

Implications of Conditioning in Practical Life

The contribution of Pavlov to the psychology of learning can be said to be equally important like Freud's as Pavlov as advanced certain concepts like generalisation, differentiation, withdrawal conditionings, unconditioning and experimental neuroses which have tremendous significance in life. In fact, Pavlov's discovery was so powerful that it became completely Pavlovian.

Conditioning works in every sphere of life. Bulk of learning in animals and children develops due to conditioning, language development and different habits, take place because of conditioning. Therefore, it became a key technique not only for physiology, but also for psychology, mental hygiene and therapy. Watson, therefore, remarked that the whole system oif behaviourism he has worked out in terms of habit.

When Watson found that habit is not as simple as he thought, he realized the role of conditioning in habit development. Thus, he remarked, "I had worked the thing out in terms of habit formation. It was the enormous contribution Pavlov has made and how easily the conditioned response could be looked upon as the unit of what we had been calling as habit. I certainly form that point on gave the master his due credit."

Observation of animal and human behaviour led Pavlov and Watson to believe that all our habit patterns, behaviours, attitudes, likes and dislikes, values, etc., can be attributed to conditioning. Conditioning also works as a technique for behaviour modification, elimination of behaviour problems. It is also very significant in emotional learning. Watson and Rayner (1920) believed that it is the only way by which emotions can be acquired. "Since fear or anxiety is a common symptom of mental disturbance we are led correctly to anticipate that classical conditioning figures in the development of such disorders".

Thus, the sort of dream which Pavlov had, came true to a large extent. Due to the practical implications of conditioning in life it has occupied a very prominent position in the learning psychology even today.occupied a very prominent position in the learning psychology even today.

LAWS OF LEARNING

Thorndike formulated laws of learning. Laws of learning are divided under two parts:

(1) Primary law, (2) Secondary law.

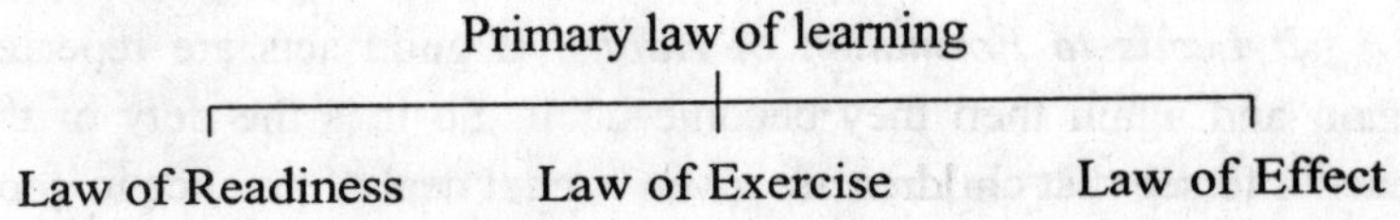

1. Law of Readiness. Readiness means a preparation for action. It is a kind of 'action tendency' aroused through preparatory adjustments,. sets and attitudes. The fulfilment of this tendency is satisfying and its non-fulfilment is annoying. Thorndike employed physiological terms in describing this law.

Learning is a matter of interest. The learner must be made ready to learn. When a person feels ready to learn, he learns more effectively and with greater satisfaction than when not ready. There are some motives, desire or purpose without which no learning is possible. So, for learning the learner must be mentally ready.

Educational Implication. This law can be effective in the following ways:

(a) To arouse the interest and attention of the students by asking suitable questions.

(b) This law is useful in arousing curiosity of the students. Curiosity is indispensable for learning.

Motivation is an important factor for learning. It is also based on the principle of readiness. If the learner is properly motivated he will be ready for the work and apply his energies vigorously.

2. Law of Exercise. This law is known as law of practice or law of use and disuse. If any activity is exercised we come to have efficiency in doing it. If it is not repeated we soon forget it. It means repetition of an activity strengthens the nerve connections and on the other hand disuse weakens the bond. In short it can be said that law of exercise as a whole emphasises the need of repetition practice and drill work in the process of learning. Children learn spellings and pronounciation according to this law.

Educational Implications. In educational field this law can be effective in the following ways:

It Leads to Formation of Habits. If good acts are repeated again and again then they become habit. So it is the duty of the teacher to see that children are given a great deal of practice in good activities.

By Practice Handwriting can be improved. Bad handwriting can be improved by practice. For this the teacher can ask the students to do regular practice.

Correct Pronunciation. It has to be learnt by practice and incorrect pronunciation can be unlearnt only by avoiding its repetition.

Bad Habits can be Eradicated. According to Dunlop Bata theory of learning, if the children are made to practice consciously, then they automatically tend to leave their bad habits. For example if a child is in the habit of thumb-sucking or nil-biting (chewing) then he should be asked by the teacher not to repeat this habit consciously. The underlying idea is that he will become conscious of this mistake and avoid the same in future.

The element of forgetfulness can be delayed or avoided because by practice the activities become deep rooted. So forgetting can be avoided to some extent.

Mathematics is dependent wholly on practice. Arithmatical tables, formulas and definitions can be learnt only with the help of practice.

Skills like music, painting, typing shorthand, athletics etc., can be developed to the maximum with the help of this law.

3. Law of Effect. Thorndike has defined this law as—"When a modifiable connection between a situation and response is made and is accompanied by a satisfying state of affairs, that connection's strength is increased, but when made and accompanied by an annoying state of affairs its strength is decreased."

It is also called as the Law of Pleasure and Pain or Law of Satisfaction and Annoyance. The word effect means the effective result of the activity. The child has to perform a number of activities. Every activity has its effect. Some activities end in pleasure and others end in pain. The activities which are associated with pleasure or satisfaction tend to be repeated again and again and the learning becomes more effective. Activities which are assoicated with pain, punishment or annoyance are not repeated and their strength is decreased. The entire system of rewards and punishments is based on this law.

Educational Implications. The educational utility of this law is as follows:

Theory of reward and punishment is based on this law. Reward should be given for desirable behaviour and punishment should be associated with undesirable behaviour.

This law is helpful in forming and developing the desirable sentiments in the pupils. Positive sentiments should be associated with satisfying state of affairs.

Problem Behaviour and Delinquent Behaviour can be improved by associating it with annoying state of affairs (punishment).

Formation of Good Habits. Good habits can be formed in children by associating them with reward, satisfaction or praise. Undesirable habits can be eradicated by associating them with punishment, dissatisfaction and blame.

Interest is directly related to this law. Interest causes satisfaction and satisfaction promotes learning and better learning gives higher satisfaction. In the selection of subjects, books, hobbies games and curricular activities pupils prefer which is interesting to them.

Memory is also connected with the law of effect. Pleasant things are generally remembered better than unpleasant things.

Control of Emotions. With its help, the teacher can control the emotions of anger and jealousy of the students.

Some times it appears that a punishment is more effective than reward. Strong punishment brings about a desired attitude towards learning.

It is also found that it is human tendency to remember certain highly unpleasant incidents better than pleasant incidents.

Secondary Laws of Learning

Secondary laws of learning are as follows:

Law of Multiple Response. This law implies that when an individual is confronted with a new situation he responds in a variety of ways before arriving at correct response.

Law of Analogy. An individual responds to a new situation on the basis of the responses made by him in similar situations in the past. He makes responses by comparison or analogy.

Law of Associative Shifting. This law is also known as the conditioned response. A response may be shifted from one situation to another which is presented at the same time. In other words any response which is possible can be linked with any stimulus.

Law of Partial Activity. According to this law the learner has the capacity to select the important from the irrelevant element in order to determine appropriate responses.

Law of Recency. It means that whatever is recently learnt by the child is retained by him. The law may be defined as 'recent acts are lasting'. Hence students should revise their courses just before the examination.

Law of Sets and Attitudes. Learning is guided by a total attitude or 'set' of the organism. The learner performs the task properly if he has developed a healthy attitude towards the task.

Law of Primacy. Learning that takes place in the beginning is the best and lasting. It is a normal saying that 'First impression is the Last impression'. It implies that pupils should make the right start and should be serious from the first day. Teacher should impress his pupils from the first day of teaching. It seems the experiences that are acquired by the child at the primary stage have lasting effect.

Law of Intensity of Stimulus. To this law, if a stimulus is strong the response will be strong and *vice a versa*. Examinations present an intense stimulus to study and hence bear a positive effect on learning.

Law of Belongingness. This law shows that if a response belongs to a situation, the learning will be more effective. Connection between stimulus and response is natural. The teacher should create natural atmosphere in the classroom and appeal to the natural tendencies of the child.

Factors or Variables of Learning

Maturation. Learning depends upon maturation. If the individual is matured to learn a particular activity, he will learn effectively. If the individual is no mature, learning will not be effective.

Readiness. If the learner is ready to learn a particular activity he will learn better and quickly.

Capacity. The greater the capacity for learning a person has, the better will be the learning.

Attention and Interest. If the learner is motivated to learn a particular task he will take more interest in the task with full attention and hence will learn that task better.

Mental Health. A child who is mentally healthy *i.e.*, free from frustrations, conflicts, anxieties and worries will learn better.

Memory. A learner who has good momory will learn quickly and effectively.

Motivation. Motives like reward, completion, level of aspiration, success and punishment etc., are powerful incentives to the learner for better learning.

Fatigue. Fatigue causes boredom and indolence and hence has negative effect on learning.

Perception and Sensation. Perception and sensation are the basis of all cognitive learning. The stronger the power of perception, the greater the amount of learning.

Food and Drugs. Food also affect learning. Poor diet, alchoholic drugs, tobacco and addictive items adversely affect learning.

Practice. 'Practice makes a man perfect' is a well known proverb. Learning is more efficient when practice is distributed at intervals over a period of time when it is considered in one period as in cramming.

Will. Will to learn is an important factor of learning, and it arouses, sustains and regulates the pattern of activity, and leads to better attention, better motivation and hence better learning.

Timely Testing. Occasional and periodical testing motivates the pupils to be regular in their studies. If the pupils are regular in studies they can learn better. Moreover through tests the learner knows his exact achievement, his accomplishment and there is little scope for under estimation.

Guidance. Guided learning is always better than unguided learning, Guidance saves times and energy of the learner, eliminates wastage and stagnation. But too much guidance should be avoided so that student may not learn the habit of remaining dependant upon teachers.

Time of Learning. Experiments have shown that there are significant variations in learning efficiency during different hours of the day. It has been established that morning and evening hours are the best hours for study. During the day there is decline in the mental capacity due to noise.

Vigorous Application. Slow learning is seldom efficient. Learning vigorously is a great asset and it pays much. The students should be taught to work whole heartedly. They must put their heart and soul while learning something.

Knowledge of Result. Knowledge of result particularly the specific knowlege of progress of the learner improves his performance, motivates him for greater learning and serves as an incentive towards increased effort.

Pleasantness of Task. Generally pleasant tasks are learnt quickly than the unpleasant tasks.

KOHLER'S INSIGHT LEARNING THEORY

According to German Getalt psychology Kohlers learning is insight. Insight is a important constituent in the solution of problems and is found in the higher class of animals and human beings. It is the best method among the methods of learning.

According to Kohler a person can deduce the solution by insight if he perceives the situation as a whole. Kohler, prepared some simple problems for experiments with dogs, hens, monkeys and chimpanzees. In an experiment a hungry animal was released from the house while some food was placed behind the fence adjoining the wall. Both the dog and the hen trotted around in the vicinity of the wall but as soon as they found the way out they made their exist and reached the food. This perception of the change in the meaning of the wall in insight. Bofore the insight the wall was an insuperable obstacle, but after insight it was not longer an obstacle but an object necessitating of new relations, the discovery of new patterns and the formation of new organisations.

The most famous experiments conducted by Kohler in relation to insight were those that were carried out on chimpanzees. Some bananas were placed outside the cage of a chimp called Sultan, who was then given two sticks so cinstucted that they could be fitted together. Sultan tried to pull the bananas with the sticks, an effort which he kept up for an hour, but he got tired of the attempt and gave it up for playing. While playing he brought the two ends together and suddenly he had an idea which resulted in his fitting the smaller stick in the hole of the bigger one. He then used the two together to draw the banana inward. The two sticks disintegrated but he fitted them together again. He then pulled in everything within reach as if he were trying out his discovery. The next day he took far less time to fit the two together. It is a peculiarity of insight that once the solution is learnt, it is not forgotten though its memory may become hazy with the passage of time.

The above experiments make it quite obvious that learning by insight has certain characteristics of its own. They are briefly as follows:

1. Insight is sudden.
2. Insight alters perception.
3. Old objects appears in new patterns and organisation by virtue of insight.
4. In insight understanding is more useful than dexterity of hands.
5. Insight is relative to the intellectual level. The higher species of animals including human beings have more insight than the members of lower species.
6. In Woodworth's opinion, insight is sometimes hindsight and at others it is foresight. The quote him, 'Foresight is seeing the way to the goal before taking it our perceiving the uselessness of a certain lead without trying it and hindsight is observing that a lead is good or bad after trying it. When the whole situation is clear and above board, there is a good chance for foresight, but when important characteristics of the situation have to be discovered by exploration and manipulation, hindsight is the best we can expect.
7. Some psychologists ray that learning by insight is associative learning. Insight appears suddenly after the manipulation of thought or objects for a small thought significant length of time.

8. If the pieces essential for the solution of the puzzle and present together when perceived, insight comes about earlier.

9. Previous experience is of assistance in sight, though its excess does not necessarily increase insight because organised perception too is an essential factor in learning.

10. Maturity also affects insight as evidenced by the smoother working of insight in older age than in adolescence.

11. The insight gained in particular circumstances is of assistance in other circumstances. A verbal formula is generally extracted by people learning by insight and this formula is capable of facile application to other circumstances.

The above mentioned characteristics of learning through insight apply both the human and animal learning. The solitary difference is the fact that a human being by virtue of his superior capacities of experiencing and understanding; observes relation between various objects quickly and sees the patterns concealed in them with alacrity. He is assisted in this by language. As a matter of fact insight occurs only when the learner perceives the related link hidden in the activity. The learning curve is altered suddenly due to insight. Insight is impossible in an extremely unfamiliar problem, because familiarity is very necessary for insight. A student of literature will have no insight in any scientific problem because he does not know even the a b c of science. When the subject of study becomes a part of life, insight becomes easier. History can be made alive by exhibitions, Geography by travelling and Arithmetic by shop accounts. Fimiliarity is also important besides the theoretical study.

One example of human learning by insight will suffice. A student of Arithmetic tries hard to solve a difficult problem of Arithmetic. He tries many methods but fails to secure a solution. He gives up and lays it aside or goes to sleep. After some time suddenly or when he is awakened the solution suggests itself and he notes it down in his note-book. When he is confronted with similar problems in the future, he will have no difficulty in solving them. The insight method is superior to imitation or conditioned response because both the later methods take more time. It is superior to trial and error in the following respects:

1. Trial and error emphasises the acquisition of motor skill but in insight mental effort is stressed upon.
2. The person keeps an eye on the goal in trial and error and all activity is goal directed, but in insight it is the unconscious mind which exerts the most while the conscious activities are either very few or aimless.
3. While insight depends upon perception, trial and error depends upon sensory motor coordination.
4. Every new problem has to be tackled from the very beginning if the trial and error method is used. On the other hand, both generalisation and differentiation are present in insight, which adds to the possibilities of transfer of learning and the use of old insight in the solution of novel problems.

Students will be permanently helped by the use of the insight method of learning in place of the trial and error method in their study and other daily activities. They will also be above to conserve their energy. Suppose that a person has to arrange furniture in a room. An average person will determine the position of the table by using the trial and error method and shifting the table from place to place. An intelligent person will take up a position from where the whole room in visible, and imagine all the possible positions of the pieces of furniture in an imagined framework of the room and then place the respective pieces accordingly. But this does not mean that trial and error method is not meant for the intelligent. But no means is this so. In many noval situations progress is not possible without it.

PSYCHOLOGY OF TEACHING AIDS OF LEARNING

To make learning very effecitve it is not only necessary to utilise the factors and techniques that facilitate learning, the teacher is to create certain conditions in the classroom that may imporve learning. These conditions are providing teaching aids, creating rivalry and co-operation, giving the knowledge of progress and success, praising or reprimanding and guiding learning.

Visual Aids. Visual aids make learning concrete and meaningful. Yoy may describe the physical features of the Indo-Gangetic plain, but motion pictures, filmstrips, maps, charts, diagrams, pictures would make your verbal description concrete. An additional meaning is attached to verbal instruction when teaching aids are used. These are simply supplementary devices and not the supplanters of what the teacher can do. The following are the uses of teaching aids:

Uses. (1) There is a belief that some students are eye-minded, some auditory-minded and some verbal-minded. Those who are verbal-minded can be easily taught through verbal instructions but for the rest visual aids are necessary. Whether the above belief is sound or not, whether pupils can be so sharply differentiated or not is not the question. The fact is that the more organs are used in learning, the more effective the learning sensory becomes. The abstract notions become easy to understand when they are presented through motion pictures or T.V. or such other teaching aids.

(2) Instructional aids provide substitutes to objects and situations that cannot be presented in the classroom. The science exhibition that is held at a far-off place cannot be brought into the science room but through a T.V. programme the whole of it can be viewed in a short period.

(3) Much of school learning involves symbols and abstractions. Language is conceptual. Arithmetic is even more conceptual. It means that the teacher who is teaching language or arithmetic will have to present varied experiences so that correct concepts may be formed. Instructional aids supply such vivid experiences.

Caution. Teaching aids are aids only. They are not to be so enthusiastically used that effort on the part of the learner is ignored. When a T.V. programme is viewed, precast and telecast work has to be done. The teacher has to connect the programme with the class work he has done previously or will do in the immediate future.

Factors that Affect Learning

There are factors that facilitate learning; for example, readiness, motivation, mental set, mental health and teacher's personality. Unless the child has reached a stage (readiness) of development and growth at which instruction becomes effective and before which instruction is relatively fruitless, we do not like to give him instruction in reading; unless we arouse (motivate) or accelerate behaviour or stimulate an activity towards a goal when there was previously no such behaviour, change in behaviour does not occur, unless the child has a temporary preparedness (mental set) to get instruction say is arithmetic, he does not learn it; unless the child's inner nature get free expression, and meets job efficiency and satisfaction, he does not succeed in learning; finally unless there is someone to mould or shape or influence child's behaviour there will be no learning.

So the factors that affect learning are:

1. *Motivation.* Motivation is at the heart of learning. It is *sine qua non* for learning. It arouses, sustains, directs and determines the intensity of learning effort.

2. *Maturation* makes speedy learning possible. The child who is physically and mentally mature learns a subject at a faster rate.

3. *Physical and Mental Development* of the child affects learning. The child who is mentally and physically not developed learns at a slower rate.

4. *Home Conditions and School Environment* affect learning.

5. *Academic Ability of the Teacher Affects* learning.

6. *Meaningfulness of Subject-matter* makes learning easier.

7. *Teaching Methods* facilitate learning children learn more by activity or by doing or by playway.

Then there are factors that make learning easy. Such factors that tend to promote learning are intent to learn, distributed effort over learning, capitalising whole and part learning, knowledge of progress, recitation, active recall, application of what is learned and activity. To make these factors that facilitate learning more effectively, we work have to improve learning conditions by giving audio-visual aids, by giving praise and reprimand, by arousing rivalry and co-operation and by guiding children properly.

Intent to Learn. The child learns what he intends to learn. When there is intent or purpose to learn, one learns rapidly and that learning is permanent. When children know what goals they are to achieve, and when they accept those goals, they become more active in the pursuit of those goals. The efforts they make are more intensive and better organised. The attention they play is more definitely focussed to the thing they are required to learn. Such learning is intentional or purposeful.

Distributed Effort. It is a simple fact that an hour spent everyday in learning a subject results is more thorough and permanent learning than the same number of hours, devoted to its study at the end of the term. Spaced or distributed effort at learning any subject results in more learning than a massed one. Spaced learning is also economical and effective. The reasons are given below:

1. Massed learning by sticking to a task for longer periods the child develops a tendency to inattentiveness. One's attention fluctuates if one tries to concentrate, on a job for longer periods.
2. Going back to a subject studied a week ago to better than studying and restudying it immediately.
3. Trying to do the same thing again and again within a short space of time is against the natural tendency to resist early repetition of an act.

It means that the study period should be short and not very long. But how short should the study period be? It depends upon the individual learner, the material to be learnt and the conditions under which the material is learnt. The more mature the individual the more capable he is for prolonged work.

In elementary school the length of the class period is kept 20 to 30 minutes and in colleges, even one hour period is short. If the material requires constant attention and is difficult to learn, shorter periods are more fruitful. In the summer we usually have shorter periods than in winter.

Long periods of study are not always fruitless. If the material is too easy, longer periods of study are recommended. Its motivation is high, massed practice is useful.

The principle of distributed effort has a great significance for the time-table builders. It is convenient for the student to learn different subjects in different periods. If the child learns mathematics in the same period on successive days, the teacher can show him how the lesson builds today upon what was learnt yesterday. The idea of distributed effort demands carrying on the same task in the same direction in a period on successive days. The principle of distributed effort indicates that since in massed learning attention begins to fluctuate, individual lessons should have variety. Even in a lesson on mathematics some time may be devoted to explaining concepts and principles and some time to their application and the rest to reviewing what has been learnt a week or two ago in the same period.

Massed practice causes boredom and boredom causes errors. Hence, distributed effort is particularly advantageous in learning many motor skills like type-writing. Proficiency in simple motor activities can be achieved in relatively short practice periods once or twice a day until competence is gained. The practice periods for younger students should be shorter than those for the older ones. Between the periods of practice certain inner co-ordinations may take place as a consequence of previous practice and present themselves in the next practice period.

Overlearning. The repetition of some matter after it has been learned to the point of one successful reproduction is called overlearning. If learning a poem, means reciting it once, overlearning it would mean continued practice after reaching a criterion level. Overlearning may be defined as applying oneself to the acquisition of a skill or knowledge beyond the point at which one can say it has been learnt.

If we have a topic when it has been learned once, it is forgotten but overlearning makes it permanent. For example, if 5 repetitions of a poem are needed to recite it, 10 repetitions would fix it in the mind for a longer time. Overlearning makes initial learning thorough and permanent.

The question arises, 'How many more repetitions would make overlearning more effective? Would 30 repetitions of a poem make it permanent when initial learning to recite takes place in 10 repetitions? It is scientifically proved that effective overlearning takes place only when 50% to 200% additional repetit ons are made. But these repetitions should not be simply unintelligent ones; they should involve reviewing the material just read, reciting to oneself, placing the material in a new context and reading similar materials in another context.

The educational significance of overlearning to the classroom teacher and the student is great. Students should be encouraged to review immediately the work they have just completed. Teachers should present material in a new context, make applications and hold class discussions.

Whole *vs.* Part Learning. Memorisation is not only facilitated by overlearning. It is also facilitated by the whole method which means that a long poem can be committed to memory by reading and rereading. If on the other hand, the poem or the passage is learnt verse by verse or sentence by sentence, it is learnt by the part method.

There are advantages and disadvantages of both these methods. A combination of these methods is suggested. When a child is required to learn a poem or a passage in prose, its meaning should first be made clear to him. Some part of it may be difficult, *e.g.*, some phrases may be hard to understand for the learner. These parts may be learnt by the part method. After that each part may be placed in total context. Such a combination of two methods may be little more time consuming, but it saves total times.

Which method should be adopted depends upon the nature and size of the material to be learnt and the intelligence of the learner. If the material is meaningful, whole method is advantageous; if the size of the material is short it is useful to learn it by part method, and if the learner is intelligent be learns a material by whole method more easily.

Recitation. Recitation again is a device helpful for retention. Recitation means repeating aloud a poem or a passage from memory. But recitation may be subvocal. Recitation, vocal or subvocal is useful to a student because it enables him to use the material before a lapse of time causes forgetting. It immediately motivates the learner by making the learner aware of the degree of success being achieved; it helps the learner to use it. It provides feedback to the teacher and tells him whether or not the class is understanding him. Recitation does not simply mean repeating what one has learnt. It also means placing the material in a different setting, applying it in a new situation, and viewing it is another perspective. The questions given at the end of a chapter in a book and meant to provide opportunities to recite.

Recitation to be an effective technique for facilitating learning should be more than restatement of the printed word. It should mean sensing of information in new context. Teachers can make this technique more effective by employing discussion or conversation or presenting problems before students so that they may make a functional use of knowledge.

Active Recall. While reciting one uses certain cues; for example, when we recite the subject-matter presented in a chapter we make use of the paragraph headings. These headings serve as cues for recitation. While recalling one has to recollect material without the help of such cues. For example, in completion type of items one has to recall because there is nothing to help him, but in matching type items one recites with the help of cues given.

Active recall is a challenge to the learner. It requires him to recollect, or reconstruct the material without cues, hints or guides. The more the amount of active recall used in learning, the greater is the speed, precision and permanence of learning, Once a student makes it a habit to recall actively what he has learnt, learning becomes easy to him. He notes headings, emphases, and illustrative material to make an active recall.

It means that teachers should advise children to be active and vigorous while studying a chapter. They should be encouraged to recall what is learnt just after learning it. They should be encouraged to seek answers to questions such as these, "What have we studied similar to this?" "How does it relate to our lesson of the last week?" A few extra moments spent in active recall will be more economical than re-reading the same material later.

Applying What is Learned. Application of what is learnt is a really useful technique to facilitate speed, precision and permanence of learning. Information is made functional when it is applied. Making applications encourages the use of learning. Making use of knowledge provides a purpose for learning and yields reinforcement.

The classroom teacher has in teaching as well as in testing situations, a very great scope for applying what is learned. After presenting principles in any subject-field, their applications should be encouraged. For example, after teaching theorems in mathematics, their application in solving problems may be stressed; after teaching rules of grammar, the teacher may emphasise on writing sentences and essays using those rules; after giving information in civics, he may lead his students to solve problems faced by the community.

Students can be encouraged to apply for themselves the knowledge gained in the classroom in student government, community projects, work experience.

Activity is Essential to Learning. By activity we do not mean simply muscular activity. One has to be mentally active if one wants to learn speedily, precisely and retain it permanently. When the child listens to the lecture given by the teacher he is mentally active, but he is mentally more active when he recites and discusses. Listening as a process may be derogated but here too the listener has to accept or reject the ideas presented. In a traditional school where the child sits and listens, he does not learn effectively. In a progressive school in which activity is involved in the learning process, there is a better learning, provided the activity is meaningful. Even where the school is not in a position to provide such an activity, children may be encouraged to make use of insight and understanding.

THORNDIKE'S TRIAL AND ERROR THEORY OF LEARNING

Trial and Error Theory of Learning. For nearly half a century, one learning theory dominated all others in the U.S.A. despite many attacks on it and the rise of its many rivals. It is the theory of E.L. Thorndike (1874-1949). This theory was given by him in 1898, in his book the *'Animal Intelligence'*.

The basis of learning accepted by Thorndike in his earliest writings was association between sense impressions and impulses to action. Such an association comes to be known as a 'bond' or a 'connection'. Because it is these bonds or connections which become strengthened or weakened in making and breaking of habits. Thorndike's system sometimes has been called a 'bond' psychology or simply 'connectionism'. As such it is the original S—R Psychology of learning.

To quote **K.P. Pandey**—Thorndike's theory of learning is based on the following three elements:

(a) The Stimulus element which involves an environmental event.

(b) The response element which indicates a behavioural act.

(c) The formation of a connection or bond which implies that every stimulus is linked with some kind of response and thus makes for the building block or structure of behaviour. **Pandey** in his book "*Advanced Educational Psychology for Teachers*" further states that the *formation of a bond* (S-R bond) is the key expression in describing the learning theory of Thorndike. When an oganism is said to have learned something, it is essentially the formation of a connection or bond between a stimulus and a response.

Connectionism has two phases:

First phase was before 1930.

Second phase was after 1930 because Thorndike made important changes later on the basis of experiments. We shall examine this theory as follows:

There are four characteristic features of Trial and Error Learning :

1. There is some sort of a motive that arouses or sustains the activity. This motive may appear in the form of need, a problem or a goal. Essentially the equilibrium of the organism is disturbed and this impels the organism to react to the situation in an effort that comes to terms with it.
2. Several different kinds of responses are made.
3. Finally there is a progressive integration and establishment of the reaction by which the goal is achieved.
4. There is progressive elimination of superfluous unsuccessful or wrong form of activity.

The essential point in trial and error is the second point—the process by which the correct response is identified through trying various responses until a solution which permits the attainment of goal is achieved.

The Puzzle Box Experiment. Thorndike studies the character of Trial and Error learning in a number of experiments on cats. A favourite device was his puzzle box used years ago by him for his studies of animal learning.

In one of the experiments a hungry cat was placed in the box and the door was closed. A fish was placed outside the box. The cat was given 100 trials, ten each morning and each afternoon for five days. The cat was fed at the end of each experimental period and then was given nothing more to eat until after the next session. In after opening the door in any trial by jumping or by chance, he went in immediately to the food, he was allowed a small bite. A complete record was made of the cat's behaviour during each trial.

It may be mentioned that besides these cat's experiments which became so common and cheap, it has trained some classical experiments performed by Ebbinghaus on memory and by Brain and Harter on Telegraphy. But these experiments of Thorndike are different from Ebbinghaus experiments w.r.t. two points and those points are that of : *(i)* Motivation, *(ii)* of Reward and punishment. He aid that the world cannot ignore reward and punishment and motivational factors.

As early as 1913, Thorndike wrote, "Both theory and practice need emphatic and frequent reminders that man's learning is fundamentally the action of laws of readiness, exercise and effect. He is first of all an associative mechanism working to avoid what disturbs the life processes of the neurons. If we begin by fabricating imaginary powers and the faculties or if we avoid thought by loose and empty terms or if we stay lost in wonder at extraordinary versatility and inventiveness of the higher forms of learning, we shall never understand man's progress or control of his education."

Criticism. A serious limitation of this theory is its lack o understanding. Thorndike did not consider understanding important He merely assumed that it would follow as a natural result of wel organised learning. He believed that insightful learning, though it di occur, was infrequent.

Educational Implications of Trial and Error Theory

1. *Effect of Motivation.* It is the most important factor in all learning. Motivate the child.

2. *Exercise Patience.* Learning by Trial and Error theory is always gradual. The teacher must exercise patience with the child if the child does not show any progress immediately in any learning situation.

3. *Make Learning Meaningful.* Effect of belonging to a thing should be exploited.

4. *Place of Exercise.* Exercise has its own place in education and learning. Repeat, give a sufficient drill in some tests.

5. We must learn basis things needed for it in any learning.

6. This theory has drawn our attention to the principle of learning by doing. You will learn only when you do a thing.

S-R BOND THEORY OF THORNDIKE

One of the most accredited among all the current theories on the law of learning is the one presented by Thorndike, in America. Talking of its importance Tolman says, "The psychology of animal learning, not to mention that of child learning has been and still is primarily a matter of agreeing or disagreeing with Thorndike or trying in minor ways to improve up him. Gestalt psychologists, conditioned reflex psychologists, sign gestalt psychologists, all of us here in America seem to have taken Thorndike, overtly or covertly, as our starting point."

Thorndike first presented his theory in his book '*Animal Learning*' published in 1968. The clearest form of his theory is seen in the three volumed treatise '*Educational Psychology*'. His theory may be understood in a systematic way with the help of three major laws which are as follows:

1. Law of Readiness.

2. Law of Exercise.

3. Law of Effect.

Writing on the subject of the importance of his laws in the action of learning Thorndike says, "Both theory and practice need emphatic and frequent reminders that man's learning is frequently the action of the laws of readiness, exercise and effect." Accordingly, in Thorndike's opinion, man's learning takes place according of these laws.

He drew a learning curve for men and animals and concluded from it that usually the methods employed are similar in both classes of creatures. Until 1930, Thorndike laid particular emphasis on these three laws.

Law of Readiness

The law of readiness describes those situations in which the person who learns either invites the object of his learning or rejects it. Readiness include all those preparatory adjustments which immediately precede the action. Reminding the learning of his past experience mental preparation for the understanding of new things, diverting his attention towards the subject to be learned, the altering of the environment to suit the learning, are all included in learning. This readiness creates a desire for learning and turns the learners's mental attitudes towards the suject to be learned.

In Thorndike's the view law of readiness is active in three following conditions:

1. When a conducting unit is prepared to go into action, its work is quite satisfactory because nothing is done to alter its working.

2. When a conduction unit is forced to act while it is not prepared to do so its behaviour is of a nature calculated to excite anger.

3. The inactivity of a conduction unit which is ready to behave, may be unsatisfactory and any reaction may arise is connection with that deficiency.

Law of Exercise

The second law, of any consequence in human and animal learning is the law of exercise, which is based on the laws of use and disuse. The repeated application of an activity fixes it firmly in the mind while on the other hand no psychological reference is intended. The relation is weekened through continuous disuse. Whenever there is an appropriate situation, the activity which is firmly entrenched might take place. This law, taking a cue· from this universal experience, emphasises repetition in the activity of learning. Repetitive application of the activity results in the formulation of a habit in the muscles and the nerve fibres of the brain so that there is a facility in its execution in time of need. The element of understanding in repetition was not adequately stressed in Thorndike's law of readiness. For example, it is a rule that if repetition in the memorising of a poem is complemented by an attempt to understand and mutual relate the different stanzas, the learning may be affected with ease. Not so with Thorndike, who considered the mechanical repetition of learning individually sufficient. This type of memorising becomes rote learning highly undesirable thing, and the forgetting of one line resuls in the forgetting of the rest while the recollection of the important makes a clear understanding of the subject-matter and constant renewal quite as important an constant repetition. Thus, Thorndike's mechanical repetition came in for a lot of criticism and he reached by effecting modifications.

Law of Effect

The meaning of the law of effect is the effect of learning in answer to question as the success or failure of learning has very significant bearing on the law now under study. Success brings with it satisfaction and along with it a strengthening of the relation of the facts. Failure increases dissatisfaction and the absence of the relation amount the facts weakness them. Thus, we may compare success to a reward or failure to a punishment and desire to repeat success or avoid failure or the inevitable antecedants.

In 1932, Thorndike propounded a new theory on the basis of his experiments about the law of effect, and this he entitled "Spread of effect." This novel theory postulates that by the activity of learning adjustments are not left unaffected. For example, the son of a businessman is ahead of his class in arithmetic because he has already learnt some accountancy in connection with sales in the shop.

In 1935, Thorndike made some modification in the law of effect, based on experimental findings. He now said the influence of reward or punishment is not equivalent and neither it is paradoxical. The effect of reward is for more influential than that of punishment, the strengthening of associations due to reward is not paralleled by the demoralisation caused by dissatisfaction as possible in order that he may learn with success . Encourage the child when he does some thing and congratulate him besides rewarding him with object of desires in order to bring desirable spirit in his learning.

Importance of the Major Law

These major laws enunciated by Thorndike are of great practical importance. Very few of us realise the effect which reward, encouragement, praise etc., have on learning. These theories are of importance not only in the teaching of others but also in personal activity to be learned should be created in the learner, be it oneself or some other, because the learning will be greatly expedited. And the meaningful practice of the learnt activity will help its retention in no small measure.

Subordinate Laws

Other five subordinate laws were also mentioned by Thorndike in relation to the three major ones studied above. Though a methodical explaination of true laws as given by Thorndike his later expositions sometimes contain their description while at other occasions they are lacking in it. He does not consider these subordinate laws to be of equal importance with the three major ones mentioned above. These five subordinate laws are:

1. ***Multiple Response.*** The first subordinate law is called varied action. A person seeks to solve a novel problem placed in front of s in accordance with his instincts and learned behaviour, because .s search in conditioned by these two. There are many multiform nd diversified responses in behaviour which guide a person in ttaining success and makes learning possible. The learner reaches ıe solution by the variation in the response.

If the activities are not multiform the person would never get ıe correct solution. The theory of learning by trial and error if ɔunded on multipurpose response and diversified reactions. If a erson adopts a particular method of approach but does not change it ı case of failure and gives up his attempts or if nothing new uggests, that person will never learn anything.

2. ***Set or Attitude.*** This is the second law of learning. Learning s conditioned by the attitude and set of the creature. The response of ı person in a specific situation is dependent upon his permanent ıdjustment in a particular culture. On seeing a figure or idol a Hindu :hild will bow his head but a Muslim will not pay any respect. Both hese responses are affected simultaneously by current tendencies. In an extraordinary situation, the worshipper may even throw the status. The set or attitude decides not only the response of the person but also the object from which he will derive satisfaction or classification. A first class student cries on scoring 50 per cent marks, while a third class student feels delighted with the same score. The reaction of a student on scoring certain number of marks depends upon the set, attitude and the tendency present in him at the time.

3. ***Prepotency of Elements.*** The fourth subordinate law of learning is the prepotency of elements. Every problem has some fundamental proponent element. The learner gets greater success if he bases his response on those elements, though this depends on the insight and capability of the learner. This kind of capacity is of great help in though learning. The insight, into a mathematical problems, of a student of this particular subject cannot be equalled by that of a

student of languages into the same problem because the student of mathematics will grasp its fundmentals with consummate ease.

4. *Response by Analogy.* This is the third law of learning and is called the law of assimilation. A person will respond in a manner similar to the one in which he has behaved previously if he finds that similarities between the previous situation and the new situations are none too numerous, the response will be similar of that in the first.

5. *Associative Shifting.* This is the first and last law of learning. The title quite obviously indicates that the position of the response of the learner shifts. This shifting is done in respect of the basic stimulus or some related associative stimulus. To take an example, a dog starts salivating when he sees food, and approaches the bearer with his tail wagging. The result of constant repetition of this phenomenon is that dog wags his tail on the mere perception of the man and the shape of dish. Thus, the response originally directed to the food is now aimed at the man and the dish because both these objects are associates of the main stimulus, the food. Thus, an associative shifting in the response is observable.

All the law subsidiary and main, presented by Thorndike are important in learning, both for the teacher and the student. They are applied comprehensively in education though all the psychologists are not agreed upon the truth and usefulness usually attributed to them.

The above described laws of learning are not intended to convey the impression that Thorndike's attention was confined only to the laws. Actually, Thorndike paid even greater attention to the practical aspect education and made attempt to absolve the difficulties to the teachers and taught alike. Thus, Thorndike attended to the specific aspects of learning and did not rest content with a general description of the activity. He has mentioned many factors which may assist in learning but which are not implied in and cannot be derived from his laws of learning. For example, he has stressed the following five things which assist in the progress of learning:

(i) Interest in the work,

(ii) Interest in improvement,

(iii) Significance,

(iv) Problem Attitude,

(v) Attentiveness.

To these five. Thorndike added two which in his opinion, are not indisputable. These are absence of irrelevant emotion and absence if worry. In this way, he encouraged practical experience and measurements. He himself conducted experiments throughout his life and made continuous progress in his theory. He is fundamentally a behaviourist, not with-standing his acceptance of the effect of introspection of human being and he frequently used subjective words. He encouraged the psychological revolution in the field of education and emphasised the study of elements according to specific situation.

❐

9

Physical Growth and Development

Generally both the terms 'growth' and 'development' are used interchangeably though they differ in their meaning to a great extent.

The term 'growth' usually implies increase in size, weight, height, etc. It is in terms of growth is bodily features.

'Development' is a much broader term than 'growth'. It includes growth also in it. It refers to overall changes in the individual. Growth is one of its parts. Development includes changes in intelligence, understanding, attitude, interests, personality and character traits.

Characteristics of Development

1. Development is the product of heredity and environment.
2. Development is a continuous process.
3. Development of various traits are correlated.
4. Development proceeds from general to specific.
5. Development can be predicted.
6. Rate of development is not even throughout.
7. Development follows a sequential order. It is a step by step process.
8. Rates of development of different aspects are different.
9. Every child has his own rate of development.

Various Aspects of Growth and Development. These can be named as follows:

(a) Physical growth and development.

(b) Intellectual or mental growth and development.

(c) Emotional development.

(d) Social development.

Various Stages of Development. Following are the various stages of development which have been commonly accepted:

Name of the Stage	*Period and Approximate Age*
1. Prenatal (Prebirth) Stage	From conception to birth.
2. Infant Stage	From birth to three years.
3. Childhood Stage	From 4th to 12th years or to the on-set of puberty.
(a) Prechild Stage	From 4th to 6th years.
(b) Early-childhood Stage	From 7th to 9th years.
(c) Later-childhood Stage	From 10th to 12th years.
4. Adolescence	From the on-set of puberty to the age of maturity (generally from 13th years to 19th years).
5. Adulthood	From 20th year or the age of maturity till the age of productivity—55 years.
6. Old age	From the end of productivity till death.

Educational Implications and the Role of the School. The teachers and parents should not expect a child to achieve something suddenly. They should provide suitable environment for the child for his proper development. The schools should provide different curricular and co-curricular activities so that these suit the students with their specific needs and traits. If a teacher finds any abnormality in the pattern of development of the child the case should immediately be referred to the guidance of counsellor. The teachers should provide learning materials and activities that will facilitate the development of different aspects at the proper time. If a teacher has the adequate knowledge of the rate of development of a particular child he can easily control the behaviour of the child. The school should realise the importance of individual differences while providing instructional materials and other activities. The child with the knowledge of child development becomes more practical and understanding. He knows what to expect from a child at a particular stage. Knowledge of development aids the teacher to find out learning readiness.

In a democratic climate of the school children display mutual understanding, tolerance, a sense of responsibility and disciplined conduct. A school provides suitable social environment for the development of a social beings who are socially efficient.

General Remarks. The characteristics, physical as well as mental, of all the stages as given above are too well marked and distinct that an infant is quite different from a grown-up child or an adolescent and similarly an adolescent differs from an individual of any other stage. The tastes and interest, and temperaments and inclinations, physical features and emotional attitudes of an individual of one stage differ from those of the individuals of other stages quite apparently and basically.

Still we cannot divide the whole life of an individual into distinct stages different from each other in watertight compartments. There is always a continuity of development in him from birth to adulthood. The child himself or his relatives and friends who come into contact with him everyday do not notice any abrupt and sudden change in him at any time. Growth is quite gradual continued and normal and it cannot be detected during the process of development.

It should also be noted that the characteristics of one stage are not entirely absent from those of any other stage. The difference lies in the prominence and domination of certain characteristics. The infant is imaginative and the adolescent again takes refuge in day-dreaming. But day-dreaming is not absent from the mind of an individual entirely at any stage. Similarly, other emotional impulses or intellectual trusts are, always there, but they are less or more prominent on different stages.

These changes do not appear in all the individuals in definite years of age. All children do not turn to be adolescent in the 12th year and all the adolescents do not develop to be adults in the eighteenth or nineteenth years of the age. Development depends upon many factors such as individual, physical features, sex, climate, social environment, food, habits and so many other environmental influences. Hòwever, an average individual is expected to develop at various stages at specific ages.

DIFFERENT STAGES OF DEVELOPMENT

Different stages of development are as follows:

(i) *Infancy,* from birth to two years.

(ii) *Early childhood,* from two to six years.

(iii) *Later childhood,* from six to twelve years.

(iv) *Adolescence,* from twelve to sixteen or sventeen years.

(v) *Adulthood,* after 18 years.

(vi) *Old Age,* period after the age of 58 years.

Infancy

It is a very improtant period of a child's life. It may be considered as the basis on which the future structure of a child's life can be constructed. This structure too depends on careful guidance and supervision.

According to **Ruth Strang,** "One can determine how a child stands in relation to life, a few months after his brith." "During the first two years of his life the child lays the foundation for his future."

According to **F. Goodenough,** "One-half of an individual's mental structure had been attained by the age of three years."

(a) Physical Development. It is the period of rapid growth in size and weight. The new-born child is 18 inches in size and weights about seven pounds. Changes in the proportion of the body are visible. The head which seems enormous of birth seems small now, as legs and trunk lengthen. The hands and the jaw develop. The muscles of the child also develop. He starts using his fingers by holding things, standing, walking and running.

(b) Emotional Development. He cannot show specific emotions like anger, fear, joy as the adults do. It takes time to develop them. As the children grow up and reach the age of two, there is differentiation of emotions. Anger is the most common emotion of this age and is aroused when adult force is used to restrict the freedom of the child. It is sometimes used as a device for gaining the attention of adults. Children also show at this stage the emotion of joy. They express it on seeing familiar faces generally of adults and also show affection for parents and nurses.

(c) Social Development. The social development of the child essentially depends on the parents. If the parents are well inclined towards him, the child starts developing a healthy social personality; whereas an absence of such a relationship may injure his personality. He may develop anxiety, depression and feeling of insecurity.

Educational Significance of Infancy

1. The child at this stage should be provided wooden blocks and other play material which he may handle with ease and which do not require any special skill.
2. He should be given enough freedom in his movements. He should not be protected too much, otherwise he will not be able to develop his normal personality.

3. The child should feel secure in the family and the parents should treat him well.

Early Childhood—(from 2 to 6 Years)

(a) Physical Development. During this period the child attains height at the average rate of about three inches per year. At the age of six years he comes to have a height of 3 1/2 feet. The weight of the child also increases. The proportions of the body also change. The head grows very slowly. This is also the period of developing finer muscular co-ordinations.

(b) Emotional Development. At this age the child shows off his emotions. The young child will cry and throw himself on the ground, if his wishes are frustrated. He also fights with the children of his age. Another emotion of this stage is fear. The child is afraid of many things and situations as he develops his intelligence. He is also curious at this stage to know about the various things of the universe.

(c) Social Development. He makes friends with other children and tries to get on well with them. Sometimes he also quarrels with his friends which is a normal form of behaviour. Children also disobey their parents which is also a healthy sign. "A child who never says no and always does as told is not growing satisfactorily." Children also sometimes compete with each other at this stage. They also sympathise with each other in case of distress.

(d) Mental Development. He wants to know something about the universe. He is always asking questions. He also tries to handle the various objects of the universe and tries to understand them. It is after seeing and handling the objects that he builds up 'Concepts' about them. He is able to judge distances when he runs, walks and climbs.

He follows conversation. He also develops his vocabulary and expresses himself in short sentences. Children who have superior intelligence are able to express themselves well in comparison to average children.

(e) Moral Development. The child has no idea as to what is good or bad. He considers things good or bad as his parents explain to him.

Educational Implications of Early Childhood

Early childhood is considered to be "an ideal period for learning." **Watson** thinks, 'the scope and intensity of learning during this period exceeds that of any other period of development." The following points should be kept in view by the educator while planning the education of the child at this stage.

1. *Proper Atmosphere.* A healthy, peaceful and secure atmosphere should be provided for the child. This is necessary both at home and the school.

2. *Developing the Endowments of the Child.* A child takes birth with certain natural endowments. The educator should try to locate them and plan for their maximum development.

3. *Proper Treatment.* The child has to depend on others for the satisfaction of his requirenments. Hence he should always receive an affectionate, sympathetic, and courteous treatment from others. An atmosphere of fear and repression will not allow the child to develop properly.

4. *Satisfaction of Curiosity.* Every child is curious to know the details of his social environment. The parents and the teachers should try to pacify this need of the child by answering the questions asked by him.

5. *Developing a Social Sense.* Efforts should be made by the teacher to develop a rational social sences in the child. The Child starts developing a social sence by the end of this stage.

6. *Developing Self-Sufficiency.* The infant depends on others for the satisfaction of his needs. The child has to do everything himself. The educator should try to develop a spirit of self-sufficiency in the child and should provide him opportunities so that the child is able to do most of the things himself.

7. ***Encouraging the Instinctive Development of the Child.*** The child at this stage is guided by his instincts. The teacher should not try to suppress the instinctive development of the child. It should be sublimated in the best interests of the presonality development of the child.

8. ***Learning by Doing.*** The child is active by nature. This ought to be satisfied through the use of activity method which advocates learning by doing.

9. ***Formation of Good Habits.*** This is considered to be the most flexible age of the child. Steps should be taken towards the formation of good habits by the child.

10. ***Use of the Play-Way.*** Play is natural to the child. Let him play and learn. This will make learning easier and acceptable to the child.

11. ***Sensory Training.*** There are five senses of the child. These should be properly developed at this stage. This sensory training was also emphasised by Madam Montessori.

12. ***Use of Stories and Pictures.*** Children at this stage are interested in stories and multi-coloured pictures. They should be made to learn by using story telling method and with the help of multi-coloured pictures and charts.

Later Childhood—(from 7 to 12 years)

(a) Physical Development. The development is slow and uniform. The child at the age of 12 it about 55 inches in height, which means an annual increase of 2 to 3 inches. Boys are slightly taller than girls. Body proportions change considerably and the overall appearance of the child also alters. The nose becomes larger and the lower jaw also increases in size. Arms, legs and trunk increase in length and look thinner. This rather gives 'an ugly look' to the child. He also builds up fine muscular co-ordinations and improves many muscular and mother skills. Boys show superiority to girls and special interest in games and skills requiring physical strength, while girls are superior to body in skills involving the use of finer muscles, such as drawing, painting, sewing, etc.

(b) Social Development. At this stage the child is engaged in social give and take. Sometimes he is teased and bullied by others and he also teases and bullies others. He attaches great value to friendship and takes part in games and excursions. Now he is fairly independent in his behaviour. He moves with his friends and comes to have a 'group' spirit. Sometimes he may assume the leadership of the group as well. Boys and girls make their separate groups. The children also come to have a knowledge about their caste, religion bias and prejudices.

(c) Emotional Development. The child now comes to have a control over his emotions. His emotional behaviour is guided by a rational expression. He is still jealous, may be of his younger brothers or his class-fellows. He may tease and make fun of those children who are the objects of his jealousy. He may be afraid of things but tries to look brave. His expression of joy is expressed by a smile. He satisfies his curiosity by asking questions from the teacher and by studying books.

(d) Mental Development. Children develop their mental power by studying in the schools, reading books, and by visiting places. They develop their reasoning power, memory, attention and sensory discrimination during this period.

Children also judge their own actions and criticise the actions of others and in this way they come to have their own opinions. In religious and racial matters they take up the opinions of their elders. They also take up the aesthetic standards of their elders.

Their vocabulary increases by leaps and bounds. Now they are able to speak and write sentences of more than average length.

(e) Moral Development. To him the moral code is now determined by the group to which she belongs. He considers that stealing is generally bad. He judges the actions of others accrodingly. He has a strong sense of fair—play and justice. Sometimes conditions in the family play a very important role in determining these attitudes.

EDUCATIONAL IMPORTANCE OF LATER CHILDHOOD

This period of childhood is the time when the basic outlook, values and ideals of the child are finally shaped. Hence it is duty of the parents, teachers and the society to plan for their proper development. The School, however, has a very important role to play. The following points should be kept in view by the teacher.

(1) ***Proper Physical Development.*** Well-organised evening games and sports should be provided for children so that they are able to have a proper physical development. The teacher should see that every child takes part in these games. Morning physical training may also be organised for resident students. In the new educational pattern of 10+2+3, physical development is being highly emphasised by educators.

(2) ***Proper Provision of Extra-Mural Activities.*** Hidden qualities have to be found out and properly developed. This is possible only if a large number of extra-mural activities are provided in the school. This will enable the child to choose those activities in which he is interested. In the organisation of these activities democratic ways should be adopted.

(3) ***Provision for Excursions and Scouting.*** Children start developing surplus energy at this stage. They are interested in adventure and roaming about here and there. It is, therefore, necessary that suitable provision should be made for excursions and outings for them. The scouting should be organised in the school to satisfy this need of the child.

(4) ***Planning for Proper Social Development.*** Children develop the 'group spirit' at this stage. In order to direct it in the right channels it is necessary that group games on a group competition basis should be arranged. It is a period of competitive socialisation. It is throguh these group competitions that the child will develop various qualities like discipline, self-control, sympathy and co-operation.

(5) ***Developing the Creative Instinct.*** Children want to create something new. This creative trend should be properly utilised for educational ends. The teacher should provide opportunities where children are in a position to satisfy their creative instinct.

(6) ***Satisfying the Acquisitive Instinct.*** Children want to acquire those things which they like. If it is not properly directed they start stealing. They should, therefore, be encouraged to collect those things which have an educational value.

(7) ***Proper Emotional Outlet.*** This stage, however, is considered to be a unique stage in the emotional development of the child. It is possible only if proper outlets for the emotional expressions of children are provided. The teacher should not try to suppress these outlets. He should try to redirect them in the right channels. He should place examples of greatmen of the world before them.

(8) ***Moral Training.*** The child at the age of eight years starts accepting the moral values of the society in which he lives. Therefore, it is necessary that some moral training should be provided. Instructions may be provided which have a moral value for the child. A democratic approach should be followed as morality is something which springs from the heart of the child.

(9) ***Learning though Self-Activity.*** Children like activity. It comes to occupy a more important place in the educational system when it originates from the children themselves. Self-activity leads to self-expression, thus leading to self-realisation.

(10) ***Teacher's Role in Academic Development.*** The teacher has a very important role to play in the mental development of the child. His role may be in the following directions :

(a) Children are interested in language learning. They may learn two or three languages at this stage.

(b) Children should be encouraged to choose those subjects which have a functional value. Preference should be given to those subjects which are useful in life.

(c) Interests of children differ and change. Hence, it is necessary that their text-books should have different types

of lessons. They may include adventurious stories, biographies of greatmen, drama, dialogue, etc.

(d) It is the duty of the teacher to make necessary changes in the curriculum and methods of teaching.

ADOLESCENCE STAGE
(Period From 12 to 16/17 Years)

The term 'Adolescence' is derived from the Latin word 'Adolescere' which means 'to grow to maturity.' This is a period lying between childhood and maturity. Thus, it is a period of change, when the individual is neither a child nor an adult. The changes which take place are physical, sexual, emotional, social, mental and moral.

A harmonious development of adolescence means full adult height, weight, stature and strength, and complete sexual maturity; the proper adjustment of the adolescent in the society; he also takes up his duties and responsibilities; the complete development of his mental powers and emotional stability and economic independence and professional competence.

Physical Development

Height and Weight. Growth is rapid just before and during the early years of adolescence. Both boys and girls develop their height and weight.

Bodily Proportion. Different parts of the body grow at different rates and reach their final size. Arms and legs grow longer and hands and feet grow much bigger.

Sexual Development. This stage is the development of sex maturity. The pituitary glands secrete 'gonadotropic' hormone which finally stops bodily growth and leads to sex maturity. The sex glands of male produce spermatoza which leads to the development of sexual growth. In the same way, female sex glands are called the ovaries which produce 'Ova' sex harmones.

Emotional Development. This is the period of increased and changed emotions as the instincts of the child attain maturity. His feeling also undergoes a great change. He is sensitive and easily offended. He feels he is all alone, unloved, and in a world which is hostile.

He is required himself to adjust to the new situations and behave as the new adult. He may face emotional difficulties. He is not able to control his emotions and this leads to temper outbursts. Sometimes he is happy and sometimes he is sad, sometimes he also suffers from emotional moods. He may also indulge in day-dreaming.

Love is also predominant feeling in this period. This is due to the development of sex instinct. This love may be of most selfless kind. Adolescents are prepared to sacrifice every thing simply to gain the love of another child. In the later period of adolescence this love is directed to the opposite sex. The adolescents also direct love towards great men, which is known as hero worship.

Social Development. At this stage the adolescent is self conscious and lacks confidence and is very modest. He wants seclusion. All these things disappear as he develops. He starts choosing his own friends and chooses them on the qualities they possess. Gradually he forms small group. He takes part in various social groups as a member of these groups. Thus he gains experiences which are valuable to him in adult life.

In this period adolescents also come in conflict with parental demands. They demand independence of action whereas their parents treat them as children and hence they come in conflict with them.

Moral Development. At this stage the child develops his critical ability and judgement. He also comes across various individuals and thus he does not accept religious principles without criticism. He becomes conscious of the idea of right and wrong.

Mental Development. At this stage the span of attention increases. Memory, reasoning and judgement also increase. He understands and appreciates, poetry, music, art, literature and mathematics.

ADULTHOOD STAGE (PERIOD AFTER 18 YEARS OF AGE)

Adulthood period is the longest of all the periods or stages of life. It is characterized by an all round maturity—physical, intellectual, emotional and social. At this stage the individual develops into a functioning member of the society and acts according to social and moral standards. He is self-reliant and accepts responsibility for this decisions and actions. He develops ability to think rationally and intelligently, ability to understand the world and to make maximum adjustments.

OLD STAGE (PERIOD AFTER 58 YEARS OF AGE)

This stage starts from 58 years till death. At this stage one spends one's most of time in worshipping, social service and excursions.

PRINCIPLES OF HUMAN DEVELOPMENT

Developmental psychology studies human development, the study starting not with the infant's birth but before it, while it is in embryonic form within its mother's womb. The child's development within the womb is a very important phase of his entire development. Hence, there have been origination in the form of a fertilised ovum. Gradually and continually, this fertilised ovum shows signs of structural development, the ovum cells multiply in number and increase in size. These cells are of two kinds, the germ cells and the somatic cells. The germ cells help the germ cell plasm to develop various physiological parts such as bones, muscles, nerves, etc. Beside changes in structure, the functions of the embryo also take on variety and complexity. Functional development occurs with the addition of new activities. While the human being is in the embryo, the structural and functional developments take place in the nature of two mutually supplementary aspects of total development.

Psychologists have divided the embryonic development of the being into several states. These states and a brief mention of them are given below:

1. Germinal Period. The period beginning with conception of the child and lasting for a period of two weeks is called the germinal period of the being's development. During this period of the being exists in the form of a fertilised ovum, not being given any external nutrition. The form of the fertilised ovum is that of an egg, and its cells are equally divided.

2. Embryonic Period. The period from the third to the eighteenth week of pregnancy is called the embryonic period, during which the embryo gets nutrition from its parent. As a result, its form undergoes rapid change. In the change there is a sac related to the ovum and it is situated between the cells that lie in between Omniotic sac and Yolk sac. In this the cells lying next to the omniotic sac are called the ectoderm cells. The cells of the first kind prove of help in the development of the digestive and the respiratory systems, while the latter or second kind of cells lead to the development of the nervous system and the skin of epidermis. The mixing of the two kinds of cells leads to the development of a new layer called the mesoderm. Development of the two kinds of cells leads to the creation of muscles and bones. Cell's structure which is originally flat and convex, gradually spread out. Every cell has its own peculiar position, and if it is changed, its characteristic features will also undergo some change. For example, if it would originally have developed into skin, it will develop into the muscles of the eye on changing the cells. Certain chemical substances are also of importance in the separate and individual development of the cells. These chemicals are called organisers. Besides these, the development of the embryo is influenced by the use of the light, electrical field, X-rays, and other chemical rays.

3. Fetal Period. In the development of the being, this state begins, with the eighth week, and in it a number of cells increase, following which their size improves. Change in this stage is very rapid.

As has been pointed out above, the child's development during pregnancy is characterized by two types of development, the structural and functional. The following two laws are accepted in respect of structural development:

(a) Law of Caphalocaudal Development. According to this law, in the development of the embryo, the development starts with the cephalic portion or the head and gradually proceeds to the tail portion. In this way, this law of development the direction of the bodily development. This law applies to growth as well as differentiation.

(b) Law of Proximo Development. According to this law, the progress in development is more rapid in peripheral parts situated in the centre.

In structural development, the structure of the nervous system is a very important one. In this development, the first layer of the ectoderm cell turns inwards to form the neural tube, the major portion of which, the spinal cord and the upper part develops into the brain. In the fifth week of development, the medulla, cerebellum and the mid-brain become distinctively visible. The nervous system develops very rapidly during the fetal period. Mucles, being to be formed even before the nerves and sensory organs. Almost all the sensory parts develop in the being before the delivery or actual birth. The development of vision starts with the second week, and continues even after pregnancy. Receptors concerned with olfactory reach maturity in pregnancy in the case of some children. Taste cells develop in the third month, that, is during the fetal period. Besides this, during pregnancy the being attains the power of feeling sensations of pressure on the skin.

SOCIAL DEVELOPMENT

The concept of social development *lies in the concept of socialisation*. To understand that, we have to understand socialisation.

At the time of his birth, a child is very selfish. He does not know about sharing his joys and toys with others. Round the age of two, he realises that he is just a little man in the complex order. Others also matter and that he alone does not matter. Giving and taking starts. This we call socialisation and social development. Social development never takes place *in isolation*. A child left in jungle will not be social. It is as a result of interaction that social development takes place. That is why schools exist. A man gone throught schooling is a better socially developed man as compared to one who never went to it.

Various authorities have also defined social development. Few are quoted below:

Freeman and Showel, "By social growth and development we mean increasing ability to get along well with oneself and others."

Hurlock, "It is attaining of social relationship."

In nutshell, socialisation means:

(i) contact with people—its beginning,

(ii) dealing with people and learning from them,

(iii) It is a conscious activity. It does not take place automatically.

SOCIAL DEVELOPMENT DURING VARIOUS STAGES

Babyhood. Boby deals with adults in his/her immediate environment. According to Mrs. E. B. Hurlock, the important patterns of his social development during this age are:

2nd month. On hearing a voice, the baby turns his head.

4th month. Stops crying when talked to and makes movements in anticipation of being lifted.

6th month. In touch with the adult 'talks' to adult.

2 years. The baby likes to do things independently and runs around for the adults—he can bring the newspaper lying at gate when asked to and when the baby is in mood. Learns to imitate adults.

Up to this age, babies indulge in what is known as parallel play.

Early Childhood (2–6 Years)

1. Becomes active members of the group. He participates in group activities.
2. 'Parallel play' activity is no longer there.
3. Social development during this stage depends much on his relationship with his parents. He can become *likeable* individual if relationship is not cordial he will become *assertive.*
4. He has many friends.
5. He shows preferences for friends.
6. His *patterns* of social behaviour are—*(i)* Aggression, *(ii)* Quarrels, and *(iii)* Selfishness.

Latter Childhood (6–12 Years)

(i) This is called school going age.

(ii) The number of friends increases mainfold—permanent associations are formed. Social interaction is at its maximum.

(iii) The child is capable of dealing with many social situations.

Gang Age. Later childhood, social development-wise is also known as gang age. Formation of gangs is the peculiar feature of social development in this age.

Gang means small group or a spontaneous local group. It is formed by children themselves. It is not authorised from outside.

Gang has a leader who issues commands.

Gang has a code of ethics.

Gang has secret language.

Gangs disband after sometime.

Girls gangs are smaller and firmer.

Gangs meet at a secret place or hide out.

Activities. The activities of the gang are mostly anti-social—teasing old men, bullying small children—stealing fruit from neighbour's garden, fights with other gangs, tearing posters, throwing stones in neighbour's courtyards etc. They also play cards and go to pictures together.

Sex Dfferences. It is at this age sex differences come in. Boys and girls become conscious of their sex and they tease one another.

(i) Social activities depend upon sex.

(ii) They are conscious of social approval and disapproval.

Adolescent Age (12–16 Years)

1. ***Independence from Parents.*** The adolescent at this stage seeks independence from his parents. He is critical of them.

2. ***Peer Group Relations Assume Greater Proportions.*** The friends of child matter. It is the peer groups that shape the behaviour of adolescent. Company at this age matters.

3. ***Hetrosexual Relations.*** Boys begin to take interest in girls and vice versa. Both make themselvess attractive. Hence all sorts of beauty aids are used.

4. Friendships is a matter of mutual interest and not of nearness. Two adolescent brothers can have different friends.

5. Sentiments develop during this period.

Role of the Teacher in Social Development. The role of the teacher is very important in social development of the child. His role begins when the child enters the school. The following points highlight his role or educational implications of this topic:

1. ***Practice What You Preach.*** Teachers should practise what they preach. Things go wrong when they say one thing and do another.

2. ***Consistent Bebaviour.*** Teachers should be consistent in their social behaviour towards children. Inconsistency creates problems for them.

3. ***Opportunities.*** In schools and colleges, there should be maximum opportunities for give and take, for "hitting and being hit." Let there be maximum outings, camps, trips. It socialises the child. The teacher should be liberal in it.

4. ***Self Government*** in school will not only socialise the child but also make him responsible.

5. ***Avoid Harsh Discipline.*** Control will breed scandals. Understand it.

6. ***Mass Media*** (newspapers, magazines) which have bad influence (like some film magazines) on the development of child intellectually and result instunted. Social growth be not allowed to influence them. *Direct* the child along healthy lines.

7. Allow the child to display social responsibility. Let him receive guess at a function.

8. Parents and teachers should take children to parties. It socialises them.

IMPORTANCE OF DEVELOPMENTAL TASKS

The above discussion makes quite clear the importance of developmental tasks in the life of man. Briefly, their significance is as follows:

1. **Direction to Individual.** The list of tasks appropriate to various stages of life given earlier clearly shows to an individual what the society expects from him at various stages of life.

2. **Prediction about Future.** The knowledge of the developmental tasks tells a person in advance as to what physical and mental changes to expect in future. For example, the middle aged person who knows that will be his state of affairs after retirement, he can prepare in advance for all exigencies. He can save more or start side-business to be taken up fully later on. It is always difficult to make adjustment with new situations and this gives rise to great deal of tension. However, if one is mentally prepared for the change, difficulty will be less.

Facts Helping Adjustment

The development psychologists have found out certain facts which would help a man to make better adjustment. Following are the significant facts in this regard:

1. *Childhood is the Foundation of Life.* It is well said that the coming events send their shadows before. A strong foundation laid in the childhood will surely ensure happy and prosperous adulthood. It is generally found that the physical and mental characteristics observed in the childhood persist throughout. An honest child is likely to grow an honest adult. A study of fat adults has revealed that in childhood they were over-protected. As Alder has shown, alone child displays specific characteristics throughout his life. Similarly it also matters whether the child is first or last. The roles children play in their family later on determine their basic personality traits. If the experiences in childhood are positive and favourable the child grows into a healthy, moral and happy adult; but if these experinces are negative the child tends to develop abnormalities. The causes of a number of mental diseases are to be found in childhood experiences. The most important influence upon the child is that of his parents. If the child is taught to be tidy and clean, it develops in them a habit of cleanliness. Besides if there are some inborn defects in the children they can be best rectified in childhood. The child is a tender creeper. He must be zealously cared for and good habits inculcated in him. This will help him to become a healthy and moral adult.

2. *Development is Dependent upon Maturity and Learning.* In the past there was a controversy among the psychologists as to what is more crucial in the development—maturity or learning. Some opted for maturity and the others regarded learning to be the crucial factor. Now it is settled beyond doubt that there is an interaction between the two. It is also proved that in the absence of certain level of maturity there can be no learning. The interaction between maturity and learning can be seen in three ways. It tells us about individual differences. It tells us why some individual cannot learn beyond a certain point. Thirdly, we know what age is most appropriate for a particular type of learning.

Educational psychologists have made special investigation in this regard. Upon the basis of these studies individual differences have been noted. No two persons are equal and same. Individuals therefore differ in tense in their reaction. A situation which may be ridiculous for some may be serious for others. Briefly, differ in their level of maturity and learning and they therefore have in different ways.

CHARACTER DEVELOPMENT

To quote Professors **Sharma** and **Narula**, "Character is the end of all social development. It is the height of all that individual can think of."

Character formation thus is one of the most important aims of life. All systems of education in the world must meet at this point. Even Gandhiji stressed the importance of education building character or building of character through education.

Woe to the nation which has men and women of weak character.

What is Character? You talk to an Indian and ask him what he understands by character? His concept is a funny concept. Character to us is sex—sex-loaded or sex oriented or sex dominated. And bad character *is egg, meat and wine*! This is in fact not the exact or learned or psychological definition of character.

Various authors have tried to be fine character in their own way. Some selected definitions are given below:

Ross. Ross defines character as, "just organised self." You orgnise your instincts and sentiments.

Kolesnik. "It is acquired component of personality which inhibits impulses of an immoral or unsocial nature and disposes an individual to act in accordance with relative principles."

McDougall. "Character consists in proper organisation of sentiments."

Francis F. Powers. "Character is one's constancy in conduct trained, outer and inner, in conformity with group in which he lives."

Four representative definitions have been given above. The best definition comes from the pen of **Cronbach** when he says, *"Character is defined as the way you make choices.* How yours action affects the welfare of others." This is the crux. At the same time, you do not have to sacrifice your interests. You have to be normally selfish.

Character thus is a stable organisation of needs/motives/ sentiments in relationship to others.

Marks of Good Character. (Test yourself!)

1. Consistency is the hallmark of character. He sticks to his stand.

2. ***Reliable.*** A good character is reliable. You can depend upon the person for his word.

3. ***Some Marks of Personality.*** Some known personality traits such as cheerfulness, optimistic (Netaji Subash Chandera Bose was the greatest optimist India ever produced) are found in men of strong character.

4. A man of good character is courageous. (India suffers from this crisis!)

5. A man with good character is not influenced by the opinion of others. His decisions are his own.

6. He has strong master sentiment.

7. He has great powers of intellectual judgement.

8. He is emotionally responsive. He cannot sit still in a situation.

9. Simplicity is another mark of man of good character.

CHARACTER AND PERSONALITY

Personality is a bigger term. It includes character.

Personality is sum total of good and bad. Character is moral (good only) estimate of an individual.

Factors which Influence Character

These are also known as determinants of character. As a result of survey of literature the various factors emerge:

1. ***Physical Factors Like Health.*** It is said that good food determines good health and good health determines good character. A man with good health has powers of resistance.

2. ***Intellectual Factors Like Intelligence.*** Intelligence helps to discriminate between good and bad. Intelligent man is fearless and truthful. These are hallmarks of character.

3. Social factors like home, sohool and other social agencies, Company influences.

4. ***Moral Factors Like Religious Education.*** Religious education is missing in Indian schools—may be because of this reason that immorality has increased in post-independence India.

5. ***Sex.*** Sex is another determinant of character. Females fall earlier or quicker to temptations.

6. ***Creativity.*** Creativity or ability to invent ensures good character of man. You are busy thinking and inventing. You have no time to waste it.

7. ***Will.*** Character is closely related to determination. Will plays an important role in formation of character.

RELATIONSHIP OF INSTINCTS AND CHARACTER

Instincts are the movers of behaviour. They are innate dispositions. They form the basis on which character is formed. It is again not the raw instinct that leads to the formation of character but the sublimated form that leads to formation of character example. If sex instinct exists in one in raw form—uncontrolled form, it will make one a criminal, a sexual offender but if is sublimated, one can be a poet, a musician, and artist—sublimated form of instincts thus is the foundation of character.

Levels of Character Development

All leading authors have quoted from Croanbach in this connection. Various other views on development of character are also available but that is the popular version which is being discussed here.

There are five levels of character development:

1. *Amoral Stage.* This stage lasts up to first two years. The child is not aware of what is good and what is bad that is why this stage is called the amoral stage, *i.e.,* is not aware that his actions disturb others.

2. *Self-Centred Stage.* Then the second stage begins. The Child is aware that his actions sometime disturb others but it cannot help it. This stage lasts up to 8 years (2–10 years). The child knows that plucking flowers from neighbour's garden is not good but she/he does it.

Some children when they grow into adults remain fixated at this level. They live as misers.

3. *Conforming Conventional Stage.* This is the third stage. There is no age limit. Even adults operate at this level. The best example given by Croanbach is—while in Rome, do as Romans do. Why come in conflict with the society or with the established norms?

4. *Irrational Conscientious Stage* comes next. These people hold values of life clear emotionally rather than rationally. Best example—Yudhisthir from *Mahabharta*. People who stick to values emotionally are maladjusted. On the other hand, they are very happy.

5. *Rational Conscientious Stage.* This is the highest level of character development. Every one should try to operate at this level. Here the values of life are held clear rationally rather than emotionally. *Example*—Killing in war is bad but even then you are free to kill in self-defence.

Drever's Theory. Drever has divided the development of character into three stages. The basis of this development is Feeling. The three stages are:

(i) The stage of crude emotion,

(ii) The stage of sentiment, and

(iii) The self regard stage.

McDougall and others have also their own views.

Educational Implications

Both the Secondary Education Council (1952-53) and Indian Education Council (1964-66) have laid great importance on the development or building of character. The S.E.C. has even suggested a scheme of character education. **Kilpatrick**, the American philosopher has also suggested a scheme of character education.

Some hints in this connection are as follows:

1. *Teacher.* Teacher himself should be man of sound character. Sound character is a matter of being caught than taught.

2. *School Atmosphere.* It is again the duty of the teachers working in schools to keep the school atmosphere as pure as possible. It is easy to preach but it is very difficult to practice. Whatever the preachings, teacher's actions in school be good, in mutual regard so that the atmosphere is not polluted. They should be fair in dealings with the students.

3. *Sublimation of Instincts.* It is the duty of teachers again to modify, sublimate, reform the instincts of the students. It is also the duty of the teachers to strengthen the determination of students.

4. *Sentiment of Self-Regard* should be developed in students.

5. *Great Men and Their Lives.* Teachers and parents should make their children familiar with the lives of great men. **H.W. Long** fellow—the famous English poet has remarked:

"Lives of Great Men, All remind us,

We can make our lives sublime."

6. ***Co-curricular activities*** and participation in these activities lead to building of character.

7. ***Live Out Emotions.*** It leads to sound building of character.

8. ***Celebration of Days.*** Important religious and social functions should be celebrated in the school. Through these we acquaint the students with moral and spiritual value of society.

9. ***Reward.*** Children when they carry out some good deed. Example helps.

10. Motivate children.

11. ***Strengthen Physical and Mental Health of Students.*** It plays a great role in shaping one's character. Someone has lightly remarked:

"If health is lost, something is lost.

If wealth is lost, nothing is lost.

If character is lost, everything is lost."

Nevertheless:

Character plays an important role in life. Without men of character, nation is doomed—personalities are incomplete.

CHARACTERISTICS OF DEVELOPMENT

The English word adolescence is derivative of the Latin 'adolescere' which means to grow to maturity. This age begins from twelve and continues till the age of twenty. In the words of **Jersild,** "Adolescence is the period through which a growing person makes transition from childhood to maturity." Adolescence, in the opinion of most educational psychologists, begins between the age of 12 and 14 years. Compared to boys, girls enter the period of adolescence a couple of years earlier. According to **Dr. Jones**, adolescence is the recollection of infancy. It parallels the states of infancy and childhood in being patterned into two conditions, the first of growth and the second of maturation.

1. State of Growth

In this state, the adolescent is seen to be very active and unstable as well as disturbed. He gives the impression of being somewhat lost, and is subject to repidly, warying moods of dejection and elation, enthusiasm and deep lethargy, etc. The main thing concerning this period in life is that the adolescent is no longer a child but an adult, though the society in which he lives continues to treat him as a child. Secondly, he climbs down from the dizzy heights of imagination that he reached in his infancy and childhood and steps firmly into the real world. Both these factors engender in him a constant fear of reproof and criticism at the hands of others. He often becomes helpless and pitiable, shy and repressed. This does not indicate that he runs away from the real world, but that he tries to modify it according to his own notions. In efforts of this kind, relation and dejection are only natural, and it is for this reason that the adolescent is often seen wearing a look of anxiety.

2. State of Maturation

By the time he enters this stage, he has calmed down a bit and shown signs of stability. He carves a niche for himself in his society, and gradually his tendencies, habits and activities become stable and regular.

Mental Characteristics of Adolescence

In adolescence the individual is so transformed that he wears but inwardly he seeths with revolt and pent up anger which sometimes leads him to run away not only from school but even from the home a new and unrecognised look. Mental changes in this period of life find their best expression in the works of poets as they depict the mental states of young men and women. Adolescence exhibits the following mental characteristics generally:

1. *Development of Mental Abilities.* In adolescence the individual's nervous system becomes more strong with the result that his mental activities show greater tenacity and system. Ability to think, to solve problems, to differentiate and evaluate are some of the more prominent characteristics and abilities that he exhibits.

2. *Sexual Development.* From the psychological viewpoint, the most significant characteristice of the period of adolescence is sexual development. According to Dr. Jones, the repressed sexual force of infancy, that continued latent through the period of childhood, once again wakens and the individual passes through various stages of sexual development. The truth of the matter is, that even if it not the only tendency, sexual tendency is undoubtedly the most prominent and stable tendency to be found in adolescence. Hence, to disregard it is to make a fatal mistake as it is the most harmful form of negligence conceivable. The development in this sphere is so rapid that his entire personality appears to be coloured by it. Sexual development in adolescence finds its expression in attraction towards strangers, rather than towards parents as in the case of infancy. It announces its presence even in such small activities as the young boy's anxiety and nervousness, biting of fingernails, putting a pencil in one's mouth, tying knots in handkerchiefs, etc. Both physical and mental teachings in this age can use the sexual tendency as an important force.

3. *Hero Worship.* Generally speaking, adolescence evince a strong tendency towards hero worship, though the criterion of heroism is not the same in all children. Possession of any quality that attracts an individual child the most is sufficient qualification for a man or woman to become its ideal. While one child may regard a wrestler as hero, another may profess allegiance to a scientist, yet another may be devoted to film personality or a political leader. In schools some teachers impress their students considerably with the result that they come to be tenderly and affectionately regarded by them, also being imitated by the tender children. Sometimes, this hero worship turns to love. It is not till considerably later that the young man turns his thoughts to his own heroic qualities, when he begins praising them. The tendency to hero worship can be turned to good account by inculcating a proper character and personality in the child's mind.

4. *Extroversion.* In this period, the child once again regains his extrovert flambuoyancy, taking deep interest in his surroundings and other individuals, their activities and conflicts. In school, too, he likes to take part in all kinds of activities. And it is a matter of joy with him if he can spend the larger part of his time in the company of his friends. Various individuals become engaged in programmes of social service and welfare. In this manner does the adolescent announce the interest that he takes in the real world. This interest can be usefully exploited to ingrain, in him such useful qualities as self-dependence, self-determination cooperation, discipline, honesty and the quality of maintaining good relations with others or developing the social instinct. This is the age in which the foundations of good citizenship can be deeply laid.

5. *Religious Feeling.* Many adolescents become positively and deeply religious in this period of their lives. One can often observe them loving God in some one image, talking to him, sacrificing themselves to him and praying to him. India is particularly productive of such specimens since, for one, the religious tendency is deeply ingrained in the people's mind, and for another, in Indian society young boys and girls meet great leaders and famous personalities on very rare occasions. While religious tendency protects the young inexperienced child from many bad habits, it sometimes helps in making him somewhat impractical. Teachers can help to create a healthy attitude towards religion.

6. *Gregarious Instinct.* Adolescents are always acutely desirous of being among their friends, of praising them and of improving their relation with them. Often, they form definite groups in which each adolescent has his specific status and a role to suit him. This status and role plays an important part in determining his status and role in adult life.

7. *Excessive Imagination.* Although the adolescent is as much in this world as any other living being, yet he is prone to much imaginary flights into the world of fancy. The smallest thing can persuade him to temporarily abandon the world of reality and turn to the imaginary world. Such excessive imagination manifests itself in the strong tendency towards daydreaming, but some gifted children express their creative and aesthetic imagination through literature, music and painting, besides other arts.

8. *Lack of Stability and Adjustment.* It has been pointed out earlier, too, that in his adolescence the growing individual is at the threshold of his life, although he is rarely if ever considered an adult by his serious. From the psychological point of view, he takes himself seriously enough not to consider himself a child and likes to be treated as an adult. Evidently, he shows considerable instability and lack of adjustment. His adaptation, to his environment is upset by such small considerations as the growth of pimples on his face or the presence of other small physical deformities. In fact, it is a stage in which he learns to lead adult life in every sphere and direction. Hence, the presence and continual development of problems is only natural. And these problems are susceptible to ready solutions if the seniors are prepared to extend their sympathetic cooperation and guidance.

9. *Excessive Sentimentality.* The adolescent is very sentimental and emotionally unstable, although at this age his mind is fairly well-developed. Of the many feelings that drive him, the strongest are the desire to win praise and self-respect, any injury to or repression of them leading to serious malformations and even open rebellion. Sentimentality can be turned to good use in developing culture qualities in the adolescent.

10. *Personal Interests.* In adolescence, as the individual develops both in mind and body, his interests vary. Progressively the boys and girls develop the interests of their adult counterparts. Girls show this development in such interests as the use of various cosmetics, efforts at appearing very beautiful, reading or taking interests in romantic novels, love stories, dramas or poems, participating in music, art and acting programmes etc. Boys manifest their approaching adulthood in the form of various active games, running around, doing acts to valur, developing a vocation that they are to pursue in their adult life. Both boys and girls task constant interest in their addled life. Both boys and girls like to mix with the other sex and maturing it to fruition through conversation, intimacy, letters and romance.

11. *Development of the Mind.* In adolescence, the mind develops rapidly. The cells of the nervous system increase rapidly and the chemical composition of the nerves also undergoes a change. In this way, the mind and the nervous system rapidly mature. In this period along with physical and mental development, practice helps to develop mental abilities. Linguistic ability also registers improvement during this period. In his adolescence the child develops the vocabulary that he possesses. His vocabulary reveals general intelligence. Mental development, too reaches its apex in adolescence. Despite the inevitable individual differences that are invariably persent, mental maturity achieves its completion normally by the age of twenty. Practice or experience contributes considerably to this maturation. Normally, the individual's intelligence continues on the same level or, on other words, even in different ages the intelligence quotient of an individual remains more or less the same.

ADOLESCENCE

The term adolescence is derived from the Latin word Adolescere, which means to grow to maturity. It is a critical stage of development which lies between later childhood and maturity, emerging from childhood and merging into adulthood. During this period of development great physical and mental changes occur. Therefore, the stage of development is a period of uncertainly when everything is in a ferment. **Stanely Hall** defined adolescence as "a period of great strain, stress and storm and strife".

Not a Sudden Growth. Adolescence in not a sudden spurt of growth. The new traits and tendencies do not appear suddenly. No individual sleeps at night as a child to get up as an adolescent in the morning. Growth comes in continuity. There is a continuity of development from infancy to early childhood, from early childhood to later childhood and then to adolescence. No two stages in the development are clearly marked off. Even the adolescent himself does not feel any sudden change. Endocrine glands were already working but they are more active now. However, sex glands now are active. This is a significant change in this stage and it affects the whole organism.

Time at the Advent of Adolescence and Duration. The physical signs of adolescence occur between the ages of 12 and 18 in India. But there are differences due to sex, climate, race and individual constitution. Generally boys grow to be adolescent in their thirteenth year while the girls in their twelfth year. The individual differences are always there. The duration of adolescence ranges between five and eight years.

Physical Characteristics of the Stage

1. Rapid growth.
2. Growth not uniform and proportionate.
3. Different rate of growth of boys and girls.
4. Increase in modern activities.
5. Sense of clumsiness.
6. More significant growth of reproductive organs.

Mental, Moral and Emotional Characteristics

1. Sex-consciousness.
2. Self-consciousness.
3. Imaginative Activity.
4. Development of Special Intellectual Interests.
5. Contrasting Mental Moods.
6. Revolt to Authority.
7. Moral Awakening—No Acceptance of Sermons without critical evaluation.

PROBLEMS OF THE STAGE

The adolescent is a problem-individual. There are many problems around him and he needs help and guidance for their solution at every step. The following problems are the most significant in this stage.

1. Excessive Energy. Adolescence is the stage of excessive energy. In-take of food is increased in this stage and general health is also improved. The result is excessive energy. The adolescent needs more activity for catharsis of excessive energy. Our traditional schools do not provide such physical activity. Consequently, the adolescent is restless. Various activities act as sublimation for the adolescents and they feel relieved.

2. Misunderstandings Concerning Sex. With the advent of adolescence the gonads come into activity for the first time. The appearance of secondary sexual characteristics is due to the same. They produce emotional upheaval in the adolescent. The first appearance of menstrual course or nocturnal emission bewilders and shocks the adolescent who is quite ignorant about it. The school should supply right kind of information regarding sex at this stage. Due to ignorance about sex, many promising personalities are doomed.

3. Aggressiveness or Withdrawal. When an adolescent cannot adjust himself with the world, he grows to be aggressive or withdraws from the field and his personality is arrested. If the conflict is too serious, he regresses. The school should provide ample opportunities to the children to express themselves properly. Cocurricular activities, scouting student self-government and changed methods of instruction can go a long way in enabling the adolescent to adjust himself with the world.

4. Rebellious Attitude. The adolescents are no more children. They should be recognised as young men and women in the school as well as in the home. Their craving for independence should be satisfied to some extent. They should be given some responsibility. They turn to be very obedient if they are trusted. But things do not work so smoothly in ordinary schools and homes. Their sense of independence and responsibility is seldom recognised. The result is rebellion against authority.

5. Physical Awakwardness. Most of the adolescents have the feeling of physical clumsiness. Consequently their movements stand to be awkward and unbalanced. They may be corrected in the playground and on the stage. Games and dancing will give them harmonious and balanced movements. Social service at the occasion of festivals etc. and practical work can help the children in this respect.

6. Excessive Day-Dreaming. Day-dreaming is normal at this stage but when it grows to excessive it may be injurious as far as development of personality is concerned. The teacher should note that the adolescents are active and busy in their studies and other aspects of school life. The children indulging in excessive day-dreaming should be encouraged to be constructive and creative.

Role of the teacher in solving problems and proper physical, mental, emotional and social development of the adolescent:

1. *Proper Physical Development.* The teacher should plan for this aspect in the following manner:

(a) by organising various types of physical exercises, sports and games,

(b) by imparting a proper knowledge about physical and health education.

(c) by organising various types of extra curricular activities.

2. *Proper Mental Development.* The mental development of the adolescent should be according to the following lines:

(a) It should be according to the ability and aptitude of the pupils.

(b) They should study both arts and science subjects.

(c) Excursions to various places may be organised.

(*d*) Modern methods of teaching should be used to teach various subjects.

(*e*) They should be entrusted with responsibility so as to develop a feeling of responsibility in them.

(*f*) All the school teachers should try to impart him necessary guidance as and when required.

(*g*) The teacher should keep in view that there are individual differences among students. Every child should be able to find out subjects of his choice.

3. *Proper Emotional Development.* The emotional development of the adolescent should be as follows:

(*a*) The teacher should try to sublimate the lower emotions of the child.

(*b*) A healthy emotional atmosphere should be maintained in the school.

(*c*) The teacher should pay due regard to the personality of every child.

(*d*) The teacher should try to avoid frustration among the adolescents.

(*e*) The adolescent should be imparted proper knowledge about sex. If this aspect is properly attended to it would lead to a better emotional development.

4. *Proper Social Development.* The social development of the adolescent may be as follows:

(*a*) He should have a knowledge about social relations and he should know the art of group-living. Various group activities may be organised.

(*b*) The **Kothari Commission** has emphasised the instruction of moral and spiritual values. We should try to impart a right and rational knowledge of various religions to the adolescent. Leaving him to his own resources would be dangerous for social development.

(c) A right and rational attitude towards democracy should be developed in the school atmosphere. This would enable the child to develop his own philosophy of life.

SOCIAL PROBLEMS OF ADOLESCENTS

Adolescence is a period in which a number of social problems crop up. The social contacts of the person expand from infancy to maturity. In infancy a child's social contacts are with one person, usually its mother. From the early childhood onwards the mother-child relationship normally expands as the child comes into contact with the other members of family. When the child moves outside his family circle, he establishes contact with other children of his own age. These children form his peer group. When he takes admission in the school the peer group expands because now the child is free to choose his own friends and associates. Here he meets his teacher. As he enters adolescence he becomes a part of the gang, whatever be the stage of development of other people from his social environment. Adolescence is the stage of development which produces a number of problems for the person. These problems arise out of the adolescent's adjustment with following social groups:

(a) family;

(b) school;

(c) associates of one's own sex; and

(d) associates of the other sex.

Social Problems Raised by the Parents. During adolescent years the boy or girl tends to develop interests for groups outside the family. The youngsters commonly have misgivings about the changes that are taking place in their interests. On the one hand, they feel joy in being dependent upon their parents and on the other, the experiences with their peers are also pleasant. The peer group attracts them a greater force, because it offers them esteem and status which is either lacking in the family or is not got there at all.

Parents generally complicate the problem by placing demands on the adolescent sons or daughters. When they come to know that the relationship between them and their children is about to change, when they find their children are becoming more rebellious, less responsive, and less involved in the life of the family they feel threatened. Every father or mother thinks that his son or daughter is a psychologcial extension of himself, and when the adolescent slips along into the outside world, he or she feels that he or she is losing a part of himself or herself. As the adolescent becomes more independent he needs not so much care, direction, and attention of his parents, which parents still think necessary for his existence and well-being. The emotionally insecure parents are unable to face and accept this fact. The adolescent may feel the need of parental love, care and attention at certain times, but he is so proud of himself that he does not want to accept these things. He looks upon any form of dependence as a sign of weakness. This is the reason why there is a conflict going on between the adolescent and his parents. The conflict is of the approach avoidance type; it is so because he wants love and direction, at the same time wants to be strong and self-sufficient enough not to need love and direction. The adolescent resolves such a conflict by making decisions which are not in his interest and defends them stubbornly and rebelliously in the face of all adult opposition.

The loyalities of the adolescent are now divided between the family and the peer group. This division causes tension and anxieties in the adolescent and creates differences between him and his parents. The struggle that goes on within the adolescent is seldom known to most parents. The struggle is caused by his attempt to live in accordance with a double standard composed of the expectations of his parents and those of his associates.

How to Solve Social Problems Raised by the Family. Social problems which have a root in the relationship between the adolescent and his parents arise because the two do not understand each other sympathetically. The parents believe in the efficacy of greater control and direction. Whereas the adolescent believes in less adult control and greater opportunity for independence. The adolescent wants more independence but he also wants his parents to tell him what to do. The parents want to give more direction and control but at the same time require him to think and act for himself. There is dilemma, and the inconsistency is not soluble and therefore it creates difficulties for both.

The mutual problems should be discussed by the parents and the adolescents frankly. It is very unfortunate what and whenever the two parties try to clarify the issues through discussions heated arguments are advanced by each to defend its own point of view.

The adolescent who is in conflict tries to seek social satisfaction outside the home, but he does not get sufficient success in his attempt. If he wants to become successful outside the family he should have emotional support and acceptance within the family.

Problems of Adjustment with the School. The average adolescent tries to run away from home, though economically and vocationally he is yet not able to leave it. It is the school where he can be away from home for a particular length of time in the day. It is in the school also where he can mix with associates in the study-hall, in the classroom, on the playground and on the streets. If the school does not organise social gatherings like excursions, outings, trips, and if there is no arrangement for social develpoment, the adolescent does not find the school a satisfactory place, consequently, he becomes a truant.

If the school wants that the pupils should find joy and satisfaction, pleasure and happiness it should organise social activities in its premises. These activities, if wisely directed, tend to develop social maturity in the adolescents. Maximum participation in co-curricular activities like evening games and sports, plays and dramatics and student councils will inculcate better social interests, skills and attitudes.

Social Problems of Adjustment with Associates of One's Own Sex. Why does a boy belonging to upper class or higher caste family not like to mix with the one of lower class family? Why is a particular boy not popular? Why does a boy like a particular boy and not others? These are some of the problems raised when the adolescent tries to mix with the associates of his own sex. So long as he is a child he does not have such problems. Children of different socio-economic status work and play with each other. But the social distance increases in the adolescence period.

In the society of adolescents there are many who are not popular, who do not belong, and who are occasional. It is strange to find isolates everywhere. Isolates are boys and girls who regard others their best friends but are disregarded by them. The adolescents who are thus rejected become quarrelsome or unduly sensitive. On the others hand, those who are liked seem to be cheerful, humorous and lively.

Social Problems of Adjustment with the Other Sex. The adolescence is the stage when interest in the other sex is developed as a result of certain physical developments. The perennial topics of conversation among boys or among girls are sex and the opposite sex. They try to learn about sex from each other; often, they do help each other but such help is fraught with difficulties. Hence, there is a need for sex education at this stage. It is this stage when the youngsters try to discover the other sex. At first the boys and girls do not know what to make of each other and how to get along together. The boy now sees the neighbour girl in a new way. She is now really a different person from what she was when both of them were of twelve year's age. If he develops healthy relations with her he is in a happy position. If he does not achieve a satisfactory adjustment to the other sex, he may have difficulties in marriage. He may have other social problems also. The boy who cannot establish happy relations with girls may withdraw from their associations. If he becomes too interested in the other sex and goes too far he may cause scandal. If the adolescent boy withdraws from association with girls he will become mentally unhealthy. Marriage becomes either impossible or likely to be unhappy for the introverted youngster who does not have healthy normal associations with the other sex.

Adolescent girls try to attract adolescent boys. The increasingly do thing which may catch and sustain the attention of the other sex. They are more active because of their earlier sex maturity. Many girls, who find the boys of their own age sexually not so mature and responsive, try to seek attention from older boys. As sex maturity among boys and girls occurs at different ages, in a complicated and rapidly changing social situation the adolescents find it difficult to make social adjustment with the other sex.

Education and Social Maturity. The teacher who has to guide the adolescent facing social problems will have to understand the social liabilities and assets. He has to find out the relationships between the adolescent on the one hand and his parents, the peer group, and the school on the other. The teacher has to make a close study of the quiet, commonplace youngster who is rejected by his group or the other sex. If the teacher wants to understand the adolescents and develop them socially he may do the following:

(a) Know the settings and backgrounds of the adolescents.

(b) Make an appraisal for their social status.

(c) Plan a broad social programme to meet the needs of all.

(d) Teach them an informal applied Social Psychology directly or indirectly.

The first step in helping the adolescent achieve social maturity is to gather information about his settings and backgrounds. It is, therefore, necessary that the teacher should try to find out whether or not a particular boy or girl takes part in social activities, whether or not he or she belongs to a team, a society, or a council. Early or late maturing, higher or lower socio-economic status of the family may be influencing his or her social maturity. The teacher has to investigate the causes of social maladjustment. He should then plan a social programme comprehensive enough to meet the needs of all adolescents.

As some of the problems arise in the school environment, he may produce good social atmosphere in the school for adequate social development. But most of the social problems arise out of the school, in the family, in the group, in the relations with the other sex. To solve these problems an active co-operation of the parents and the society has to be sought so that desirable social adjustment may be fostered. Regular P.T.A. meetings, conferences between parents and adolescents, healthy associations of one sex with the other, active participation by both boys and girls in the school and community functions may go a long way in helping the adolescents achieve social maturity.

The teacher teaches his subject; the boys or girls learn it. But of greater importance than teaching and learning of the particular subject in the classroom is the development of social maturity. The first thing needed for that is a good-humoured, relaxed, friendly, social climate in the class. Where socialised activity programmes as group games, scouting and guiding, debates and dramatics, run regularly and where students take part in them freely, social maturity is developed as desired. Social adjustment or social maturity may be developed through a direct or indirect instruction in informal applied social psychology.

It is said that adolescents are inept and out-of-place socially. There is little doubt about it. Some adolescents do lack in social skills considered desirable by adults. This social out-of-placeness is, however, due to their lack of experience and self-consciousness. The educational implication of the fact is that adult judgement should be allowed to measure their eptness or ineptness in social skills. The adolescents should be provided with experience in social skills. When the youth is given a chance to express himself in the class, he expresses himself in the public.

EMOTIONAL PROBLEMS OF ADOLESCENCE

A Conflict between Empathy and Self-concern. The emotional problems of the adolescent are caused by his growth in the ability to interact with and respond to others accompanied by conflicting developments. On the one hand, he tends to develop a kind of self-concern; on the other, he becomes more aware of the needs and feelings of other peoples. The ability to understand the feelings of others is known as empathy. There is an inverse relation between self-concern and empathy. The greater the sense of self-concern, the less the empathy. The adults may not care at all about their self-concern and may not empathise with others, but adolescents do so. The adolescent behaviour is dogmatic. The adolescents show rigidity, narrowness and egocentricity while dealing with others. It is now thought that they develop these characteristics as defense mechanisms against feelings of insecurity and anxiety.

Insecurity and Anxiety are Caused by Thwartings. The adolescent feels a great deal of insecurity in his relations with others and particularly with adults. The society hopes and expects that he should behave like an adult but not too much like an adult. The adolescent is also eager to play adult behaviour but he does not know whether he has gone too far or not far enough. This state of affairs causes a sense of insecuirty and anxiety. The problem could have been solved, had the society placed before him definite standards of teenage behaviour.

The anxiety is also caused by the fact that the adolescent is living in two kinds of societies—teenage society and adult society. The behaviour that satisfies one irritates the other. Therefore, the adolescent is living constantly in a state of tension. Anxiety is caused also by a number of thwartings. Take for example sex. Autosexual behaviour is frowned upon in our society and sexual relations are forbidden to adolescents. Certain forms of sexual activity are punished by law and by adult society. This causes anxiety.

Sexual Problems. Ideally, the adolescent is supposed to wait until a certain age when economic independence has been achieved and marriage and subsequent monogamous, heterosexual activities are condoned. However, throughout adolescence models for non-conventional behaviour are many and stimulation for sexual activity is generally strong.

The society imposes limitations on sexual expression and creates problems for the adolescents. It regards even simple sexual urges as immoral and reprehensible. When the individual reaches his middle teens he is able to perform all the adult sexual functions. But society wants that he should postpone sexual expression, until marriage, There is freedom in print, as shown in many novels and stories. There is freedom also on the stage. Still most people speak of sex with embarrassment indicative of anxiety. Hence, the adolescents do not get clear answers to their problems regarding sex.

The sexual activity in the males is strongest during ten years and gradually declines after 20. This heightened male sex drive creates further problems for the adolescent boys. Although during these years, the desire of sexual activity is at its height there is no approved way in which it can be satisfied. The male adolescent tries to get some relief through masturbation. The solution of these sex problems becomes necessary in school and colleges. A compulsory programme of sex education has been suggested so that the adolescent may be better informed about sex and may be better able to discuss sex problem objectively and bravely.

Personal Problems. The adolescent is faced with many emotional problems. He does things which he later regrets. He wishes he were more popular but he finds himself ignored, isolated and rejected. He worries about little things but he cannot find answers to them. He wants to improve his prestige and position but fails. He needs to develop self-confidence but he is not given ample opportunities. He is easily hurt. He is not sure of himself. He hesitates to assume responsibilities. In short, he remains in a continual tense emotional state. Adolescence has, therefore, been regarded as the period of stress and strain.

Stress and Strain as Caused by Cultural Factors. The adolescent is subject to pressures. Many of his difficulties are caused by culture in which he lives. The conditions that culture imposes upon him are responsible for stress and strain. He feels that he does not belong, that he is different, that others view him with suspicion and hostility.

"In this world of human affairs" says Tagore there is no worse nuisance than a boy at the age of fourteen. He is neither ornamental nor useful. It is impossible to shower affection on him. If he talks with a childish lips he is called a baby; and if he answers in a grown-up way he is called impertinent. In fact, any talk from him is resented. Then he is at the unattractive growing age. His voice grows hoarse and breaks and quivers; his face grows suddenly angular and unrightly. It is hard to tolerate even unaviodable lapses in a boy of fourteen. The lad himself becomes painfully self-conscious. Yet at this age the lad most craves for recognition and lòve. But none dare openly love him for that would be regarded as undue indulgence. So with scolding and chiding he becomes very much like a stray dog that has lost his master.

❐

38. Indian National Congress **(New)** 450/-
39. Indian Polity **(Revised Edition)** 295/-
40. New Comparative Government **(Revised Edition)** 295/-

Advanced Study in the History of Modern India

41. (Volume-1: 1707-1813) 225/-
42. (Volume-2: 1813-1920) 325/-
43. (Volume-3: 1920-1947) 175/-
44. Handbook of Nutrition & Dietetics 250/-
45. Development of Education in India 195/-
46. A Text Book of Environmental Studies 195/-
47. Teaching of History 175/-
48. Administrative Thinkers 195/-
49. Research Methodology 175/-
50. Curriculum Development 195/-
51. Teaching of Science 175/-
52. Teaching of Mathematics 175/-
53. Principles of Educational & Vocational Guidance 195/-
54. Child Psychology 175/-
55. Abnormal Psychology 175/-
56. Indian Education in Emerging Society 195/-
57. Human Resource Management 175/-
58. Higher Education and Global Challenges 175/-
59. Teaching of Geography 175/-
60. Teaching of Social Studies 175/-
61. Teaching of English 175/-
62. Education for All The Indian Saga 175/-
63. Value Education in Global Perspective 195/-
64. Teacher Training 175/-
65. Public Administration 175/-
66. Public Relations & Integrated Communications 195/-
67. Educational Psychology 175/-
68. Introduction to Educational Technology 175/-
69. Textbook of Food and Nutrition 175/-

Unit No. 220, Second Floor, 4735/22,
Prakash Deep Building, Ansari Road, Darya Ganj,
New Delhi - 110002, Ph.: 32903912, 23280047, 09811594448
E-mail: lotus_press@sify.com, www.lotuspress.co.in